TEACHER TRAINING LIBRARY
NORTH CAROLINA SCHOOL FOR THE DEAF

WITHDRAWN
L. R. COLLEGE LIBRARY

CARL A. RUDISILL LIBRARY
LENOIR RHYNE COLLEGE

N. C. S. D.

907.12
St4p

104651

WITHDRAWN

DATE DUE			

PROBING THE PAST

PROBING THE PAST

A Guide to the Study and Teaching of History

LESTER D. STEPHENS
University of Georgia

CARL A. RUDISILL LIBRARY
LENOIR RHYNE COLLEGE

Allyn and Bacon, Inc.

Boston · London · Sydney

© COPYRIGHT 1974 BY ALLYN AND BACON, INC.,
470 ATLANTIC AVENUE, BOSTON

ALL RIGHTS RESERVED

*No part of the material protected by this copyright notice may
be reproduced or utilized in any form or by any means,
electronic or mechanical, including photocopying, recording, or
by any informational storage and retrieval system without
written permission from the copyright owner.*

LIBRARY OF CONGRESS CATALOG CARD NUMBER: 73-80550

ISBN: 0-205-04196-5

Fourth printing ... August, 1977

907.12
ST4P
104651
april 1978

PRINTED IN THE UNITED STATES OF AMERICA

FOR FAYE, KAREN, AND JANET

Contents

Preface

This book is intended for teachers of history—both those who are already engaged in the profession and those who are preparing themselves for that career. It is based on a personal conviction that history is a subject worthy of study in secondary schools, but it is also grounded on the belief that instruction in history must be improved if the potential value of the subject is to be realized. The volume will obviously reflect my own point of view, and I have not hesitated to express my ideas from time to time. Nevertheless, I feel that I should stress at the outset two of the notions which undergird my work.

First, I strongly subscribe to the idea that history should be taught as a subject in its own right and not merely as a part of integrated social studies. I am not opposed to the teaching of other social studies, nor do I believe that history deserves an unduly disproportionate share of the social studies curriculum. Other social studies are as valuable as history in the school program. I simply do not endorse the view that history ought to be made subservient to its sister studies, and vice versa. Second, I believe wholeheartedly that to teach history well, the teacher must possess a thorough understanding of the nature of historical inquiry. I am persuaded that a great deal of incompetent teaching in history is the result of inadequate grounding in the knowledge of how the historian goes about his business. Too many people feel that a pinch of inspiration and the ability to read a history book are the only requisites for teaching history. Granted, both are essential, but they are insufficient without an understanding of what history is. It is to this end that I have devoted so much space to Part I. In writing this section, I simply tried to remember at all times that I was addressing myself to people who care enough about history to devote their lives to teaching it. I can only hope that my synthesis will aid them in improving instruction in history.

In Part II I have attempted to follow up on some of the ideas presented in the initial section by suggesting some approaches to the teaching of history. The reader should remember that they are only suggestions, not prescriptions. Hopefully, they will initiate ideas for the teacher. Through my years of teaching history in a secondary school, a college, and a university, through my experience in teaching "methods" of teaching history at the university level, and through my contact with secondary school teachers and college teachers whom I have observed teaching, I have seen these suggested approaches work. Some of them are original; others have come from the minds of highly effective teachers whom I have had the good fortune to know. All of the suggestions in Part II are based upon the arguments set forth in the previous chapters. Thus, it is important to read Part I first.

I believe in no magic formula for good teaching, and I support the idea that successful teaching takes many forms. In my judgment teaching is not a science but an art which varies with the style of the individual. That does not mean, however, that "anything goes" in the teaching of history. Teachers of history should continually reflect upon the nature of their subject, and they should remain open to new approaches to instruction. I hope that this book contributes to those ends.

Many people had a hand in the shaping of this book, some of them indirectly, of course. I am grateful to those writers and thinkers whose ideas on the nature of historical inquiry stimulated me. And I wish to acknowledge my debt to those teachers who, because of their ability, have inspired me to reflect upon their approaches to teaching. Some individuals had a more direct hand in forming the book, and I must express my appreciation to them.

Helpful comments upon an early draft were offered by Professors Carl Gustavson, Derwyn McElroy, Horace Montgomery, Bruce Sandberg, and Waltraut Stein. To my fellow historian Dr. Alf A. Heggoy, with whom I am joined in a mutual society for professional criticism, I am grateful for a valuable review, and to Dr. William C. Merwin I am obligated for criticisms through the eye of a master teacher. I am greatly indebted to Eric R. Lacy for going that proverbial last mile to subject the entire manuscript to a thorough-going analysis; his thoughtful criticisms and constant encouragement were invaluable to me. Any mistakes which may remain are my own responsibility, of course. The interpretations and views with which my colleagues and critics disagreed and which I nevertheless persisted in holding to cannot be charged against any of these individuals. I am only thankful that they defend my right to express my own views.

I wish to thank Mrs. Carolyn Burt for typing the manuscript; her diligence and professional skill made my job easier. Above all, I am indebted to my wife, Faye, for her encouragement and understanding; she deserves credit which cannot be adequately expressed in words.

L.D.S.

PART I

In Pursuit of the Past

CHAPTER 1

The Nature of History

Over a half century ago Henry Ford declared that "history is more or less bunk." [1] When he uttered his statement, Ford probably struck a sympathetic chord among many school children of his own day, and today many students would most likely still agree that Ford was "telling it like it is." History is not the most popular course in secondary schools, colleges, or universities. Yet almost every school and college requires some formal study of history.

In 1827 the states of Massachusetts and Vermont instituted compulsory instruction in national history. Other states followed suit, and by the end of the nineteenth century "the place of history in the school curriculum was . . . thoroughly established by law. . . ." [2] Obviously state legislators and school officials had become convinced that history deserves a place of importance among the basic school subjects. And in our own day school authorities have not altered their confidence in history as a vital subject of study for school children and college students alike.

But unfortunately the authorities often have only a vague notion of the nature of history as a discipline. Their definition of history usually takes the form: "It is a record of the past."

[1] Interview with C. N. Wheeler, *Chicago Tribune* (May 25, 1916), p. 12.
[2] Bessie Louise Pierce, *Public Opinion and the Teaching of History in the United States* (New York: Alfred A. Knopf, 1926), p. 6.

And indeed history is that, but it is much more too—as we shall attempt to demonstrate. To restrict the definition so narrowly is to entertain the complaint that history is no more than just "one damn thing after another."

This is neither to argue for a simple definition nor to contend that history is essentially esoteric. Too many historians have believed the former, and as a consequence we have been inundated with a multitude of short and simplistic definitions of history. On the other hand, numerous philosophers of history have presented us with abstruse and involved explanations of what history is. Our purpose here is to examine the nature of history in order to gain a better understanding of that subject as a discipline. And if one is to devote himself to a lifetime of study and teaching in history, it seems only reasonable to expect that he give some serious thought to the nature of his discipline.

DIMENSIONS OF HISTORY

Perhaps a good place to begin is with the previously mentioned popular definition of history as a record of the past. But immediately we are compelled to elaborate and explain. What do we mean by a "record," and does the "past" refer to all previous events and happenings? First, a record generally refers to a written record, though of course we now have some oral records, such as the Columbia University Oral History Collection. A record is not, however, *ipso facto* history; for if it were, we would have to consider the cuneiform clay tablets of ancient Mesopotamia as history, while in reality they are only evidence or traces from which the historian constructs an account of the past. Moreover, the records do not normally provide a continuous story, another important characteristic of history that will be discussed later. One of the reasons for this narrow view of history may stem from the conception of history as a written record, hence history as what is written or recorded in a book.

Next, we must explain what is meant by the "past." History is not a record of all the past. In the first place, we cannot reconstruct the whole record of the past, for much of the essential evidence is presently unavailable, and some of it has left no traces at all. Furthermore, we are not interested in everything that has happened in the past. Primarily, though certainly not exclusively, we are interested in those aspects of the past which have significance for present society, or at least those which have some value or relevance for specific organizations or groups. Nor are we usually interested in that part of the past which does not deal with men and their relationships with society. While such scholars as geologists and primatologists are interested in the phenomena of the earth's formation and physical evolution, the historian is concerned with *man* in the past as he interacted with other men in a physical environment and in a societal context.

Just as each individual possesses a memory of his past, so societies and nations have a memory of their past. Thus, history may be defined as "organized memory." [3] To provide meaning for our personal lives, we must "organize" the memory of our personal history; and the same is true for societies and nations. This organization consists of both a record and a story. In other words, "The narrative of past experiences, active and passive, is for societies what memory is for their individual members." [4]

History is also a story. We need some sense of order, of organization—and this we find in the "story" of history. The story must always unfold with some sense of chronological sequence, else it is not truly a story and certainly not history, since both time and sequence are important characteristics of history. Even in the most analytical type of history, the time and sequence features are present, no matter how the historian may choose to present the story. But history is not just any story: It is one reconstructed on the basis of certain evidence. If it were not, it would be more properly labelled myth or fiction. The key to understanding the difference between history as a story and other nonhistorical stories is the manner in which the story is reconstructed. Thus, history may be defined as "any integrated narrative, description or analysis of past events or facts written in a spirit of critical inquiry for the whole truth." [5]

[3] Henry Steele Commager, *The Nature and the Study of History* (Columbus, O.: Charles E. Merrill Books, 1965), p. 3.
[4] G. J. Renier, *History: Its Purpose and Method* (New York: Harper & Row, 1965), p. 19.
[5] Reprinted by permission of the publisher from Allan Nevins, *The Gateway to History* (Lexington, Mass.: D. C. Heath and Company, 1946), rev. ed. (Garden City, N.Y.: Doubleday, Anchor Books, 1962), p. 39.

From the characteristic of history as a story we can move directly to a related feature, that is, history as explanation. History as a record of the past or as a reconstructed story may be interesting, but it would serve no useful purpose if it did not attempt to *explain* the past. "The historian tells us not only *what* happened, but *how* it happened, and this *how* includes both *what* and *why*." [6] This does not imply that the purpose of history is to teach moral lessons, but rather that any history which provides no explanation of why and how would be incomplete and leave us with many nagging questions about the reasons men acted as they did and why events took a particular turn. History as explanation, then, helps us to understand the origins of certain problems, events, or phenomena, and how they have come to be as they are.

Another significant, yet entirely different, way of looking at history is to perceive it as a special mode of inquiry. Though historical inquiry is similar to the scientific mode of investigation and closely akin to literary research, it nevertheless stands apart as a particular type of discipline. History is a *study* of the past, and as a *study* it entails a method. The historian approaches his subject with an understanding that he must attempt to find out what really happened and why or how it happened, realizing fully that no matter how thorough his search, he is faced with a number of tough problems. History, said Lord Acton, "is not only a particular branch of knowledge, but a particular mode and method of knowledge in other branches." [7] It is a way of searching for truth, and as such it cuts across—or better, underlies—all other disciplines or types of knowledge. It eschews acceptance of common beliefs, standard assumptions, or, for that matter, scholarly interpretations, when not subjected to a critical eye. This must not be taken to imply that historical inquiry leads to unbounded skepticism but rather that it promotes a healthy attitude of "uncertainty about what is to be accepted as truth [and] not a belief that anything might be true or that everything may be false or that knowledge is impossible." [8]

[6] Philip Bagby, *Culture and History* (Berkeley: University of California Press, 1963), p. 38; italics in original.
[7] Lord Acton. Quoted in Herbert Butterfield, *Man on His Past* (Cambridge: Cambridge University Press, 1955), p. 97.
[8] G. Kitson Clark, *The Critical Historian* (New York: Basic Books, 1967), p. 128.

Yet another dimension of history is what we may call history as thought, that is, a mental attitude about the past. We cannot avoid thinking about the past—either in a personal way or as a member of a particular society. As human beings, we reflect only superficially. "We are," as Pieter Geyl reminds us, "always trying to state past reality in terms of certainty, but all that we are able to do is to render our own impression of it." [9] Thus history is thought; but, as suggested earlier, it is different from mythic thought because it is disciplined thought. Historical thought is perceiving the past in an ordered and critical way, seeking insofar as is possible to think objectively. To view history as a type of thought is not to equate it with thought *per se*, however, for such a position might advance the notion that each mind constructs its own history. Though, as R. G. Collingwood suggests, the only way one can reconstruct the thoughts of men in the past is "by re-thinking them in his own mind," [10] we should not conclude that history is whatever any man thinks about the past. Instead, we should view history as a way of thinking about man's experiences in the past.

Finally, history is change, particularly those changes affecting man in society over a period of time. The social sciences share with history concern over change in man's operations in society. History, however, takes change over time as its focal point of inquiry. At the same time history recognizes the presence of continuity in man's affairs. Though we may not wish to go as far as the Spanish philosopher José Ortega y Gasset, who held that "History is a system, the system of human experiences linked in a single, inexorable chain," [11] we should nevertheless view history as *happenings* which are always in some way or other connected with previous and subsequent events. Men in societies do change, but they do so in no certain way. Thus, history deals with change, but it is not purely haphazard: The links of the chain are always there.[12]

[9] Pieter Geyl, *Debates with Historians* (Cleveland: Meridian Books, 1958), p. 41.
[10] R. G. Collingwood, *The Idea of History* (New York: Oxford University Press, 1956), p. 215.
[11] José Ortega y Gasset, *History as a System* (New York: W. W. Norton & Co., 1941), p. 221.
[12] An excellent illustration of history as both change and continuity can be found in Carl Gustavson, *A Preface to History* (New York: McGraw-Hill, 1955), chap. 6.

Considering the sundry features of history, to attempt a one-sentence summary definition would be simplistic. For practical purposes, however, we need at least a brief definition as a working guide. Thus, we will define history as a mental construct of the past based on evidence which has been carefully subjected to tests of validity and then critically and systematically ordered and interpreted to present a story of man's interaction with other men in a society. Though at points it may blend with myth, history differs from myth in that history constantly quests for the truth and does not assume that truth has been immutably revealed. Moreover, history confines itself to natural activities, avoiding queries into supernatural phenomena.[13] History is always character-ized by critical inquiry and helps to explain how and why change occurs as well as what "actually happened." We will say more on this point later.

This definition is restricted because it confines history to what is written and thought about the past. It does not include history "as past actuality,"[14] that is, the total cumulative experience of man, or all that has been said and done by man in the past. In other words, we intend to deal with history only as the activity and the product of the mind and pen of a person who calls himself a historian. We do not intend to consider it as though it were the entirety of man's past.

With these considerations in mind, we can now elaborate upon the nature of history and provide an even fuller descrip-tion of its characteristics and forms.

HISTORY AS ART AND SCIENCE

Is history a science? This question was argued with consider-able fervor by historians of the late nineteenth century. The controversy has abated in the twentieth century, but the question continues to reappear from time to time. Receiving impetus from the scientific spirit which pervaded the intellec-

---

[13] The historian is interested, of course, in the activities of man as they emanate from man's belief in supernatural powers. What the historian attempts to discover, for example, is what man *believes* to be true about God, not whether the concept of God is in fact valid.

[14] Charles Beard, "Written History as an Act of Faith," *American Historical Review*, 39 (January 1934): 219.

tual world of the latter part of the nineteenth century, historians began to think of their task as no less scientific than that of the natural and physical scientists. Even the contemporary literature reflected the scientific *Zeitgeist* (spirit of the time). Following the demise of Romanticism such writers as Gustave Flaubert and Thomas Hardy wrote their novels in a meticulous, precisely detailed, and "realistic" style. And among historians the phrase of the German historian Leopold von Ranke that history was to be written *wie es eigentlich gewesen* (as it actually happened) became the watchword.[15] Historians such as Henry Adams, J. B. Bury, and Henry Thomas Buckle employed their talents in the search for laws of history, and Bury confidently affirmed that history is "a science, no less and no more." [16]

Though the issue of whether history is exclusively a science or purely an art is no longer as heatedly debated as it once was, we can profit from looking at the question because it is itself an important step in the development of historical writing and can therefore help clarify the nature of history. Although the scientific school of history has been rejected by most recent historians, it did in fact make its contribution to a further refinement of the nature of history. We have come to understand, for example, that historical inquiry is scientific in its method or approach. What we must be careful to guard against is categorizing history as solely a science or exclusively an art. In point of fact, history is a combination of both art and science.

At this point, then, let us examine history as it qualifies for each of these appellations. First, history is a science to the extent that its method of inquiry is scientific. If the historian fails to apply the rigor of the scientific method to the study of his topic, he is engaging in the construction of myth or the writing of fiction, not in the production of history. Above all, the historian must strive for objectivity.[17] Just as the scientist must refuse to close his mind to any possibilities, the historian

[15] As with the ideas of many other powerful minds, this dictum was carried to extremes by Ranke's followers.

[16] J. B. Bury, "The Science of History," in *Selected Essays of J. B. Bury*, ed. Harold Temperly (Chicago: Argonaut, 1967), p. 22.

[17] Total objectivity (strict impartiality, complete freedom from bias) is, of course, impossible, since the historian is human and inevitably possesses a frame of reference. This will be discussed more fully in chapter 3.

must steadfastly refuse to regard any historical subject as too sacred for investigation, and he must consider any topic as potentially open to critical examination.

Moreover, the method of the historian is scientific in that it requires him to subject all facts to tests of validity, all hypotheses to the most careful and searching examinations, and all generalizations to systematic and thorough criticism. Summarizing the historian's method, Allan Nevins has noted that the historian

> collects his data fairly, observes it systematically, organizes it logically, and tests its parts thoroughly. Then by inductive logic and the use of hypothesis he reaches provisional generalizations, and only when he has carried out a final search for new data, and made fresh tests, does he commit final conclusions to paper.[18]

Since history deals with the past and is therefore not susceptible to "experimentation," the comparison of the historian's method to the scientific method must not be overdrawn. History does not qualify as a science which can be subjected to verification under laboratory conditions. Taking this limitation into consideration, G. J. Renier cautions us that strictly speaking "the methods of science are not those of history," and he reminds us that what the historian and the scientist share in common is the spirit of "intellectual honesty" in which they approach their work.[19]

Yet science and history appear to be similar at another point, namely, in the outcomes of their research. Each is concerned with discovery of general propositions. But in this regard they are also different: Science seeks general *laws,* while history, at best, seeks tentative *generalizations.* True enough, even the laws of science are not immutable—as we have discovered in the instance of quantum physics; but there are no real laws of history. What history provides is generalizations, and they are statements about the past, not those which are applicable to the present and the future.[20] Neverthe-

[18] Reprinted by permission of the publisher from Allan Nevins, *The Gateway to History* (Lexington, Mass.: D. C. Heath and Company, 1946), rev. ed. (Garden City, N.Y.: Doubleday, Anchor Books, 1962), p. 29.

[19] Renier, *History: Its Purpose and Method,* p. 154.

[20] A detailed discussion of generalizations and laws in history is provided in chapters 4 and 5.

less, both the historian and the scientist seek to draw general conclusions from their investigations. They are seeking explanations of cause-effect or antecedent-consequent relationships, that is, the "why" of phenomena. In effect, each attempts to abolish error, correct misconceptions, and enlarge our understanding of how things have come to be as they are.

Though the historian is interested in determining regularities and uniformities wherever they may exist, these are minor concerns to him—principally because he recognizes that each historical event is unique. Thus, to speak of history as a predictive science is erroneous. History as a predictive science is further hampered by the fortuity of some events, making guesses about the future a hazardous business. Added to this is the problem of ascertaining significance of factors in history.[21] How much weight should the historian give to such a force or factor as nationalism in outlining the causes of World War I? How can he measure the impact of imperialism, of entangling alliances? The historian, in other words, must deal with factors or forces, institutions, and the minds of men; and once he enters these realms of abstraction, he is hard put to demonstrate empirically that these intangibles exerted such and such an amount of influence on the course of events.

History is more than a mere aggregation of facts which, by being put together, explain the "whys" of historical events. What historical investigation requires is genuine involvement on the part of the historian—that is, he must "put" himself into the time and mood of the age of which he writes. Then, through following the rules of inductive logic, he must interpret the facts in order to arrive at a reasonable generalization. How absurd is the assumption that one can merely determine the facts of, say, Mesopotamian myths and then let them speak for themselves! Could we even begin to comprehend how the Sumerian mind conceived its city-states as microcosms or models of the perfect city-states in the supernatural or macrocosmic world unless we were informed by the interpretation of a historian who is in tune with the meaning of the myths to those people? History must deal with cultural forces, with

---

[21] J. H. Hexter argues against the concept of factors in history, identifying it as a fallacious "assumption of the conservation of historical energy." See *Reappraisals in History* (London: Longmans, Green & Co., 1961), pp. 26–44.

ideas, with human beings—and these prevent history from ever becoming a full-fledged science.

Although history may be considered a science within the bounds we have described, it may also be considered an art. Even though the artist must have some knowledge of scientific matters—hues, durability of materials, and so forth—he differs from the scientist in the pursuit of his inquiry: He is free to employ imagination, to allow for considerable selectivity of factors, and to employ his intuitive powers. As Henry Steele Commager notes,

> History must rest on statistics, embrace details, exploit drama, but it should control all of these ingredients as an artist controls the ingredients of his materials and elements of his subject—control them, master them, penetrate them with meaning and suffuse them with imagination.[22]

To classify history as an art does not mean that it can neglect accuracy of presentation. If this were true, history might be defined merely as a branch of mythology. Reacting to the kind of history which had been written with "a laxity in representing facts," [23] Bury roundly rejected the notion that history is an art, declaring that accuracy in historical writing did not come of age until the era of science had begun. Certainly, Bury's condemnation of inaccuracies is laudable, though his announcement that history is only a science is a better clue to the age in which he lived than it is to a realistic definition of history. In spite of his adamant statement, however, Bury did not write his own histories as science: They contain something of the qualities of art, as all good history must.

History may be viewed as an art to the extent that it is a written reproduction of the past. Written in narrative form, it is an art in the same sense that good literature is an art. History, as Sir Lewis Namier notes, is more like a painting than it is a photograph of the past.[24] Since the past has already occurred, it cannot be recaptured exactly as it happened, or even if it were totally recaptured, as in a photograph, we would

[22] Commager, *The Nature and the Study of History*, p. 8.
[23] Bury, "The Science of History," p. 7.
[24] Lewis B. Namier, *Avenues of History* (London: Hamish Hamilton, 1952), p. 8.

not know it because we have no way of determining that it is an exact and precise picture. The historian, then, must paint a picture of the past, but he does so with the goal in mind of painting it as accurately as possible, and so he differs from a mythographer who does not attempt to recollect his picture on the basis of carefully scrutinized evidence. Naturally, one historian's painting may differ in varying degrees from those of others because paintings of the past represent a collage of events and impressions shaped into some kind of pattern or meaning, i.e., into some kind of interpretation. This is true because facts have no meaning of their own, and the painting represents the individual historian's own perception of reality. Hence, some historical paintings are quite similar one to another, while others vary appreciably. Of course, we must not stop here, for still another historical painter, living in yet another age, may have a perspective which will allow him to synthesize the previous pictures into a more comprehensive and still more realistic one.

Good history is shaped with all the care and craftsmanship shown by the poet, the novelist, the essayist, the dramatist: It contains all of the richness and color of any literary work. And as with any work of art, history which is drab, prosaic, and devoid of aesthetic value often merits the little attention it is likely to receive.

So we may say that history is both art and science. And perhaps it is something else too. Since it is concerned with man and his relationships to his fellow man and consequently to human beings of the past who have in one sense or another made him what he is today, history may qualify as one of the humanities as well. History links us inexorably to the men and women of the past—to their art, literature, and thoughts, to the immeasurable collective experience of mankind. Without disparaging the value of the natural and the social sciences, we can state unreservedly that those branches of human knowledge cannot sufficiently satisfy all of man's needs. Eschewing the mystical, we must recognize that man does possess a spiritual side to his nature. Man is immediately conscious of himself and of his fellow countrymen, but without history his perspective is limited. History makes us aware of life and its aesthetic qualities, of our heritage, of our bond with all men in every culture and in every time—in short, of the human-ness of man. Emptied of this broadened outlook, shorn of history, man *qua* man would revert to a barbarism of the spirit. History alone will not prevent parochialism of this sort, but it is a necessary requisite to a broadened perspective of our common bonds with other men. Because its subject is mankind, history is universal.

TYPES OF HISTORY

History has many faces, and happily it is always willing to allow us to view its varying countenances, to see something other than its unrelieved mask of narration. Let us, then, examine the many faces of Clio, muse of history.

History may be categorized as primarily narrative or analytical. We must exercise caution on this point, however, for the former is never completely devoid of the latter, and rarely is complete analysis possible without some description. Both categories are in keeping with our previous discussion of the nature of history, but not all historians agree on the value of each type of history. Page Smith, for example, contends that

> Great history, the history that has commanded men's minds and hearts, has always been narrative history, history with a story to tell that illuminates the truth of the human situation, that lifts spirits and projects new potentialities. The detailed, analytical history that is the standard product of our academies has little to say to the ordinary man.[25]

While Smith's argument contains an element of truth, it is somewhat exaggerated. Smith assumes that history can be easily dichotomized and, further, that one type is more useful than the other. Both types are in fact essential to the fulfillment of the role of history, though certainly we must concede Smith's point that analytical history rarely captures the attention of the "layman." This weakness, however, may stem more from poor craftsmanship in the writing of analytical history than from the alleged power of narrative history.

Now, taking as our base that history is primarily either

[25] Page Smith, *The Historian and History* (New York: Alfred A. Knopf, 1964), p. 142.

narrative or analytical, we may classify it in other ways as well. Bearing in mind that the various types of history are not mutually exclusive, history may be written as accounts (narratives) or studies (analyses) of periods of time, topics, ideas and institutions, nations and regions, problems or issues, and the role of influential individuals in history (biographies). Each of these types may serve as the organizing structure of a historical work. Each type is useful, however, *only* as a means of organizing history, since to allow them all in a single work of history is both untenable and humanly impossible.

One of the most common ways of organizing historical accounts is periodization. College history courses and textbooks, for example, are frequently organized by time periods —"Nineteenth Century Europe," "An Economic History of the United States, 1900 to the Present," "The Russian Revolution and the Rise of Stalin, 1881–1927," "Problems in Diplomatic History, 1776–1898," and so on. Obviously, periodization is inextricably intertwined with other types, that is, national history (United States, Russian), ideas (Social Darwinism, the Renaissance), influential individuals (Bismarck, Stalin), topics (economics), and issues (problems of diplomatic history). This is unavoidable, of course, inasmuch as *time* is a distinguishing characteristic of history. The point is, periodization is a matter of convenience; it is of necessity arbitrary. The historian must work with his materials in manageable chunks. Thus, even though each of these periods contains certain characteristics, none is to be taken as absolutely fixed with specific dates for both beginning and end. The "Age of Reason," then, is merely a label, and to separate it entirely from its roots and to suggest that it ended precisely in a given year is to violate the notion of historical continuity. Certainly it may be set off by dates and studied as a period of change, but it did not exist independently of events prior to 1650, nor did it stop abruptly in the year 1800.

Topics likewise provide a basis of organization.[26] Hence, historians have written *The Economic Development of Western Civilization, A Diplomatic History of the American People,*

---

[26] Topics are here distinguished from ideas and institutions on a somewhat arbitrary basis, since in reality there is no thoroughgoing distinction. For purposes of discussion we have taken topics in a broad sense (e.g., economics, diplomacy, religion) and ideas and institutions in a more restricted sense (e.g., freedom, Darwinism, materialism).

The City in History, and so forth. The primary advantage of topical history is that it affords a way of looking at the impact and development of particular aspects of culture and politics over a period of time. Again, this is a manageable division of history and one which permits the historian to specialize in a limited area of study. Through such studies as these, history can show another of its faces. It is only *one* face, however, and to designate a specific topic as *the* way to view history is to impute validity to only one aspect of history's features.

The history of ideas has come into its own in recent years. This is greatly encouraging, for history is shaped as much by the thoughts and loyalties which compel men to action as by man's overt actions themselves. Crane Brinton has demonstrated the significance of ideas in his *Ideas and Men: The Story of Western Thought* and also in his *A History of Western Morals.* On a more popular level Herbert Muller has traced the development of the concept of freedom in his trilogy, *Freedom in the Ancient World, Freedom in the Western World,* and *Freedom in the Modern World.* And Richard Hofstadter has treated significant ideas in his *Social Darwinism in American Thought* and his *Anti-Intellectualism in American Life.* Needless to say, this kind of history requires special insights on the part of the historian. One of his particular problems is that of capturing the spirit of the time about which he is writing. Moreover, he must also relate ideas to the larger context of history. How, for example, did liberalism develop as a nineteenth century ideology, and how did it relate to religion, politics, and economics? Particularly difficult in this respect is the problem of understanding the effect of ideas on the common man, primarily because records are often scarce for other than literate people. Who, for example, wrote on the subject of liberalism? Was it not the John Stuart Mills rather than the factory workers or the farmers? And, finally, the historian must exercise caution in ascribing a single idea to a given culture at a given time. To do so is to stereotype a culture and to ignore the fact that in most groups conflicting ideas exist among the various subgroups.

Rarely has the historian attempted to write a universal history. Few men have been bold enough to attempt such an undertaking. On the popular level Will Durant and his wife Ariel have achieved a near likeness in their ten-volume work, *The Story of Civilization,* and the scholar Arnold J. Toynbee has written a multivolume account titled *A Study of History*, to cite only two examples of efforts to compress the whole of man's history into a unified treatment. Historians by and large, however, deem it unwise to take on such a demanding task. Instead they elect to study a nation, region, or at best some larger cultural entity such as Western Europe. Thus we have the histories of England, France, Germany, the United States, Europe, Latin America, and the Far East—though more frequently even these are restricted to limited periods of time. National histories are indeed quite useful and necessary—useful because they provide an in-depth study of a particular cultural entity and necessary because they provide a base for both societal and individual identity. This is the kind of history taught most commonly in the schools of our country and indeed in most, if not all, other countries. Aside from its merits, however, it often contains seeds of a dangerously narrow provincialism, especially when one nation is treated in isolation from other countries and cross-cultural influences and more especially when it is bent with the overweening bias of nationalism. This is not to suggest that we can—or for that matter, *should*—completely avoid giving some attention to an ethnocentric point of view. Instead, it is intended to point up the hazards of national chauvinism, which in its most blatant forms is antithetical to the spirit of genuine historical inquiry. In chapter 3 we will explore in greater detail the matter of national bias in historical writing.

Another type of history focuses upon interpretations of controversial issues or problems. Typically these "problems" or "issues" include questions of causation and impact or influence. There are, for example, conflicting interpretations of the role of the frontier in American life and of the question of guilt for World War I; and debates continue over older questions, such as the reasons for the decline of the Roman Empire and whether Martin Luther was a reformer or a revolutionary. These issues, which excite the attention of a number of historians, are important because they often involve questions which have some meaning for us. Thus, this type of history promotes critical inquiry and leads to further analysis of historical materials.

Finally, history has a face we often call biography, the study of the lives of significant men and women in history. Biography qualifies as history, however, only insofar as men are not isolated from the greater context of historical events: When the subjects are treated more or less in isolation, it does not represent a type of history—that is, at least, as we have defined it. Some examples of biographical writing which qualify as history include R. R. Palmer's *Twelve Who Ruled*, Alan Bullock's *Hitler: A Study in Tyranny*, and David Donald's volumes on Charles Sumner. Biography as history must not be taken to imply, however, that Thomas Carlyle was correct in stating that history is principally the story of "Great Men." [27] Certainly so-called great men have influenced the course of events, but, as we have previously noted, to ascribe historical happenings to any *one* factor is to embrace an untenable position of determinism—and this is no less true of the "great man" theory than of any other monistic interpretation.

HISTORY AND MYTH

In previous instances we have referred to the similarities and differences between history and myth. Our comparisons, however, were fairly general and incomplete. Thus, because history and myth are often intertwined, we should examine the two more fully.

For the purpose of discussion we shall define myth as "a large, controlling image that gives philosophical meaning to the facts of ordinary life; that is, which has organizing value for experience. A mythology is a more or less articulated body of such images, a pantheon." [28] Thus defined, a myth is a mental construct, and it may include an image of such stories as the creation of the world and of man, an image of man's (or a people's) relationship to the cosmos, or an image of life-binding symbols. These images have the power to motivate, to explain the unknown, and otherwise to give meaning to individuals and to societies and nations. Joined together, they constitute a mythology.

In virtually every instance these images are tied to a memory of the past, whether by direct or vicarious experience. Such memory of the past differs from history, however,

[27] Thomas Carlyle, *On Heroes, Hero-Worship, and the Heroic in History* (New York: D. Appleton & Co., 1852), *passim.*
[28] Mark Schorer, *William Blake* (New York: Henry Holt and Co., 1946), p. 27.

because it remains unexamined, uncriticized, and closed to probing inquiry. Nonetheless, the image or the memory is valid for its subscriber; hence, it is not a "myth" but truth to him: It becomes myth, that is, a fable, only after he has ceased to accept it.

Man as an animal of extensive memory must have some knowledge of the past. How accurate, how rigorously examined that knowledge is will depend upon the individual, of course. That anyone can ever attain perfection in this regard is unlikely, since every man must surely construct images for certain matters which are either unknown or unexplained. And perhaps each of us must engage in both "mythical thinking" and "critical thinking," to borrow a distinction from Peter Gay. But, while we must admit of the necessity—or perhaps at least the persistence—of the former, we cannot promote the value of history unless we "regard critical thinking as essentially superior to mythical thinking." [29]

The validity of a myth generally can be neither proven nor disproven in any empirical sense because it is a personal, a private image. History, on the other hand, must stand the test of scrutiny: "It is public, self-corrective, never complete, and in this sense, scientific." [30] A myth is purely subjective and esoteric; thus the "evidence" upon which it is based is assumed to be unquestionable. History, though partially subjective because of the nature of the human mind and of historical facts, attempts to be objective and public, and its evidence must be corroborative in an empirical sense. The evidence for myths is received or revealed, while that for history must always be confirmed in human records and remains.

The problem which is presented to us by this distinction, of course, is that the human mind is involved in the process of locating, sorting, and analyzing historical evidence. And because it is, historical interpretations are not purely objective and detached. Thus a shadow of mythic influence is ever-present in even the most rigorous analysis of man's past. The best we can do, perhaps, is to recognize the problem and constantly strive to attain the goal of seeing the past as it actually was.

[29] Peter Gay, A Loss of Mastery: Puritan Historians in Colonial America (New York: Random House, 1968), p. 121.
[30] Gay, A Loss of Mastery, p. 121.

As several historians have noted, the problem of distinguishing critical thinking from mythic thinking about the past has been peculiarly difficult in the United States. One reason for this unusual circumstance is simply that this nation has had a relatively short life. "Other nations," argues C. Vann Woodward, "were born with the heritage of a long and misty prehistoric past that served as a limitless source of myth and legend." Thus, Woodward continues,

> Myth-hungry and legend-starved, the Americans set about peopling their wilderness with folk-gods constructed from their own history. The tall tales and credulous minds of the American frontier were fruitful sources of myth. . . . Political hagiography preceded political biography in America, and the two were sometimes confused.[31]

Many American historians of the nineteenth century obliged this quest for roots in the past. It is not as though these historians deliberately constructed a mythology of the American past. They sought to reconstruct our past as accurately as possible, but they were products of their own age. Hopefully, however, we have moved closer to the goal of critical thinking about our past, though we have by no means perfected the distinction between historic thinking and mythic thinking. The two remain intertwined, but the maze is at least less confused now than in a former age.

In the so-called Third World today, however, the problem of mythic thinking in reconstructing the past is still acute. As David Gordon notes, the newly independent countries of Africa and the Middle East are passing through "a sort of adolescence" in their historical conception:

> The use and misuse of historical heroes and incidents as symbols, and of unifying myths to combat the colonizer's historiographical pretensions and the myths of rivals, as well as to "reanimate" a people to a sense of its historical value through such media as historical textbooks, have produced much historical reconstruction that is fanciful and extravagant.[32]

[31] C. Vann Woodward, *American Attitudes Toward History* (London: Oxford University Press, 1955), p. 5.
[32] David C. Gordon, *Self-Determination and History in the Third World* (Princeton: Princeton University Press, 1971), pp. 128–29.

This stage, which resembles that of our own country in the nineteenth century, is probably unavoidable. As these people search for the roots of their own past and seek to rid themselves of colonial influence, they tend to be less critical in their historical research. Their search for their own identity is centered upon the glories of the past, and only time and an increased sense of self-worth will allow their historians to apply the canons of critical inquiry. Only in the future will they become capable of transcending mythic notions of their past and be able to examine it critically while preserving the necessary symbols of their heritage. It will hopefully become a kind of inquiry which joins in the endeavor to see the universal qualities of humanity and thus become *history*.

CHAPTER 2

Historical Evidence

The historian employs the scientific method in his inquiries into the past. This method requires that he proceed through a series of steps. First, he perceives a problem, which may take the form of something unknown about the past, or an incomplete or unsatisfactory (at least to him) explanation of a historical event, or an interpretation which has now come into question. The problem usually grows out of his reading and probing into various sources. Then, after further reading and reflection, he formulates a hypothesis or a *tentative* answer to the problem. Next, he collects facts and data to test his hypothesis, after which he analyzes and interprets those facts and data. Modifying his hypothesis in accordance with the direction in which the facts lead, the historian finally draws conclusions or generalizations from his findings. This is, of course, an idealized or theoretical model, and it is certainly overly simplified. In actual practice the historian employs certain mental processes which permit him to move back and forth among these steps, and typically he works without conscious attention to the particular steps. The general pattern is the same, however, for every historian. To forego it would be to write history in the less critical, nonscientific style of Herodotus, and not after the more careful, rigorous manner of Thucydides. Undergirding the entire process of historical research is the historian's willingness to abide by the rules of internal criticism, to be intellectually honest, and to seek the truth.

In the day-by-day application of the scientific method, the historian confronts numerous problems which require his careful reflection. If we are to fathom some of the difficulties encountered in application of the historian's method, we must examine some of those problems.

FACTS AND INFERENCE

History does not exist apart from facts: They constitute the basic substance from which the historian constructs his work. Unfortunately, however, facts about the past are not building blocks, neatly stacked and ready to be cemented into place. Perhaps they are more like clay than bricks: They are substantive, to be sure; but they have not been hardened in the kiln of certitude.

What is a historical fact? An answer to this question may seem simple enough; a fact about the past is an event which actually happened, anything which is true or real. This common definition is a necessary starting point, but it is not entirely sufficient—it is only a partial answer to our question.

Perhaps we can illustrate our point through examples. We accept as a fact that Alexander the Great was wounded in the chest by an arrow while storming the Malli fortress in the year 326 B.C. We also accept as a fact that a rifle will fire a bullet which can wound or kill a man. But it is evident that the nature of these two facts is different. They differ specifically in the character of their "provability." Can we *prove* that Alexander was wounded, and can we *prove* that a rifle will fire a bullet which will wound or kill a man?

In the latter case the fact is generalizable: A bullet fired from a rifle *can* wound or kill any human being today, as it could yesterday and as it can tomorrow. We do not require a demonstration of its lethal effect because knowledge of the fact is common and widespread. Daily police reports affirm the fact. In the instance of the wounding of Alexander the Great, however, we are dealing with a particular fact: It happened in the past to a particular individual and in a particular situation. Unlike the fact about the rifle, the fact about Alexander the

Great deals with a unique event, and it cannot be repeated. Knowledge of the wounding of Alexander, moreover, is based not on repeated daily reports of the same instance but upon the statement of one man who recorded it more than 2300 years ago. Thus the problem of proof is one of determining the accuracy and truth of the report of the recording agent. As contrasted with the daily police reports, do we know if the report was made soon after the storming of the Malli fortress? Was the report written by someone who was actually a witness? Was it recorded by someone who was willing to tell the truth? All of the questions lead us into the nature of historical evidence, about which we will say more later.

In one sense there are no facts in history. Instead there are only vestiges or traces of the past. Historians may say that a civilization once existed on the island of Crete, but such a "fact" is actually inferred from certain tangible traces. For example, archeologists have uncovered the remains of the palace at Knossos. A magnificent structure of brick and limestone with great columns supporting its roof, the Knossos palace is tangible, visible evidence of an early civilization. It is not itself, however, a fact, but merely a vestige from which we build many facts. What facts we have of Cretan social and religious life are inferred from both the marvelously detailed and well-preserved frescoes on the palace walls and from the clay tablets found on the island. Thus, we my infer that these people conducted ceremonial bullfights; their women wore attractive dresses and coiffured their hair; they constructed a sanitation system; and so on—all based on the traces which remain for our observation even to this day. We face greater difficulty, however, in determining when that unusually well-advanced civilization flourished, and we must be content to accept from inferential constructions that the Cretan civilization reached its highest point *circa* 1750 to 1500 B.C.

Historical facts, then, are a little less solid than many people ordinarily suppose. We may take this problem a step further by suggesting that historical facts are also to an extent subjective in nature: Because "they exist in the mind of the historian, they change their character with each historian." [1] Idealist historians, represented by the Italian Benedetto Croce

[1] Henry Steele Commager, *The Nature and the Study of History* (Columbus, O.: Charles E. Merrill Books, 1965), p. 48.

and his English disciple R. G. Collingwood, argued that historical events are merely products of the human mind. Perhaps this was an extreme position, but we must at least recognize that a certain amount of subjectivity pervades the so-called facts of history. For instance, we may ask, "What are the *facts* of the Reformation?" A German historian may come forth with certain facts about the Reformation, an Italian historian may submit other facts, and an American historian may proffer still others. A Lutheran historian may speak of the facts of the *Reformation*, and a Catholic historian may muster facts on the *Protestant Revolt*. We are, of course, merely demonstrating here some corollary aspects of the problems of writing history—namely, frame of reference, selection, and bias—and we shall have to discuss these more fully later. Suffice it to say, however, that historical facts "do not exist for any historian until he creates them, and into every fact that he creates some part of his individual experience must enter." [2]

Establishing dates often presents a difficult problem for historians. This is particularly true in the case of ancient history because the records are often indefinite with respect to dates.[3] How does the historian establish the fact that such and such an event occurred in a given year? For example, that Jesus was not born in the year 1 A.D. is rather common knowledge. Probably he was born in either 4 or 6 B.C. For convenience we might simply add the two dates, get the average, and state that Jesus was born in 5 B.C. and be done with it. Unhappily, no such statistical manipulation can be justified. The historian must study the evidence, the traces, the vestiges, and decide which of the two dates is accurate—but this does not exclude the necessity for engaging in some logical, or even intuitive, hypothesizing. Fortunately, whether Jesus was born in 4 or 6 B.C. makes no great difference, though precision becomes much more crucial, even to the point of days and hours, in more recent history, as in the case of determining the facts of mobilization of armies, invasions, and

---

[2] Carl L. Becker, "Detachment and the Writing of History," in *Detachment and the Writing of History: Essays and Letters of Carl L. Becker*, ed. Phil L. Snyder (Ithaca: Cornell University Press, 1958), p. 12.
[3] The problem does not disappear in recent history. For example, in his account of *The Last Days of Hitler*, Hugh Trevor-Roper illustrates some of the difficulties he encountered in establishing the dates and chronology of the final events which transpired in Hitler's underground bunker.

declarations of war at the outset of World War I. Surely enough, the events occurred at a specific time, but the fact of their occurrence can at best be only approximated in the mind of the historian.

Even more difficult than establishing the ordinary facts of history, such as dates, is the problem of ascertaining motives. We cannot lightly dismiss the place of motivation in the lives and activities of historically important men and women, no matter how hard we may try to write it off as an impossible task. To be sure, the nature of the facts of motivation must remain inferential, and they must be based on demonstrable evidence. An illustration of this problem has been given by Erik H. Erikson in his brilliant psychoanalytical study of Martin Luther:

> Judging from an undisputed series of extreme mental states which attacked Luther throughout his life, leading to weeping, sweating, and fainting, the fit in the choir could well have happened in the specific form reported, under the specific conditions of Martin's monastery years. If some of it is legend, so be it; the making of legend is as much part of the scholarly rewriting of history as it is part of the original facts used in the work of scholars. We are thus obliged to accept half-legend as half-history, provided only that a reported episode does not contradict other well-established facts; persists in having a ring of truth; and yields a meaning consistent with psychological theory.[4]

Here we have certain demonstrable facts, such as Luther's "weeping, sweating, and fainting," but they are meaningless without inference. To the psychoanalyst they suggest a particular pathology, though to the theologian they may suggest not a mere human state but divine direction. At any rate, we are faced again with the problem of facts.

In a court of law eyewitnesses sometimes offer conflicting testimony. Both judges and lawyers have been confronted with this problem a sufficient number of times to know that conflicting testimony of eyewitnesses does not necessarily mean that one or the other is lying. The plain truth of the

[4] Erik H. Erikson, *Young Man Luther* (New York: W. W. Norton & Co., 1958), p. 37.

matter is that all of us do not see events and objects in the same way. We perceive matters differently according to our frames of reference, our bias, our predilections, or even the position from which we view an object or event.

Whenever we consider the subject of perception, we are forced to accept the fact that it is the human mind which tells us what we have seen or witnessed. And as the biologist Agnes Arber reminds us, "we see *through* the eyes, rather than *with* them," and "the mind . . . has the power, not only of modifying but of rejecting the data offered to it." [5] Three brief examples will help to reinforce this point. The first is typical of several psychological experiments on perception, and it deals with three photographs. In the first picture three potted plants dominate the foreground, and a table is seen in the distant background. Thus, it appears to one that he is looking into the window of a room with the potted plants on the window ledge. Next, a close-up photograph of the table makes it appear to be of ordinary size. In the third picture, however, the head of a woman has been photographed over the table. After a brief start, one is made aware that the table is a miniature and that it appeared to be large only because of the perspective of the camera lens. Perceived as it was in the first two pictures, the table is made in our eyes to be something other than it really is.[6]

A second example is taken from an account of a naval battle in World War II. The noted American historian and naval officer Samuel Eliot Morison reports that after a Japanese-American sea battle he and other men on his ship witnessed what they believed to be three Japanese ships burning and sinking. Accordingly, the commanding officer reported that three Japanese ships had been destroyed. Not until the end of the war did Admiral Morison learn the facts, however. From Japanese records he discovered that only two ships were ablaze and that one of them had actually broken into two parts and sunk. The other ship, though on fire and heavily damaged, managed to limp back to its base. Thus the observers had seen "three burning and sinking ships" silhou-

[5] Agnes Arber, *The Mind and the Eye* (Cambridge: Cambridge University Press, 1954), p. 116.
[6] E. H. Gombrich, "The Evidence of Images," in *Interpretation: Theory and Practice*, ed. Charles S. Singleton (Baltimore: The Johns Hopkins Press, 1969), pp. 41–42.

27

etted against the night sky.[7] The eye and the mind had recorded that impression as fact.

A staged experiment serves as our final example. Over a half century ago a fictitious event was carried out in the presence of a gathering of scholars in a large meeting hall. The spectators had no knowledge that the incident had been carefully planned in advance. In the city where the group was gathered, a masquerade ball was taking place. "Suddenly the door of the hall opened and a clown rushed madly in, pursued by a negro with a revolver in his hand. They stopped in the middle of the hall, reviled one another; the clown fell, the negro leaped upon him, fired, and then suddenly both ran out of the room. The whole affair had lasted barely twenty seconds." After the incident the members present were requested to write out an account of it for a report to investigating authorities. Of the forty reports submitted, only one contained fewer than 20 percent of errors, and twenty-five contained more than 40 percent of errors. In more than one-half of the reports, some details were fabricated.[8] Quite obviously people encounter difficulty in reconstructing accurately the facts about past events; our perceptions, then, may be "true" to us but not necessarily true to reality.

The human mind is likewise capable of accepting facts of a supernatural nature. We have on record numerous accounts of individuals who report that they have actually *seen* a supernatural or miraculous occurrence. Moreover, these people offer as proof of the event the testimony of an independent witness, that is, someone else who saw the same thing without benefit of prior prompting from the original observers. It would seem, therefore, that the test of independent observation has been met, for, after all, the historian often corroborates his facts by checking the testimony of one witness against that of another. What remains to certify such evidence, however, is the question of possibility. Thus, even though independent witnesses may claim to have viewed the appearance of an angel on the field of a battle, the historian would

---

[7] Interview with Samuel Eliot Morison by William F. Suchman. Recorded as "The Faith of an Historian," A Time for Ideas Series, The Academic Recording Institute, n.d.

[8] A. van Gennep, *La Formation des Légends*, as cited in Thomas Spencer Jerome, *Aspects of the Study of Roman History* (New York: G. P. Putnam's Sons, 1962), pp. 32–33.

reject it as an actual occurrence. In other words, "The whole body of reliable human experience is against the possibility of the thing affirmed." [9] This is not to deny the validity of the belief of the witnesses but only to disallow the probability of such a supernatural phenomenon.

The problem with historical facts does not end here, however. Given all the foregoing limitations, historians are beset also with a "paradox." As Commager notes: "There are too few facts, and there are too many." [10] The historian of the ancient Near East, for example, is confronted with a paucity of facts about the Sumerians, and his work is largely restricted to relatively few cuneiform tablets and artifacts. The historian who writes of early Central American Indians is likewise faced with a dearth of evidence, at least with respect to some segments of Indian life. He must sometimes depend on the accounts given by early Spanish explorers, which naturally carry their own built-in limitations. Other historians are likewise faced with the problem of too few facts, as in the case of facts about the nonliterate classes of society. Until fairly recent times we have had very little knowledge of the ordinary man. Robert S. Lopez, a medieval historian, reminds us that

> It is always difficult for a historian to know what is going on beneath the upper strata of society and outside urban centres; for peasants are a slow, silent people. The furrow their plow drives deep and unregarded through the countryside alters it noticeably only in the course of centuries. The few writers of the barbarian age are not concerned with everyday life. The most they do is to tell us sometimes of the sudden calamities which transform the monotonous misery of the nameless masses into despair.[11]

Even in our own time the historian of recent events is often troubled by the scantiness of facts. The assassination of President John F. Kennedy is a case in point. On the one hand the amount of evidence related to the assassination is huge, but on the other hand the absence of certain facts about the

[9] Fred Morrow Fling, *The Writing of History* (New Haven: Yale University Press, 1920), p. 105.
[10] Commager, *The Nature and the Study of History*, p. 48.
[11] Robert S. Lopez, *The Birth of Europe* (New York: M. Evans and Co., 1967), p. 51.

event prevents us from stating flatly that we have solved the mystery. The investigating authorities have been able to establish about as much as we may ever know about the case. Yet, some nagging questions linger, and they probably always will. Though many individuals have sought to present an airtight, convincing case, none has wholly succeeded. It is a matter of reality thus to recognize that "in many of a nation's affairs, as in many of an individual's, truth can never be known, and even the important questions cannot be settled one way or another beyond a reasonable doubt." [12] This is, as John Kaplan reminds us, "a most upsetting statement. . . . But it is a sign of maturity to recognize that even the most important of issues often cannot be resolved to a certainty." [13]

The paucity of facts will always be a problem to "explorers of the past," suggests Marc Bloch, for the past "forbids them to know anything which it has not itself . . . yielded to them." [14] In effect, then, the facts of the more remote past are largely preselected for the historian by virtue of being the only ones extant.

The other extreme is too many facts. When one considers how many facts have become available during the last century, he cannot help being overwhelmed.[15] To write the history of any significant segment of the most recent times requires a stupendous grasp of sources. Hence historians have tended to move toward specialization, and only rarely does a historian appear on the scene to undertake a universal history. This is both good and bad: On the one hand it permits the historian to do a more thorough job of research, while on the other it encourages a narrow perspective. The only solution to the problem of too many facts is selection. The historian must narrow his focus to the most significant facts, and immediately he is faced with the need to establish criteria: significant by whose standard? significant for what and for whom?

Selection in the writing of history is nevertheless unavoid-

[12] John Kaplan, "The Assassins," *Stanford Law Review*, 19 (May 1967): 1151.
[13] Kaplan, "The Assassins," p. 1151.
[14] Marc Bloch, *The Historian's Craft* (New York: Random House, 1953), p. 59.
[15] In the United States the holdings of the National Archives alone "amount to 1,895,807 cubic feet of textual records (probably over 2,000,000,000 pages of writing), 3,620,000 still pictures, 1,551,000 maps and charts, 64,900 reels of motion pictures, 34,300 sound recordings, and thousands of reels of microfilm." H. G. Jones, *The Records of a Nation* (New York: Atheneum, 1969), p. 75.

able. Thus, we must remain constantly aware that some facts have been omitted, certain ones have been emphasized, and the historian has of necessity ordered the facts into some kind of pattern. Contrary to popular opinion, the historian does not merely uncover existing facts which of themselves tell the story of history. Facts, then, are next to worthless until someone does something with them—and the job of the historian is to make them tell the truth as fully as possible.

Perhaps our discussion of historical facts has led to a pessimistic view about the writing of history. Hopefully, this has not been the case. The intention of the discussion is to promote a critical understanding of the nature of facts. History, to reiterate, could not exist without facts, but historical facts are not characterized by the certitude we often ascribe to them. They are not manna from heaven. They are human constructs, and they are to be used to further human understanding, to lead man to truth, however tentative that may prove to be in the long run. The historian bases his work upon facts, but he also recognizes the problems attached to them.

HYPOTHESIS AND THEORY

After the identification of a problem, the second step in application of the scientific method is the formulation of a hypothesis or a statement of possible relationship among the data or facts. It is, in other words, a guess or a hunch about the conclusions which will be found. The hypothesis is a starting point, and it is to be verified or refuted, depending upon the support of all available evidence.

In the natural, physical, and social sciences, the hypothesis usually plays a more crucial role in scientific investigation than it does in history. Unlike the experimental sciences, historical inquiry does not strictly lend itself to the scientific model of investigation. The historian is in most instances searching for the unique and particular case, not for the general and universally applicable principle or law.[16] The

[16] Not *all* historical inquiry deals with the unique event. For example, comparative history attempts to isolate the uniformities of certain societal and political institutions. Moreover, a growing number of historians are applying

31

"problem" for the historian is to find out what happened and why an event occurred as it did. Hence his hypothesis tends to be a "working" hunch which serves merely to get him started on his way and to guide his inquiry. He will, then, be compelled to modify his hypothesis as the evidence "leads" him. His goal, therefore, is less to verify or refute a hypothesis and more to reconstruct the past as accurately as possible.

Nevertheless, most historians begin, either consciously or unconsciously, to formulate a hypothesis in their investigations somewhere early in their encounter with the evidence. In the most basic kind of study, the researcher is simply trying to answer the question: "What happened?" But as he proceeds to answer the question of why an event occurred as it did, the historian finds it helpful to develop a working hypothesis to guide him in a coherent and systematic fashion. His hypothesis, however, is not an *a priori* judgment, for such would be no better than the opinion of any other man. Usually he "develops a guiding idea to propel him along his route, a hypothesis ahead of the facts, which steadily reminds him of what to look for." [17] The development of this guiding idea must not be taken to suggest, however, that a hypothesis, even a *working* hypothesis, is an infallible guide to the truth. As Allan Nevins has observed, the use of a hypothesis involves certain risks:

> The principal dangers in the use of hypothesis are three. The first and most frequent is the temptation to let bias, or prejudice, or what we fondly call "conviction," supply a ready hypothesis which we abstain from testing rigorously. . . . A second danger in the use of hypothesis lies in the temptation toward oversimplification. . . . The third danger is the tendency of excessively clever writers to reject the obvious hypothesis merely because it is obvious, and to present instead some explanation which will give them a reputation for independence, ingenuity, and subtlety.[18]

theoretical models from the social sciences to their investigations of the past. A good example of the latter may be found in David Hunt, *Parents and Children in History* (New York: Basic Books, 1970), in which Hunt applies certain hypotheses from psychoanalytical theory to his study of family life in seventeenth century France.

[17] Jacques Barzun and Henry F. Graff, *The Modern Researcher*, rev. ed. (New York: Harcourt, Brace & World, 1970), p. 179.

[18] Reprinted by permission of the publisher from Allan Nevins, *The Gateway to History* (Lexington, Mass.: D. C. Heath and Company, 1946), rev. ed. (Garden City, N.Y.: Doubleday, Anchor Books, 1962), pp. 242–45.

Abuse of the hypothesis leads to the production of questionable history, but careful use of it can aid in the investigation of the past.[19]

The term "theory" is often used interchangeably with hypothesis. It is not at all unusual, for example, to hear the statement, "I have a theory about that. . . ." In reality what the speaker usually means is that he has either a hypothesis or an opinion about this or that subject. Perhaps, then, it will be helpful to distinguish between theory and hypothesis. A theory is much broader and more encompassing than a hypothesis. We may think of a theory as the roof of the Pantheon, supported by the individual columns of hypotheses and generalizations which are erected on the basis of evidence. In science, theory would also be supported by general laws, but these are lacking in history. A theory, in other words, can be constructed only after many smaller investigations have been conducted. Thus, we may correctly speak of Walter Prescott Webb's hypothesis that conflict with the Plains Indians resulted from cross movements—that is, the Indians moved northward–southward while American settlers moved westward. On the other hand, we may speak of Arnold Toynbee's theory of civilization which is a broadly encompassing notion consisting of numerous hypotheses and generalizations. All in all, though, a theory of history—just as a theory of science—must always be compatible with new discoveries, or it stands in need of modification. In general, theory has not played an important role in historical research.

HISTORICAL SOURCES

During the United States presidential campaign of 1964, a book appeared under the alluring title of *None Dare Call It Treason*.[20] Purporting to purvey certain historical truths in order to show how the United States has fallen into the hands

---

[19] For an excellent discussion of the use of hypotheses in historical research, see Allen Johnson, *The Historian and Historical Evidence* (New York: Charles Scribner's Sons, 1926; reprint ed., Port Washington, N.Y.: Kennikat Press, Inc., 1965), chap. VII.

[20] John A. Stormer, *None Dare Call It Treason* (Florissant, Mo.: Liberty Bell Press, 1964).

of Communist conspirators of one sort or another, the author relied heavily on much unsubstantiated testimony from the *Congressional Record* and reports of the House Un-American Activities Committee. To the gullible soul the book presented a valid indictment simply because it was based on printed sources. Aside from the problem of the power of the printed page, however, the book presents an even more serious and subtle deception, namely, that the sources are *ipso facto* valid and reliable. One could say that the author of the book has documented his statements from sources which are open to the public. Yet many readers may be unaware of the fact that those sources are themselves questionable! Are the sources primary accounts, secondary accounts or interpretations, or even in some instances tertiary accounts? The historian cannot ignore this question, for he depends upon sources for his evidence. Sources must be viewed, therefore, with a critical eye. Thus the historian always must ask himself certain basic questions: What kind of source is this? Is it a valid source? Why was it created in the first place? And why has it been preserved?

Sources may be classified according to their proximity to actual events: primary, secondary, and tertiary. A *primary source* is, as the word implies, an original source, or the first in order of time; hence it is unquestionably the most important to the historian. Usually a primary source is coeval with particular men, events, or ideas, though in some instances it may be only nearly coeval, as with the Gospel of Mark, which was written about twenty years after the death of Jesus. A *secondary source* is based on primary sources, and it is derivative and interpretive. Edward Gibbon's *The Decline and Fall of the Roman Empire* is an example of a secondary source. Historians must, of course, depend on some secondary works, particularly those of reputable historians. Inasmuch as one man cannot know all that is known outside his own particular domain of knowledge, he simply cannot personally conduct research in primary sources on all topics. A *tertiary source,* such as most history textbooks, is one based on secondary sources.

The categories of primary and secondary are not necessarily exclusive. For example, a secondary or tertiary source may become a primary source if it is used by a later historian to determine the *Zeitgeist* or the spirit of an earlier period. Thus

Gibbon's *Decline* provides a clue to understanding the historian Gibbon and the Age of Reason in which he lived. The newspaper editorial or letters to the editor may be treated as secondary sources if they are taken as interpretations in their own right. On the other hand, they may be treated as primary sources if they are taken as representative of an era, as in the case of comments on civil rights in the United States in the 1950's and '60's. Still another instance would be the *Parallel Lives* of Plutarch, which may play a double role as either primary or secondary sources, depending on how they are put to use.

Historical sources may also be classified according to type. While handbooks on historical method vary in their classifications,[21] we may, for our purposes here, note four major types: material objects, written matter, aural and visual materials, and oral sources. *Material objects* or artifacts are of several kinds. The first of these is the large physical vestige, such as the Parthenon, a Sumerian ziggurat, a Spanish fortress in the New World, an ancient Egyptian boat, a Roman aqueduct, and a Mayan road. Often these remains not only are revealing in their own structure but may also contain certain visual and written matters, such as wall paintings, posters, and grafitti. Another kind of material object is the small physical article which contains inscriptions and visual imprints, such as an Alexandrian coin, a Greek vase, or a Persian tapestry. Another material object is the small utilitarian article, such as a Neanderthal fist axe or a medieval plow. Finally, in the category of material objects, we may add human remains, such as the skull of Peking man. Generally, material objects are the concern of archeologists and anthropologists; but sometimes they are useful to the historian, since he too is concerned with any kind of human achievement over time.

The second major category is the one most frequently exploited by the historian. *Written materials*—which may be recorded on clay tablets, papyri, paper, or other material commonly used at a given time—consist of several kinds also. Among the written materials utilized by historians are those

---

[21] See, for example, Barzun and Graff, *Modern Researcher*; Nevins, *The Gateway to History*; and Louis Gottschalk, *Understanding History*, 2nd ed. (New York: Alfred A. Knopf, 1969). See also Social Science Research Council, *The Use of Personal Documents in History, Anthropology, and Sociology* (New York: The Council, 1945), pp. 17–27.

35

which are intended primarily to be private, confidential, or at least restricted to a select audience. They include personal letters, personal notebooks and memoranda, military and diplomatic dispatches, commands and instructions, and official business papers of railroads, corporations, and so forth. Other written materials include public government documents, such as laws and regulations, treaties, proceedings and reports of official bodies, agencies, and commissions, census reports, and official messages of executives. Public reports of another variety are also useful to the historian; they include newspaper reports and dispatches, memoirs and autobiographies, and official histories. Some public reports are expressions of opinion, including editorials, letters to the editor, published speeches, pamphlets, and questionnaires and opinion polls.

Although written materials have long provided the bulk of evidence for historians, in recent years greater attention has been given to *aural and visual materials*. Among the aural materials are phonograph records and tape recordings. Moving picture films and video-tape (or, for that matter, live television programs) provide a source of visual evidence which no longer can be ignored by contemporary historians. And, of course, paintings, drawings, posters, and portraits are likewise invaluable as sources of information to the historian.

Finally, *oral sources* provide important information for the historian. The oral source is not new, as it served both Herodotus and Thucydides well in their histories. It is, however, becoming increasingly important to present-day historians. Oral sources include traditional beliefs and sayings, popular verse and song, and folklore, myths, and legends. They may also include true accounts which are passed on by word of mouth in the absence of a written language. Because these sources are unrecorded, however, they often prove difficult to work with. Until recent years they were handled mostly by cultural anthropologists and sociologists, but a number of historians are now busily engaged in the writing of history based on oral sources.[22]

In addition to these rather standard sources, another type

[22] See, for example, the numerous publications of Jan Vansina, such as *Kingdoms of the Savanna* (Madison: University of Wisconsin Press, 1966); Raymond K. Kent's publications on Madagascar; and W. Lynwood Montell, *The Saga of Coe Ridge: A Study in Oral History* (Knoxville: The University of Tennessee Press, 1970).

is developing. Historians have long sought to know the public opinion of people during a given era. Because the standard sources, including newspaper editorials, do not often reflect popular ideas, beliefs, and images, it is difficult to establish the viewpoints of the "ordinary man." In some instances oral sources (interviews with older people) provide a clue, and the public opinion polls of Gallup, Roper, and others are also useful. Both of these sources are limited, however, and some historians have begun to look elsewhere to determine "popular images." Melvin Small suggests that the historian can look for *sources of images* in such publications as schoolbooks, pulp fiction, comic books, fan magazines, novels, popular books on diplomacy and world politics, travel guides, and popular magazines, plays, and songs.[23]

After the historian has identified the sources which provide evidence on his topic, he then must raise questions regarding their validity. Essentially, he asks two major questions about each source: (1) Is the source authentic? (2) Is it reliable? Since a history is no better than the evidence on which it is based, these two questions must be answered satisfactorily before the historian begins to reconstruct and interpret the event which is the focus of his investigation.

The question of authenticity is answered by applying external tests to the source. What the historian wants to know is whether a document is the genuine production of its reputed originator; in other words, he must establish that it is not an altered imitation or forgery. To establish its authenticity, the historian seeks to determine who actually authored the document and when it was written. Thus, two types of external verification may be sought: (1) the nature of its physical characteristics and (2) an analysis of its contents.

In the first test the characteristics of the paper (or other material) can be chemically analyzed to verify that its weight, color, watermarks, and gloss conform to the type of material on which documents of the period in question were produced. Likewise ink and typing marks can be subjected to highly technical tests to aid in checking against forgery. In the second test the content of the document can be analyzed to detect

[23] Melvin Small, "Historians Look at Public Opinion," in *Public Opinion and Historians*, ed. M. Small (Detroit: Wayne State University Press, 1970), pp. 13–32.

anachronisms. One of the commonest mistakes of the forger is to employ language and words which do not belong to the time of the document. Moreover, the forged document is likely to betray itself in the same regard by revealing impressions which are not in harmony with the spirit of the culture from which it is reputed to have come. And if the document is in script (as opposed to type or print), it may in some cases be checked against other samples of the handwriting of the individual who is supposed to be its author, or it may be compared with samples of the writing characteristic of a given age.

Actually the problem of determining authenticity of sources is no longer as troublesome as it once was, since so much work has been performed by early historians and now by librarians, archivists, and compilers of papers and documents. Though forgery of documents does undoubtedly occur from time to time, the modern-day historian does not have to spend as much time applying the so-called "external" tests as his nineteenth century counterpart did.[24]

Once the authenticity of a source has been established, the historian must raise a second question, namely, "How reliable is the source?" In other words, the historian seeks to determine how much faith he can place in the source as an indication of truth about the event under investigation. To determine the reliability of a source, the historian must apply tests of internal criticism. Since each source has been produced by a human being, the historian attempts first to identify the author of the source. He needs to have information about two basic criteria concerning the author: (1) his ability to report accurately and (2) his willingness to report truthfully.

With respect to the first criterion, the first question is this: What was the author's proximity to the event he has reported? Certainly, it is desirable that he record from the point of view of an eyewitness, or at the very least that he provide first-hand information. And hopefully the author has reported the event soon after its occurrence rather than many years later. Mere proximity is not entirely sufficient, however. Thus the historian would also prefer to know something of the author's compe-

---

[24] The day of the forged document has not passed, however. Only recently, for example, diaries of Benito Mussolini, sold to a London newspaper, were subsequently found to be clever forgeries. See Dora Jane Hamblin, "Anyone for Fake 'Duce' Diaries?" *Life* (May 3, 1968): 73–76.

tence in observing and reporting. Did he, for example, possess any specific ability to report on a military event? Did he understand a person or a group belonging to a social class other than his own? Did he possess any special powers of observation, and did he have the ability to express himself clearly and accurately in a written account?

After satisfying these questions, the historian must then turn his attention to the willingness of the author to report truthfully. What was the author's purpose in reporting? Did he have anything at stake in issuing his report? Does he indicate a bias against any individuals or groups, or does he indicate excessive partisanship? For whom was the report intended? Was he personally involved in the event, and, if so, has he allowed this to color his report? What is his frame of reference (beliefs, educational background, cultural affiliation, and so forth)? And, finally, was the author withholding information (for such reasons as legal restrictions and fear of injury to living persons)?

The matter of perception enters the picture once again at this point. The author of a report is subject to the same problem of perception as the historian. Thus, even though he may be trying to tell the truth, he is inevitably influenced by his perceptions. The problem usually becomes more acute as the observer or reporter allows time to intervene between an event and his account of it. As an example, Otto von Bismarck was certainly in a position to know the truth about his activities in the unification of the German states. His later reflections do not indicate, however, that he always reported his role accurately. That is not to imply that he, or any writer of memoirs and autobiographies, tried intentionally to deceive, though in some instances writers undoubtedly wish to correct an earlier mistake, appear prophetic, or whatever. In many more instances the problem is more one of self-perception and poor recollection, which is naturally a common shortcoming of all men, particularly if one is writing of events which transpired four decades earlier—as was true of Bismarck.

In addition to the questions about an author of a source, the historian criticizes his source internally by checking on the logical consistency of the author's presentation and, if possible, how well it can be corroborated by other evidence. Moreover, the historian must understand the spirit of an age and the language of the time (e.g., literal and idiomatic expressions) if his inquiry into the reliability of a source is to aid him in his search for evidence. For these reasons the historian sometimes must make his case for the reliability of a source on intuitive grounds, a subject which we will examine more fully in our subsequent discussion on historical explanation.

In recent years historians, especially social and intellectual historians, have had to consider the findings of studies by social scientists. These studies may include opinion polls, questionnaire studies, and experimental research. The historian may wish to study, for example, trends in opinions of voters about certain civil rights legislation, or he may wish to study the evolution of attitudes toward race or religion. Often such studies will produce conflicting findings. How is the historian to choose among them? Or a study may not be representative of the population as a whole because of biased sampling. How, then, can the historian know? He must apply certain tests regarding sampling and statistical inference. A sampling is of little value if it is not representative; thus randomness is crucial. In other words, every person must have had an equal chance to be included in the sample; hence the historian must know if a random table was sufficient or whether some stratification of the population was a necessary prerequisite, and so on. Moreover, the size of a sample is relatively important; a too small sample would place limitations on the randomness factor. And equally important in the case of questionnaires is the number of returns; even a large, representative sample is vitiated by an inadequate number of returned questionnaires. Unhappily, far too many studies have been based on findings from a return of 50 percent of the questionnaires originally mailed. No matter that 5000 questionnaries were sent out and no matter that the sample was representative—if only 2500 of them were returned, what might have been the findings if most of them had been returned!

The first steps in moving away from myth to history came whenever men began to realize the importance of evidence in reconstructing the past. From there it was but a short step to the recognition that primary sources constitute the wellspring of true historical inquiry. Logically, then, the verification of those sources emerged as a prerequisite to using them.

CHAPTER 3

The Historian and His Work

All historical writing is shaped to a degree by the historians who produce it, and each historian is in turn shaped to a degree by his own experiences. Thus, argues E. H. Carr, "Before you study the history, study the historian," and, "Before you study the historian, study his historical and social environment." [1] Carr's admonition is another way of saying that the historian, however well trained in research techniques and however skillful in presenting the story as nearly like objective truth as possible, is a human being, a product of his society, an individual with his own unique experiences. That no two individuals are exactly alike is a fact of human nature. Each individual historian likewise is different from every other historian. Granted individual differences, how much greater are the differences of historians from one society or culture to another! Hence, some penetration into the individual and the societal make-up of the historian is a necessary prerequisite to understanding history. We should examine, then, some of the facets of the historian's mental, emotional, and psychological make-up as they impinge upon the production of his work.

[1] Edward Hallett Carr, *What Is History?* (New York: Alfred A. Knopf, 1964), p. 54.

THE HISTORIAN'S FRAME OF REFERENCE

As we noted earlier, historical facts have no meaning until someone gives them meaning. The historian selects and arranges them in some kind of pattern, he interprets them, and he draws generalizations from them. All of these actions require him to order knowledge, and this ordering we shall call his frame of reference. From the moment the historian begins to investigate and study, he brings a frame of reference to bear on his work.[2]

In order to clarify the concept of frame of reference, let us examine some of its elements and how they operate upon the historian's work. We should bear in mind, however, that these elements are not mutually exclusive and that they intertwine to make each individual historian different—in greater or lesser degree—from every other historian. Probably the most basic element in the historian's frame of reference is his underlying philosophy, that is, the assumptions and beliefs which he holds about the nature of man and the universe, the sources and nature of truth, and what is good or bad, beautiful or ugly—in short, his metaphysical, epistemological, and axiological positions. "The historian," says Louis M. Gottschalk, "cannot avoid, and therefore it is better that he should be openly committed to, some philosophy and some code of ethics." [3] Men are idealists, realists, pragmatists, or existentialists; they are supernaturalists, agnostics, or atheists; they are altruists or egoists—in short, they are *something,* philosophically speaking. The historian is no exception; hence he should be guided by the principle of "know thyself" as he writes his history. And even if a historian rejects particular "schools of history," he cannot truthfully claim to subscribe to no philosophy.

Closely akin to the historian's basic views of the nature of men are his notions about authority, politics, and symbols. Again, these operate within the historian's mind as assumptions and as such do not require proof or tests of validity. The historian as an individual living in a particular society is a

[2] The term "frame of reference" was frequently employed by Charles A. Beard. See, for example, *The Discussion of Human Affairs* (New York: The Macmillan Company, 1936), p. 122.
[3] Louis Gottschalk, *Understanding History,* 2nd ed., (New York: Alfred A. Knopf, 1969), p. 10.

political animal: He believes that totalitarianism is bad and democracy is good, or vice versa; he condones representative government and condemns hereditary kingship, and so on. Likewise, the historian holds certain views regarding authority, depending on sources and statements of men in whom he is willing to place considerable trust. And symbols also play a significant role in the lives of men; they command his loyalty, and they represent a form of security to him both as an individual and as a member of a particular society. With the "power to hold together heterogeneous manifestations of the human spirit," [4] symbols contribute to the historian's frame of reference. Again, the historian may be barely conscious of the symbols to which he subscribes, for they do not loudly intrude into his work. But they are there nevertheless, and they do influence the way in which he orders historical knowledge.

The historian is never completely isolated from his larger environment. He is in a particular culture; he normally holds citizenship in a single nation; and he is part of a specific group. No matter how hard he may try, the historian can never live a completely secluded and solitary life. As a product of Western or some other culture, he has been shaped by the prevailing mores of that culture. He has learned the habits, the customs, the way of life sanctioned by the society of which he is a part. The historian cannot escape the influence of national loyalty: The Indian historian will thus have a different frame of reference from that of the English historian, at least on certain historical issues, such as the impact of British colonialism on the nation of India. Moreover, the historian is always a member of some group or groups. It may be the group known as the academic community, or it may be a religious sect or a civic organization. Naturally the historian must be constantly aware, insofar as possible, of his loyalties and preferences in order to vitiate the effects of judging and choosing on the basis of inappropriate standards; but he will always operate to a certain extent from his cultural, national, and group frames of reference.

Thus far we have been describing the collective experiences of the historian, that is, how his frame of reference is determined by his milieu. But the historian also develops his

[4] H. Stuart Hughes, *History As Art and As Science* (New York: Harper & Row, 1964), p. 80.

own unique frame of reference. He is an individual who develops his own peculiar way of ordering knowledge. And he became the way he is by his experiential background: his home, his educational training, and his interactions with other people in the most formative years of his life. Every person, for example, possesses his own special interests—in the humanities, the arts, or the sciences; in hobbies and avocational interests; in certain types of literature; and in a wide range of preferred activities. Hence, given freedom of choice, he will select whatever suits his fancy, whatever attracts his attention and curiosity. It is no different with the historian. As a general rule, he elected to pursue an academic career in history, and he selected his own area of specialization. His frame of reference, then, is in part shaped by his interests.[5]

Similarly, the historian's frame of reference must inevitably be affected by his educational training. While he may be influenced by other factors in his academic studies, the historian is always a product of the school, the courses, and the teachers with whom he had contact. One example of the impact of education on a historian's frame of reference is the case of Frederick Jackson Turner. In his "frontier thesis" Turner argues that peculiar frontier conditions in the United States contributed significantly to the formation of the national character and the spirit of Americans. An outstanding student of biology, physics, chemistry, and geography during his undergraduate years at the University of Wisconsin, Turner's educational experience led him to employ metaphors from the biological sciences in developing his concept of a social organism. Likewise, he modified the germ theory and adapted it to support his thesis.[6]

Every historian is also a product of his own time; the moment in time when he exists always differs from other points on the continuum of the ages. This statement is not to be taken as advocating linear history, but merely to remind us that time moves on unceasingly and, with it, comes change.

[5] See Arthur O. Lovejoy, "Present Standpoints and Past History," *The Journal of Philosophy*, 36 (August 31, 1939): 477–89. Reprinted in *The Philosophy of History in Our Time*, ed. Hans Myerhoff (Garden City, N.Y.: Doubleday, 1959), pp. 175–76.
[6] See the discussion on Turner's education and its impact on his thesis in William Coleman, "Science and Symbol in the Turner Frontier Hypothesis," *American Historical Review*, 72 (October 1966): 22–49.

The modern historian, for example, exists at the moment of time when atomic and hydrogen bombs pose the possibility of a greater destructive power than man has ever before discovered; when pollution threatens man's existence; when man has been able to land on the moon and probe even farther into outer space; when the world is reduced to a small community through media of instant communication and faster-than-sound travel. Naturally, his frame of reference will differ from that of his nineteenth century counterpart. Even his vocabulary is affected by terms which would have been incomprehensible to a Leopold von Ranke or a Lord Acton.

Existing as he does in his own age, the historian struggles with the twin problems of perception and perspective. He must look back and try to see events as they actually happened at another moment in time. And while he may secure a better perspective of the Reformation or of the Roman Empire than of the Cold War and the conflict in Viet Nam, the historian's present frame of reference intrudes into his mental perceptions and understandings. Certainly the historian's "vision is distorted by a vast accumulation of ideas, values, and subsequent events." [7] The problem is further compounded by the fact that the historian himself undergoes change over his lifetime which modifies his perspective and perception. What he once magnified, he may in later life reduce to insignificance, and what he once considered unimportant, he may later elevate to a role of considerable consequence. The historian therefore must himself "be understood in terms of continuity, diversity, and change through time." [8]

A relatively new dimension of the historian's frame of reference is psychological analysis of his human subjects. The historian has always sought to explain the drives and needs of the men who have been instrumental in historical events, but only within the past few decades has he attempted a more formal psychoanalytical interpretation of historical figures. Thus, working from his frame of reference as a psychoanalyst, for example, Erik H. Erikson examined the motivations and drives of Martin Luther during the early years of Luther's

[7] Page Smith, *The Historian and History* (New York: Alfred A. Knopf, 1964), p. 144.
[8] Trygve R. Tholfsen, *Historical Thinking* (New York: Harper & Row, 1967), p. 248.

45

manhood.[9] Similarly, in a study of Karl Marx's philosophy of history, the historian Bruce Mazlish examined the psychological phenomena which helped shape the boy into the man. Such a frame of reference allowed Mazlish to organize the facts about Marx's family, religious, and medical background, to study the emotionally laden terms in Marx's poems and correspondence as clues to the psychic needs of the man, and hence to understand better his philosophy and impact on history.[10] These two studies may well provide us with some new insights, but the point here is simply that a psychoanalytical frame of reference is another way in which the historian may order his knowledge of the past.[11]

Since the historian is inescapably influenced by his individual and collective experiences, it can be argued that he should attempt to analyze his own frame of reference and acknowledge the basis on which he orders his knowledge of historical facts. Some historians have done so, and here we can cite some examples. George Rudé, author of *The Crowd in History, 1730–1848* and other works on revolution, admits, for instance, to a Marxist frame of reference. Thus Rudé says that because of his reading of Marx and Engels and his sympathy with their interpretations, he subscribes to the view that "history tends to progress through a conflict of social classes . . . [and] that it has a discoverable pattern and moves forward (not backward, in circles, or in inexplicable jerks) broadly from a lower to a higher phase of development." Moreoover, Rudé acknowledges that he learned from Marx "that the lives and actions of the common people are the very stuff of history. . . ." Elaborating even further upon the contribution of Marx (and Engels) to his frame of reference, Rudé states that "With such antecedents, it is perhaps not remarkable that I should have been drawn to the study of revolutions." [12]

Another example of a historian's statement of his frame of reference can be found in Henry Allen Bulloch's *A History of Negro Education in the South.* In the preface to his book, Bulloch states that

[9] Erikson, *Young Man Luther* (New York: W. W. Norton & Co., 1958).
[10] Bruce Mazlish, *The Riddle of History* (New York: Harper & Row, 1966), pp. 230–43.
[11] The subject of psychoanalytical interpretations of history is examined more fully in chapter 6.
[12] George F. E. Rudé, "The Changing Face of the Crowd," in *The Historian's Workshop*, ed. L. P. Curtis, Jr. (New York: Alfred A. Knopf, 1970), p. 189.

During the early years of my college days at Virginia Union University, there developed within me the feeling that segregated education had some accidental purpose. The rather orthodox value system that Union imposed upon its students—not to smoke; not to play cards; not to drink; and above all, not to refer to ourselves by that vulgar term with which racists were wont to identify Negroes—was selectively internalized, but the more fundamental belief that the system inculcated was embraced in full. It was the doctrine that the Negro college was to develop the leadership for the emancipation of the Negro American as a person. I shared this faith and sought its justification in a common denominator applicable to the development of all peoples. This was not a very diligent search, some intellectual crusade, that I waged; it was only a gnawing need to preserve and foster my self-respect.[13]

Bulloch contends that "Most Negro college students felt this need," and though numerous "Negro writers were doing so much to improve the Negro's self concept . . . [t]hey supplied no rationale that would justify the faith in Negro education which had been imposed upon us. . . ." Thus Bulloch declares that he was forced to search for a rationale and that it "came through the courses that I took at Union. In my study of the history of social thought . . . I became attached to the ideas of the German Romanticists and the generalized theories of the philosophers of history. These theories . . . inclined my private hopes toward the belief that there is a divine purpose behind human society—even behind segregated education."[14] Bulloch goes on to show how his views have been modified in recent years and how he evolved a unifying theme for his work. It is sufficient here merely to emphasize that Bulloch has revealed to his readers what role his own experiences have played in the writing of his history of Negro education.

BIAS AND THE HISTORIAN

A discussion of the historian's frame of reference leads logically to a consideration of the historian's biases. Every man

[13] Henry Allen Bulloch, *A History of Negro Education in the South* (Cambridge: Harvard University Press, 1967), p. vii.
[14] Bulloch, *A History of Negro Education in the South*, p. viii.

has preferences and dislikes, and so does the historian. Our inclination to favor or to disapprove may vary in proportion to the knowledge we possess and with the degree of our genuine understanding. But bias is ever-present, even in the best of historical works. The problem of bias is not insurmountable, however, for, as Ernest Nagel suggests, "The very fact that biased thinking may be detected and its sources investigated shows that the case for objective explanations in history is not necessarily hopeless." [15] We should at least be aware of the sources of bias as they impinge upon the craft of the historian.

A common bias grows out of the individual historian's personal predilections. This is particularly true in the case of biography. Sometimes engaging in hero worship, the historian may identify so closely with his subject that he will exaggerate the man's successes and minimize his shortcomings. One of the scholars of Hellenistic civilization, W. W. Tarn, for example, has been accused of excessive partiality in his study of Alexander the Great. The same kind of bias may manifest itself at a different level, such as that of institutions, beliefs, and movements. This type of bias we may call partisanship. It is an old vice and still a potentially debilitating one. More than five hundred years ago, the great Muslim philosopher Ibn Khaldun warned that "partisanship acts as a blinker to the mind, preventing it from investigating and criticizing and inclining it to the reception and transmission of error." [16] How often we assume *parti pris* that one school, one philosophy, one institution, or one creed is better than another!

Among the forms of bias perhaps nationalism or exaggerated patriotism has no peer. It is only natural for the historian to possess a sense of loyalty and feel a strong degree of attachment to his own country. When the historian allows himself to become preoccupied by nationalist bias, however, he is in danger of substituting propaganda for truth, and this is an unforgivable violation of the canons of historical research and writing. In late nineteenth and early twentieth century history, numerous instances of the sin of excessive nationalism can be detected. Even though it has subsided somewhat, at

[15] Ernest Nagel, "Some Issues in the Logic of Historical Analysis," *The Scientific Monthly*, 74 (March 1952): 166.
[16] *An Arab Philosophy of History: Selections from the Prolegomena of Ibn Khaldun of Tunis (1332–1402)*, Vol. I, trans. Charles Issawi (London: John Murray, 1950), p. 27.

least in historical writing, nationalist bias has not disappeared altogether. We have, for example, the spectacle of intense nationalism pervading the writing of German history textbooks as late as the 1940's, and even today the problem is severe in several countries which have won independence since World War II.[17] The problem is not confined to any single nation, of course; but in the interest of the pursuit of truth, every historian must struggle to free himself from the fetters of the "Chosen People" concept.

Bias also appears in the stereotyping of certain peoples, whether of an entire nation or a smaller ethnic, racial, or religious group. One of the potentially greatest uses of history is that of demonstrating the fallacy of the concept of a superior religion, race, or culture. Yet quite frequently the historian's personal bias will reinforce a stereotype rather than destroy it. The historian must struggle against the tendency to place labels on whole groups. H. A. R. Gibb, a scholar in Arabic history, notes that some writers encounter difficulty in shaking free of their bias against the religion of the Muslims. Their "view is coloured by the belief that Islam is an inferior religion." [18] And the English historian Hugh Trevor-Roper argues that black Africa has no history: "There is only the history of the Europeans in Africa. The rest is largely darkness, like the history of pre-European, pre-Columbian America. And darkness is not a subject for history." To attempt a history of black Africa, declares Trevor-Roper, is to "amuse ourselves with the unrewarding gyrations of barbarous tribes in picturesque but irrelevant corners of the globe. . . ." [19] Closer to home, we encounter the stereotype of the abolitionist in ante-bellum United States. According to Martin Duberman, an American historian, all abolitionists are characterized by many historians as " 'impractical,' 'self-righteous,' 'fanatical,' 'humorless,' 'vituperative,' and . . . 'disturbed.' The list varies, but usually only to include adjectives equally hostile and denunciatory. The stereotype of the 'abolitionist personality,' though

[17] See, for example, E. H. Dance, *History the Betrayer: A Study in Bias* (London: Hutchinson & Co., 1960); and Gordon, *Self-Determination and History in the Third World*, pp. 83–89.
[18] H. A. R. Gibb, *Mohammedanism*, 2nd ed. (London: Oxford University Press, 1953), p. vi.
[19] Hugh Trevor-Roper, *The Rise of Christian Europe* (New York: Harcourt, Brace & World, 1965), p. 9.

fluid in details, is clear enough in its general outlines." [20] Other examples of bias could be cited, but perhaps it is sufficient here only to note that stereotyping is a form of dogmatism which precludes the concept of individualism; all persons within a group are labelled collectively. This is not to say, of course, that groups and nations do not possess certain common characteristics, but the historian must scrupulously avoid the bias of pre- and collective judgments.

These cautions against bias are not intended to suggest that the historian should abjure his preferences entirely. "For my own part," said William Stubbs, "I do not see why an honest partisan should not write an honest book if he can persuade himself to look honestly at his subject, and make allowance for his own prejudices." Furthermore, Stubbs declared, there is no reason why a historian should not state his preference for, say, Charles I over Cromwell. In thus stating his partiality, Stubbs recognized that "I should [not] shut my eyes to the false and foolish thing that my friends do, or to the noble aspirations, honesty, and good intentions of those whom I think wrong in their means and mistaken in their ends." [21] The historian does have his favorites too, but in the interest of scholarship he does not avoid his obligation to paint the most realistic picture possible.

OBJECTIVITY IN HISTORY

After our discussion of frame of reference and bias, the question now arises whether the historian can be impartial and objective in his study of the past. The answer must be a positive and a qualified one, for impartiality and objectivity are matters of degree to the historian. The physical scientist can be reasonably objective because he can manipulate and control the materials with which he works. The geologist can also be objective because he works with inanimate substances, with objects. But if either of these scientists enters the realm of values—for example, the social implications of particular

[20] Martin Duberman, The Uncompleted Past (New York: Random House, 1969), p. 6.
[21] William Stubbs, Medieval and Modern History (Oxford: The Clarendon Press, 1886), pp. 109–10.

discoveries—his degree of objectivity or impartiality may be considerably lessened. Once one enters the domain of human activities—and that is the only domain of the historian—objectivity and impartiality are harder to attain, precisely because he is a human being looking at human events. Perhaps the truth is as Eric Dardel believes: "We ourselves are in history. It is what happens to us and our reaction to events. . . . To write history is also to realize its existence, to 'historicize one's self.' " [22] While some vestiges of the nineteenth century school of historians remain with us today, by and large the belief that the historian can be completely objective and impartial has been abandoned. Historians now realize that to stand apart, to look on as though one were suspended in space looking at a part of the world of human activity, is a fallacy of the first order. The gods, if they wish, may look on mankind with detachment, but then they are supernatural, above nature, above man. The finite historian, however, has no such ability.

Even if complete objectivity and impartiality in historical writing were possible, they would not necessarily be desirable. This may be unacceptable to the analytic mind because on the surface it allows for too much subjectivity. On the other hand, as Carl L. Becker has noted, complete detachment "would produce few histories, and none worth while. . . ." [23] The historian must involve himself in his work if it is to become viable. "He must discriminate," Page Smith reminds us,[24] for he has to select and omit according to his decision of what is significant and meaningful.

To point out the undesirability of absolute detachment, however, is not to suggest either that all truth is relative or that the historian's method of inquiry is to be compromised. Relativism which leads to unwonted skepticism is what the Spanish philosopher José Ortega y Gasset so vigorously opposed.[25] We have already noted the tentativeness of truths in history, but our alternative is not to abandon all standards of judgment and moral principles. Instead we can agree with

[22] Eric Dardel, "Personal Styles and the Study of History," *Diogenes* (Spring 1958): p. 13.
[23] Becker, "Detachment and the Writing of History," in *Detachment and the Writing of History: Essays and Letters of Carl L. Becker*, ed. Phil L. Snyder (Ithaca: Cornell University Press, 1958), p. 24.
[24] Smith, *The Historian and History*, p. 229.
[25] José Ortega y Gasset, *The Modern Theme* (New York: Harper & Row, 1961), p. 29.

Herbert J. Muller that the problem "is to maintain principle and morale in the face of ultimate uncertainty, on grounds that permit both the faith and the tolerance required by the pursuit of truth and goodness. . . ."[26] Perhaps the *real* truth exists in an absolute sense, but the historian can only struggle to achieve an approximation of the truth. Maintaining a balance between total relativism and absolute finality seems a reasonable rule for the historian. Despite the impossibility and even undesirability of complete detachment, the historian must strive constantly to expunge—or at least to keep in check—those personal factors which distort and damage the evidence. The story must be, after all, as close to the truth as it is humanly possible to determine. In the words of the ancient historian Lucian, the mark of the true historian is that he is

> fearless, incorruptible, free, a friend of free expression and the truth, intent, as the comic poet says, on calling a fig a fig and a trough a trough, giving nothing to hatred or to friendship, sparing no one, showing neither pity nor shame nor obsequiousness, an impartial judge, well disposed to all men up to the point of not giving one side more than its due, in his books a stranger and a man without a country, independent, subject to no sovereign, not reckoning what this or that man will think, but stating the facts. [27]

Although one may argue that Lucian was overly idealistic, the point of Lucian's statement is clear enough: The historian must try to "tell it like it is." And this, after all, is what constitutes humanistic history.

This brings us to the point where we must consider the arguments of the New Left or radical historians concerning objectivity and detachment in historical writing. As representative of the radical historians we may consider the views of Howard Zinn and Staughton Lynd, both of whom are accomplished historians in their own right. Zinn believes that much or most historical writing is useless because historians have subscribed too rigorously to "those professional rules which call, impossibly and callously, for neutrality."[28] By embracing

---

[26] Herbert J. Muller, *The Uses of the Past* (New York: Oxford University Press, 1952), p. 43.
[27] Lucian, *Works*, VI.
[28] Howard Zinn, *The Politics of History* (Boston: Beacon Press, 1970), p. 3.

such rules, Zinn declares, the historian loses the "urgent desire for a better world"; he suppresses his passion for humanity and human suffering.[29] Objectivity has become a fetish, prompting the historian to forget the *"quality* of events" and to spread "the cool jelly of neutrality" over his account of human affairs.[30] The historian's sin is that of detachment, in Zinn's view. And to be detached is to fail to recognize the important and subjective values of human beings. The significant needs of mankind must be the starting point of historical inquiry, according to Zinn. But although this does not imply the absence of objectivity or downgrade the historian's obligation to accuracy, he should, Zinn argues, choose to search for answers to those questions which aid us in improving the lot of mankind.[31]

The radical historian also believes that the historian's obsession with detachment has blinded him to the necessity of involvement. Caught up as he is in the past, the historian cannot comprehend that what really counts is the present and the future. There is no need to apologize, Lynd argues, if the historian "concerns himself more with the present and future than with the past." [32] In fact, Lynd believes, "The historian's first duty . . . is the sensitive chronicling in depth of the important events of his own lifetime." [33] Thus at present the historian ought to be concerned over such matters as racism and human poverty, if the radical historian is right. And furthermore, his concern must be active, and his work must aid us in finding alternatives to our present situation.

In their search for a "usable past," the radical historians have raised some important questions, and they have made several significant contributions to historical knowledge. At the same time they have forced us to re-examine the question of objectivity and detachment in historical writings. What remains to be answered, however, are certain issues about their position. Does the emphasis on subjectivity, for example, result in mere polemics? In their zeal to find a usable past, have

[29] Zinn, *The Politics of History*, p. 2.
[30] Zinn, *The Politics of History*, p. 24.
[31] Zinn, *The Politics of History*, p. 10.
[32] Staughton Lynd, "The Historian as Participant," in *The Historian and the Climate of Opinion*, ed. Robert Allen Skotheim (Reading, Mass.: Addison-Wesley Publishing Company, 1969), p. 117.
[33] Lynd, "The Historian as Participant," p. 115.

53

they become "methodologically reactionary"?[34] And once again we are brought hard back to the historian's goal, namely, to explain to us as accurately as possible what happened and why it happened. If the radical historian succeeds in attaining this goal, then so much the better for us and for history.

JUDGMENT AND THE HISTORIAN

Every man has a system of values, and while value systems vary among individuals, no one can escape his feelings of what constitutes good and evil, worthiness and worthlessness. Naturally enough, we often confuse our own notions of what is good and worthy with values *per se*. But even the criminal has values; what he treasures and holds as desirable simply is not synonymous with what society at large believes to be good and worthy. As a human being, and hence as a valuing being, the historian cannot avoid the tendency to approve or disapprove of historical actions, events, and persons. Yet we must remember that his prime purpose as a historian is not to pass moral judgment.

Some moral judgments in historical writing are subtle and appear even in descriptive accounts. Certain words tend to convey moral overtones, as for example, "massacre," "treachery," "devious negotiations," and "unfortunately."[35] Although such terms are not necessarily intended to render a moral evaluation, by their very nature they are not strictly neutral in connotation. Whether they are blatant value judgments depends, of course, upon the context in which they are used. Contrary to the argument of Philip Bagby that "we first put aside all moral considerations"[36] before we try to understand the past, many historians openly admit that some moral judgments are unavoidable and perhaps even desirable. Tolerance, replies Morison, "can be overdone. The historian has

[34] David Hackett Fischer, *Historians' Fallacies* (New York: Harper & Row, 1970), p. 314.
[35] See Ann Low-Beer, "Moral Judgments in History and History Teaching," in *Studies in the Nature and Teaching of History*, ed. W. H. Burston and D. Thompson (London: Routledge & Kegan Paul, 1967), p. 141.
[36] Bagby, *Culture and History* (Berkeley: University of California Press, 1963), p. 3.

both the right and the duty to make moral judgments." [37] And, as Barbara W. Tuchman has realistically pointed out, "To take no sides in history would be as false as to take no sides in life." [38]

Is the historian justified in rendering moral judgment upon, say, the institution of slavery? Arthur M. Schlesinger, Jr., contends that he is: "[H]uman slavery is certainly one of the few issues of whose evil we can be sure . . . it is a betrayal of the basic values of our Christian and democratic tradition." [39] If Schlesinger is right, at least on the count of "Christian values," then we may raise the question: "Should the historian indict the Apostle Paul for sending the slave Onesimus back to his master with the admonition to be a *good* slave?" Is it all right to condemn the practice of slavery in one age and to condone it in another (or at least explain away the question because the occurrence is more remote from us)? Schlesinger responds by saying "this duty of judgment applies [only] to issues . . . [and not to] men of the past. . . ." [40] Thus it is the issue, the idea, the institution we are to judge rather than individual men. But if this is the case, must the historian refrain from making moral judgments about Philip II of sixteenth century Spain and Adolf Hitler in our own century? Some historians would respond negatively to that question. Sir Lewis Namier, for example, says of Hitler: "Never before had a man so malignant attained such power. . . ." [41] And of Philip II, Cecil John Cadoux says, "[he was] a cruel and intolerant bigot." [42]

The problem of moral judgment is complicated by the context of time and culture. "But," as C. V. Wedgwood observes, "to say that those who perform evil actions are less culpable at some times and in some contexts than they are in others, is not to minimize the evil of the actions themselves." [43]

[37] Samuel Eliot Morison, *Vistas of History* (New York: Alfred A. Knopf, 1964), p. 45.
[38] Barbara W. Tuchman, "The Historian's Opportunity," *Saturday Review* (February 25, 1967): p. 31. © 1967 Saturday Review, Inc.
[39] Arthur M. Schlesinger, Jr., "The Causes of the Civil War: A Note on Historical Sentimentalism," *The Partisan Review*, 16 (October 1949): 979.
[40] Schlesinger, Jr., "The Causes of the Civil War," p. 981.
[41] Quoted in Low-Beer, "Moral Judgments in History," p. 148.
[42] Cecil John Cadoux, *Philip of Spain and the Netherlands: An Essay on Moral Judgments in History* (London: Lutterworth Press, 1947), p. 120.
[43] C. V. Wedgwood, *The Sense of the Past* (New York: The Macmillan Co., 1967), p. 48.

Certain actions we find morally abhorrent, and they are truly evil, not in any theological sense but strictly by basic human standards. Probably foremost among them are murder, torture, or any form of physical, spiritual, or mental maiming. Yet at various times and in various cultures even these have been acceptable forms of behavior.

What the historian attempts to do is "to see those men of the past in their human surroundings, and he will understand that the imperfections of both are the concomitants of that human imperfection of which he and his time still have their share." [44] The historian reaches toward the goal of intellectual honesty and endeavors to divest himself insofar as possible of propensities to moral judgment. We can accept A. L. Rowse's statement that the Germans precipitated World War I, even if we do not agree, for that is a matter of interpretation; but less defensible is his judgment that the Germans are a brutal and irresponsible people.[45] Rowse, however, is not only a historian but also a human being with strong feelings. What we must distinguish is when he, or any other historian for that matter, is pronouncing moral judgment as a man and when he is providing an interpretation as a historian.

IMAGINATION IN HISTORY

Since the facts do not speak for themselves and since the historian must construct a story from the malleable substance of evidence, imagination plays a key role in the construction of history. Imagination is a process of thought engaged in by the historian as he seeks to reconstruct the story of history and to present it with literary skill. If the story already existed, there would be no history; but, precisely because the historian must reconstruct the past, imagination is essential. It is a process of re-creation—though naturally, since it deals with the past, that is, with that which has already happened, we can never be sure that the story describes the past exactly. And the problem is further complicated by the fact that history deals with feelings, ideas, cultures, and men in given moments of time. Hence the historian must get the "feel" of history.

[44] Pieter Geyl, *Encounters in History* (Cleveland: Meridian Books, 1961), p. 273.
[45] A. L. Rowse, *The Use of History*, rev. ed. (New York: The Macmillan Co., 1963), pp. 12–13.

One of the most difficult problems of imagination is that of capturing "the spirit of the time." Our moment in time is never the same as another moment in time. It would be a mistake, then, to imagine medieval man as living in our time. To do so is to commit the fallacy of present-mindedness, to see others in the spirit of *our* time and not in the spirit of *their* time. The closer the historian comes to seeing himself as the men about whom he writes saw themselves, the closer he comes to getting the feel of their time. At best, however, he can only approximate the feel of another time, since he is in the present, in his own moment of time. Because he is constantly aware of the outcomes in history, he can never fully see through the eyes of men who could not foretell what was to happen.

We must return again to the problem of historical perspective. Something can be said for the belief that increasing distance in time allows us to catch a better glimpse of the whole, the configuration of another age. At the same time, however, the further away we are from another age, from the events, the further removed we are from the spirit of the time in which those events occurred. Perhaps it is wise, therefore, to follow Smith's advice "to show more respect for the best contemporary history" [46] and pay less heed to the power of perspective. Arthur Schlesinger, Jr., in his history of the John F. Kennedy administration, probably reflected the spirit of the time, since he was both a contemporary of and an actual participant in events of the time. The danger of partiality is always present in such instances, of course; but at least the historian is in the same, or close to the same, moment of time.

The better the historian knows the men about whom he writes, the more accurately he can portray them. But what does it mean to know Thomas Jefferson or John Adams? The historian who was their contemporary could know them in a way which a later historian could not—and only rarely does the historian know his subject in a really personal sense. In English we use the word "know" in at least two different senses: "I know that . . ." or "I know how . . ." are indications of awareness or understanding in the first instance and ability or skill in the second; "I know him," however, typically indicates a personal relationship or acquaintance. In historical inquiry the historian's use of "knowing" in the first sense

[46] Smith, *The Historian and History*, p. 198.

normally implies possession of facts and knowledge ("knowing that") and skill ("knowing how"), while in the second sense it implies knowledge *about* someone, not a personal acquaintance *with* someone. This distinction becomes meaningful when we realize that the historian is limited in how close he can really get to someone in the past.

With the advantage of hindsight comes the common error of assuming that men of the past saw themselves as we now describe them. The Christian of the seventh century is often supposed to have seen himself as a member of the Roman Catholic Church and not as simply a member of the universal church of that time. Men to whom we give credit for having begun this or that are supposed to have seen themselves as *founders*. The hardy souls who trekked westward are supposed to have known that they were *pioneers*. In short, we picture them as being aware that they were living in our past, not in their present. As a consequence we sometimes condemn them for failure to foresee the outcomes of their actions and ideas; we do not properly associate them with their *Zeitgeist*, or spirit of the time in which they lived. But they did not exist and act simply to give us a history any more than we live and act to provide a history for the generations of the twenty-first century. We are in a sense historically minded, but we live in our moment of time without too much forethought given to what later historians will say about us.

What we know of men in the past is dependent on the traces which remain today. As noted earlier, however, the men and women who have left records were not the common people; they were the literate, the people in positions of power and influence of one kind or another. They were, in brief, not representative of the entire population, though certainly they may have been representative of their own class or group. The problem of knowing the ordinary man of Jacksonian America or the common citizen of Bolshevik Russia is compounded by the scant records in which those people set forth their feelings and concerns. The historian is often left to infer from the records of literate people what the ordinary man thought about himself and about those who directed the course of his actions by domestic and diplomatic decisions.

Sometimes the influential individuals of history make a greater impact after their death than during their lifetime. Such posthumous fame may or may not be entirely deserved, but the historian's responsibility is to sift fact from fiction. Always a difficult undertaking, the historian must try to view the man as he was at a particular point in history, though of course the history of the myths and legends which grew up about the man after his death is itself a legitimate area of study. But to seize the man *as he was* is complicated by what his followers or disciples would have liked for him to be. Good examples of this problem are Jesus and Martin Luther. Was Jesus in actual life the same man as the later Gospel writers pictured him? Is the Martin Luther of later Lutheran writers distinguishable from the Luther who died in 1546, the historical Luther and not the mythical Luther? The imagination of the historian is called upon to counter fiction working against fact, and again at this point the historian is different from the myth-maker or the storyteller who is not concerned with critical inquiry but with perpetuation of an idealized image of his hero.

How is the historian to capture a man in his moment of time if the man himself changes over his own lifetime—and almost invariably the politician, the poet, the philosopher of sixty is not the same man he was at age twenty! In an essay titled "The Treachery of Recollection," Daniel Aaron poignantly notes that "The living relic is his own ancestor; and feeling a deep familial piety for his defunct historical self, he indulges in ancestor worship, tidies up embarrassing disorders of his dead past, reverently conceals his own skeleton in a hidden closet." [47] Thus the history of the individual man must take into account the man as he was at various stages of his career, and most of all the historian must not look at him solely through the rose-colored glass of the man's memoirs and old-age recollections.

Once the historian has thought through the evidence and organized it in a logically consistent manner, he is ready to bring his literary skill to bear upon its presentation. Good writing is essential to good history, and so choice of vocabulary and style is important. The historian wants to invest his work with color, and so he gives play to his imagination in the way he expresses himself, that is, in the way he tells his story.

[47] Daniel Aaron, "The Treachery of Recollection: the Inner and the Outer History," in *Essays on History and Literature*, ed. Robert H. Bremner (Columbus, O.: Ohio State University Press, 1966), p. 10.

The danger, then, is that no literary style exists which "may not at some point take away something from the ascertainable outline of truth. . . ." [48] A colorful style which distorts the truth does no less a disservice to history than a dull, prosaic style which repels the reader. Clio should be clothed with beauty of expression, but she must not be camouflaged with the cloak of inaccuracy. As the ancient historian Agathias states it: "History is not at liberty to strain or embroider the facts. . . ." [49]

Narrative history naturally lends itself more readily to artistic presentation than does analytical history, and hence the popularity of the works of such historians as Edward Gibbon, Thomas Babington Macaulay, and Francis Parkman in their day and of Samuel Eliot Morison and Bruce Catton in our own day. This is not to be taken as favoring narrative over analytical history, for the latter is as valuable as the former. Too often, however, analytical history has lost its appeal because in its written form it contains little literary imagination. Because history deals with human life, it must *capture* that life in its written style if it is to attract the attention it deserves.

[48] Wedgwood, *The Sense of the Past*, p. 70.
[49] Quoted in Pardon E. Tillinghast, *Approaches to History* (Englewood Cliffs, N.J.: Prentice-Hall, 1963), p. 30.

CHAPTER 4

Explanation and History

Once the historian has completed his research, he must present his findings. If his task were merely to trace the evidence and then write out the chronological sequence of events, the task would be less difficult than it actually is. But, as we have already indicated, the reconstruction of the past calls for more than an answer to the question of what happened. We also want to know why events occurred as they did. It becomes necessary, then, for the historian to offer an explanation of past events. Explanation involves interpretation of facts, generalizations from the evidence, and application of the concept of causation. Actually, these elements of explanation are intertwined and not separate processes. For purposes of discussion, however, we can examine them individually. Thus, in this chapter we will discuss the facets of explanation, and in the next chapter we will consider the related subjects of laws in history and of metahistory.

INTERPRETATION IN HISTORY

"I'm getting just a little tired of today's historians second-guessing the past instead of just telling us what happened," complained a syndicated columnist. Moreover, he continued,

"As Sergeant Friday was wont to say: 'All I want are the facts, ma'am.' And confound it! When I read a history of the United States, I want to know exactly what went on. . . ." [1] No one can argue against that writer's plea to know what happened. What he fails to realize, of course, is that the facts without interpretation do not constitute history. As the historian G. Kitson Clark reminds us, "History to mean anything must be more than a rehearsal of facts, it must include an interpretation of the facts." [2]

That facts are essential to history we have already noted. Mere facts alone, however, mean nothing until the historian begins to work with them. As E. H. Carr observes, "The historian and the facts of history are necessary to one another. The historian without his facts is rootless and futile; the facts without their historian are dead and meaningless." [3] It is not enough, however, to suggest that the historian bases his work on facts. "The remorseless grubbing after new facts . . . is futile *per se*. . . . Unless we are continually drawing new patterns and weaving new clothes, history degenerates into sheer antiquarianism. . . ." [4] And the moment the historian begins to select and arrange his facts into patterns, he has begun to interpret the facts. Consequently, interpretations of the facts will differ among historians according to what they select for emphasis (or choose to omit as insignificant or irrelevant) and how they choose to arrange the facts. This statement should not be taken as an indication that one man's interpretation is as good as another's or that all interpretations are of equal worth. That is patently untrue, since skill and understanding are not equally distributed among all men. But, significantly, even the most competent historians will vary in the quality of their interpretations, and thus to accept uncritically any single interpretation as certain and true for all time is to court dogmatism of the first magnitude.

The revision of interpretations is inevitable, given the conditions of historical inquiry—a point we have examined at length in preceding chapters. With the discovery of new

[1] Max Rafferty, Column in *Los Angeles Times*, September 5, 1966, Pt. II, p. 5.
[2] G. Kitson Clark, *The Critical Historian* (New York: Basic Books, 1967), p. 42.
[3] Edward Hallett Carr, *What Is History?* (New York, Alfred A. Knopf, 1964), p. 35.
[4] Bernadotte Schmitt, *The Fashion and Future of History* (Cleveland: Western Reserve University Press, 1960), p. 19.

evidence the historian has an intellectual, and perhaps a moral, obligation to revise history in keeping with the freshly uncovered facts. Moreover, he has an obligation to look at the same evidence another historian has already interpreted if he sees another way of viewing the evidence, and particularly so in instances where, say, a national or religious frame of reference has produced a narrow or provincial point of view. New methods such as quantification and new theories developed from the social sciences may provide fresh insights into the past and hence result in reinterpretation of standard explanations. Aside from these factors, history must be revised if it is to be meaningful and useful in the present. History, according to Frederick Jackson Turner, himself a great reviser, "is ever *becoming*, never completed." [5] Society changes; philosophies change; our needs and our outlook on the present change. Thus, history is rewritten as we develop different ways of looking at our past. The facts may be altered not one iota, but we rearrange them, put them into different patterns, and discard some of them while selecting others for emphasis. Such revision is not an unhappy circumstance, dogmatists and reactionaries notwithstanding. On the contrary, it indicates the viability of history. As Allan Nevins has commented:

> Were history as nearly static as some branches of learning it would be a drab affair, but it is alive in every aspect. It is most of all alive in that it is constantly being reborn like the phoenix from its own ashes. . . . While the best history has enduring elements, there is a sense in which every generation has to have history rewritten new for it, and in this fact lies much of the fascination which historical activity will always offer thoughtful men. . . .[6]

And so it is that history offers rich and fertile opportunities for studying men and their activities over time. If we bear in mind the goal of the historian, then

> History must always be rewritten because we can only approximate to absolute truth, never hope to attain it;

[5] Frederick Jackson Turner, *Frontier and Section*, ed. Ray Allen Billington (Englewood Cliffs, N.J.: Prentice-Hall, 1961), p. 17.
[6] Reprinted by permission of the publisher from Allan Nevins, *The Gateway to History* (Lexington, Mass.: D. C. Heath and Company, 1946), rev. ed. (Garden City, N.Y.: Doubleday, Anchor Books, 1962) p. 33.

63

history must be written because the story of the past is the protoplasm that keeps alive the past and shows its unity of development; the pursuit of truth must be its goal because truth must be the objective point of all knowledge.[7]

The great danger inherent in a school of interpretation, of course, is that by writing history strictly from the prevailing premises, the historian is apt to formulate a priori judgments. Thus, a historian of the Cosmic school will be guided by the tenet that the Divine Plan always determines historical events, and a historian of the Marxist school will invariably interpret history in keeping with the premise that the "history of all hitherto existing society is the history of class struggles." Numerous other schools of historical interpretation have also waxed and waned, but what they all hold in common is a tendency toward determinism, to subscribe to the theory of single causation. The Truth is always there, in their interpretation! Their Truth becomes the Bible of history. What they obviously ignore are the human factors involved in the process of writing history. In a subsequent chapter we will examine the topic of deterministic history more fully.

Apart from the broad schools of interpretation, however, the process of historical revision or reinterpretation is an enduring activity of many modern-day historians. As a case in point, let us consider briefly the shifting interpretations of responsibility for World War I, since that has continued to be one of the historical issues of our day. The popular interpretation immediately after the end of armed hostilities was that Germany was solely responsible for having initiated the conflict, and this was reflected in the "war-guilt" clause of the Treaty of Versailles. Count Montgelas of Germany, who had served as a delegate to the Versailles conference, set about immediately to exonerate Germany. Before long a serious school of revisionists took up the case in favor of removing the stigma of guilt from Germany's shoulders. Among the many revisionists perhaps the most notable was Sidney B. Fay, an American historian. In his *Origins of the World War*, which appeared in 1928, Fay presented a reasoned analysis of the problem and concluded that responsibility for the war was

[7] Lucy Maynard Salmon, *Why Is History Rewritten?* (New York: Oxford University Press, 1929), p. 30.

shared by several of the belligerents. Germany deserved no larger proportion of blame than certain other parties to the strife. The issue became dormant for a while in the 1930's but was revived upon the approach of World War II, though only for a short time. The question then received little attention until it was once again given new life in the 1950's. The Italian scholar Luigi Albertini concluded in his *Origins of the War of 1914* (three volumes, 1952–1957) that Germany was indeed culpable, not because she had planned and precipitated the strife but because she had exhorted the Austrians to strike the first blow against Serbia. And in 1961 the German historian Fritz Fischer published his *Griff nach der Weltmacht* (translated into English in 1967 as *Germany's Aims in the First World War*), which assigns a significant share of responsibility to Germany. While none of the European powers is free of "some measure of responsibility," contends Fischer, it was Germany's war aims policy and desire for world power which make it necessary to render an unfavorable verdict against her.[8] And so it is that historians continue to reinterpret this particular historical issue.

Historical revision is a healthy activity when it is done for the sake of better understanding and for the cause of truth. Unlike the revisions dictated by a totalitarian state in the interests of justifying the authority of the state, historical reinterpretations in an open society are undertaken in the interests of "telling it like it is." Historical revisionism is more than a matter of keeping historians busy; it prevents us from falling victim to the "established" interpretation, and it is entirely in keeping with an attitude of critical inquiry.

GENERALIZATION IN HISTORY

Generalization, like interpretation, is another necessary aspect of historical explanation, and the moment we reflect on the definition of history as more than a record of facts, we must accept the truth of that dictum. While the notion of generalization may appear to contradict the concept of the uniqueness of

[8] An excellent general account of the broader question on the origins of World War I is Laurence Lafore, *The Long Fuse*, 2nd ed. (Philadelphia: J. B. Lippincott Company, 1971).

historical events, it involves in fact no real inconsistency. The historian must draw on a large number of generalizations before he can even begin to make sense of his own work. He could make no progress, for example, if he could not refer to such words as war, revolution, nation state, society, radicalism, and serfdom—all general terms which suggest certain commonalities but permit individual exceptions.

Theoretically, a historical generalization is a statement or term which has been inferred inductively from a number of particular cases, instances, or events. As such, it is a natural outgrowth of the historical method of inquiry. The historical generalization suggests some regularity or pattern of events, ideas, and human actions which is of historical significance. This statement is not intended to imply that these uniformities are sufficiently stable as to constitute laws of history but only that history would be meaningless if it were concerned exclusively with factual statements.

Generalizations in historical writing serve several purposes. Chief among them is their contribution to our store of knowledge about the past. No man can hope to investigate and research all of the past; thus, he must depend upon the findings and conclusions of many scholars. Discounting the notion of sanctity or inviolability of any generalization, the historian must rely on the rich reserve of generalizations which have emanated from the works of previous, accomplished historians. Then too, historical generalizations facilitate communication. How dreadfully tedious life would be if we were required *always* to speak in terms of particulars and specifics! Finally, generalizations function as a guide to action—that is to say, they allow us to make decisions on the basis of what we may tentatively predict the outcome of a certain action to be. While this function of generalizations is undeniably limited because of the variability of human activities, it is essential to the pragmatic life we encounter in everyday politics and society.

A historical generalization can be no better than the process by which it was formulated. Quite obviously, an empirical test of the validity of a generalization is desirable. Unfortunately, historical evidence, as we have already seen, is subject to variable interpretations, and for that reason it does not ordinarily lend itself to either statistical or logical proof; nor does it permit laboratory or experimental verification. History is not written strictly in terms of the scientific method, as intuition and insight play an important role in the formulation of historical generalizations. "A generalization," remarks William O. Aydelotte, "is not simply something logically derived from the evidence, the result of hard work effectively directed. It is also a comment on the evidence. . . ."[9] And so the test of soundness of a historical generalization must be found more often than not in how well the generalization accords with the evidence upon which it is founded, how insightful the analysis of the evidence is, and the extent to which the canons of historical research have been applied.

Historical generalizations vary in degree of comprehensiveness, and they can be distinguished according to level. Of the lowest order are those which usually appear as a single word or a simple phrase. This type is sometimes called a concept, though strictly speaking a concept may include a very abstract idea which cannot be expressed in simple terms. Some historians prefer to call them "labelling generalizations," while other historians prefer to designate them as "classificatory" generalizations.[10] The term "labelling" is fittingly appropriate because it gives a name to phenomena, ideas, institutions, and time periods which possess certain uniformities, for example: "slavery," "abolitionism," "monarchy," "fascism," "the Hellenistic Period," and the "Industrial Revolution." Likewise, the term "classificatory" is apt because certain peoples, groups, and men are categorized according to common traits, habits, background, or whatever, for example: "the ancient Greeks," "Germans," "Negroes," "Buddhists," "liberals," and "autocrats." Obviously these generalizations are not peculiar to history, but history would be meaningless without them. History borrows them from everyday language and from all fields of knowledge, it bases assumptions on them, and it manipulates them as necessary in order to communicate its message.

A second level of generalization serves a connective and interpretive function. It is one of the most essential types of

[9] William O. Aydelotte, "Notes on Historical Generalization," in *Generalization in the Writing of History*, ed. Louis Gottschalk (Chicago: The University of Chicago Press, 1963), p. 167.
[10] See, for example, Arthur F. Wright, "On the Uses of Generalization in the Study of Chinese History," p. 36, and M. I. Finley, "Generalizations in Ancient History," p. 21, both in Gottschalk ed., *Generalization in the Writing of History*.

generalization, for it assembles facts and concepts into some meaningful relationship. It establishes not only how but also why certain events occurred. As an example of this type of generalization, we can cite the following statement made in reference to the frame of mind of Americans in the period immediately after the Spanish-American War:

> Once the martial fever of the short and easy war with Spain had subsided, the psychology of the American people between 1898 and 1917 was surprisingly nervous and defensive for a nation that was rapidly rising in stature as a world power. Encouraged by the eugenics movement, men talked of racial degeneracy, of race suicide, of the decline of western civilization, of the effeteness of the western peoples, of the Yellow Peril. Warnings of decay were most commonly coupled with exhortations to revivify the national spirit.[11]

One can see easily enough that these generalizations function both to tie together the events over a period of time and to interpret various facts which by themselves are relatively, if not totally, meaningless.

An even higher level of generalization is the synthetic generalization. Historians do not frequently venture into the realm of the synthetic generalization, for it is both demanding and more openly vulnerable. The synthetic generalization requires the historian to ferret out some uniformities from a mass of materials on a broad topic such as war or revolution. A noble attempt at this has been made by Crane Brinton in *The Anatomy of Revolution*. After comparing the English, French, American, and Russian revolutions, Brinton poses some "tentative uniformities" about those revolutions. He states, for example, that

> these were all societies on the whole on the upgrade economically before the revolution came, and the revolutionary movements seem to originate in the discontents of not unprosperous people who feel restraint, cramp, annoyance, rather than downright crushing oppression.[12]

[11] Richard Hofstadter, *Social Darwinism in American Thought*, rev. ed. (New York: George Braziller, 1959), p. 185.
[12] Crane Brinton, *The Anatomy of Revolution*, rev. ed. (New York: Random House, 1965), p. 250.

Similarly, Karl Jaspers generalizes that a turning point in human history, the axial age of human history, was "situated in the years around 500 B. C. E., in the intellectual development that took place between 800 and 200 B. C. E." Rejecting Hegel's contention that the advent of Christ is the axis of history, Jaspers postulated the "axial age" as that period of time when many extraordinary men and writings appeared "almost simultaneously in China, India, and the West." His generalization is a very broadly encompassing one which includes a number of subgeneralizations: "Man became aware of existence as a whole, of his self, and of his limitations"; "man became aware of consciousness itself"; the epoch "produced the basic categories within which we still carry on our thinking, and the beginnings of the world religions"; and "the age of myth . . . came to an end, and there began the battle of rationality and practical experience against myth." [13]

Synthetic generalizations are not confined, however, to comparative studies of common phenomena which occur in several different societies or nations. Some of them deal with a single nation, as in the case of identifying a national character. The American historian David M. Potter, for example, has drawn some generalizations about "the American character." [14] In the same vein, but more as an *obiter dictum,* the British historian A. J. P. Taylor has generalized that the Russians, "despite their emotional instability, present to the outer world a stolid resolution. . . ." [15]

A fourth level of generalization is suggested by the "if . . . then" statement which is not uncommonly found in history books. Speculative generalizations are less empirically based and more truly hypothetical; and they are, as opposed to the first three levels, deductively rather than inductively derived. They are not useless, however, and in fact the human condition seems to demand the right to speculate upon what might have been. How often we say, "If such and such had been modified (or thwarted, or whatever), the outcome would have been so

---

[13] Karl Jaspers, "The Axial Age of Human History," *Commentary,* 6 (November 1948). Reprinted from *Commentary,* by permission; Copyright © 1948 by the American Jewish Committee.
[14] David M. Potter, *People of Plenty* (Chicago: University of Chicago Press, 1954).
[15] A. J. P. Taylor, *Bismarck: The Man and the Statesman* (New York: Random House, 1967), p. 44.

and so." George L. Mosse has provided an example of this kind of generalization in writing about German Christians and the acceptance of Nazi ideology:

> Like science, Christianity should be absorbed into the ideology. The so-called "German Christians" noisily devoted themselves to this task. Though they were held down in favor of the established churches, which were supported by the majority of the population, *the Nazi future would have lain with the Evangelical Christians had the war been won.*[16]

Unprovable by any external criteria, such a speculative generalization must stand on the weight of the author's persuasive argument, i.e., how well he musters the evidence to prove his hypothesis. This topic will be treated more fully in another section.

Finally, we come to the generalization which approaches the nature of "law." Since it implies unvarying regularity, we may, for convenience, call it the predictive generalization. In keeping with the comment that each level of generalization is increasingly more vulnerable to criticism, the predictive generalization is usually rejected by historians. More commonly it is the brainchild of the metahistorian. In searching for the genesis and growth of civilizations, for example, the English historian Arnold J. Toynbee held that

> When a society begins to disintegrate, the various ways of behaviour, feeling, and life characteristic of individuals during the growth stage are replaced by alternative substitutes, one (former in each pair) passive, the other (the latter) active.[17]

This type of generalization will be discussed further under the topic of laws of history.

In spite of the necessity for and potential usefulness of historical generalizations, they have certain limitations. First, historical generalizations as they commonly appear in history

---

[16] George L. Mosse, ed., *Nazi Culture* (New York: Grosset & Dunlap, The Universal Library, 1966), p. xxxii; italics added.

[17] Arnold J. Toynbee, *A Study of History*. Abridgement of Volumes VII–X by D. C. Somervell. (New York: Oxford University Press, 1957), p. 373.

textbooks are stated in broad and sweeping terms, and little or no evidence is presented in their behalf. The danger of this kind of statement is that it will be accepted for truth without proper verification. Often the generalizations are drawn from the textbook writer's interpretation of other interpretations. This is particularly true in the case of books which attempt a broad survey of history, for example, the history of Western civilization. Second, generalizations are limited to the extent that they represent the personal frame of reference, predilections, biases, and individual notions of a single historian or a single school of historians. Closely related to this is a third limitation: Generalizations have their own meaning to the readers of history. And reflecting on our previous comments regarding perception, we are forced to realize that all generalizations will not be understood in the same way. For this reason so-called lessons of history are hardly ever as clear as their individual proponents would have us believe.

A fourth limitation of generalizations is language. Again, this is akin to the previous two limitations because it is largely a problem of personal understanding. The moment the historian begins to generalize, even at the "labelling" level, he introduces words and language. Thus communication of the idea of the generalization is greatly dependent upon the clarity with which it is expressed. Added to this is another problem: Generalizations are sometimes mentally converted into actuality, i.e., they are taken to be reality itself and not merely a human construct or explanation of facts.[18] As such they take on an influential character and may themselves affect the course of history. Herbert Butterfield notes this phenomenon in his comment that the course of German development from the late nineteenth century to the middle of the twentieth may have been shaped in part by German historians. "It is possible," Butterfield suggests, "for historians to mislead a nation in respect of what it might regard as its historic mission." [19] Likewise, a generalization taken as a law of history may result in unwarranted extrapolation. To do so is to lose sight of the tentative and changing nature of generalizations in history.

[18] See Trygve R. Tholfsen, *Historical Thinking* (New York: Harper & Row, 1967), p. 267.
[19] Herbert Butterfield, *Man on His Past* (Cambridge: Cambridge University Press, 1955), p. 30.

CAUSAL EXPLANATIONS

One of the primary tasks of the historian is to search for the conditions and factors behind events of the past, i.e., *why* the events came about. History without explanations of the reasons for a war, the development of a new institution, the triumph of a new religion—and a whole host of other social, economic, and political phenomena—would be barren of significance, save perhaps for antiquarians. Consequently, the historian probes behind the actual events in order to find reasons why those events occurred. Most historians are content to confine their investigations to one specific phenomenon of change, such as a war, a revolution, imperial expansion, or a social, intellectual, or political movement. A few historians, however, seek to discover explanations for the development of whole civilizations. Whatever the scope of his investigation, the historian is always concerned with an inquiry which goes beyond a description of events; his thoughts converge also on the problem of causation. This quest is followed in narrative history as well as in analytical history, though of course it is much more crucial to the latter.[20]

The story of World War I—the battles, the victories, the losses—is an interesting story. As long as it is merely a story of the events, however, we are left with a sense of incompleteness. We want an explanation of *why* it occurred, and such a query leads to a search for causes. To say that something caused something else to happen is an everyday occurrence in the world of chemistry and physics. The chemist can cause certain elements to form a compound when he brings them together in proper proportions and under certain conditions, and the physicist can cause a metal to expand by applying heat to it. Yet what we are talking about is not strictly causation but

[20] The literature on explanation and causation is extensive and frequently very involved in argument. It is beyond the scope of this book to delve deeply into the problem. For the interested reader, however, the following selected works may be found useful: Arthur C. Danto, *Analytical Philosophy of History* (Cambridge: Cambridge University Press, 1965); Patrick Gardiner, *The Nature of Historical Explanation* (London: Oxford University Press, 1961); Patrick Gardiner, ed., *Theories of History* (New York: The Free Press, 1959); J. H. Hexter, *The History Primer* (New York: Basic Books, 1971); Maurice Mandelbaum, *The Problem of Historical Knowledge* (New York: Harper & Row, 1967); Fred D. Newman, *Explanation by Description* (The Hague: Mouton, 1968); and Morton White, *Foundations of Historical Knowledge* (New York: Harper & Row, 1965).

rather antecedent conditions. Did the chemist cause the compound to result, or the physicist the metal to expand, by his action of bringing each of the materials into contact with another agent? The results could, after all, have come about without human intervention if by chance they were brought together by some natural phenomenon. Moreover, one may argue that what actually causes the reaction is not an outside agent but the atomic structure of the one interacting with that of the other to effect something different.

In some ways causation in history is similar to causation in the physical world. The necessity for bringing together reacting or interacting agents also exists in history. Again, these agents may be brought together by human design, though fortuity or chance encounters also occur in history. Moreover, the structure or make-up of certain factors in history, when brought into contact one with another, may actually have caused whatever resulted. But this is less certain than when we are dealing with physical properties. In fact, because history deals with certain intangibles—such as ideas, forces, institutions, and movements—causation must be considered as an abstraction. The interactions and relationships are not testable in the same way physical matters are: We cannot experiment with them; we cannot replicate the events, circumstances, and conditions to see if the same results will be produced.

At the immediate level we can identify the cause of an event. In the instance of World War I, for example, we can say that the assassination of Archduke Francis Ferdinand was the immediate cause of the war; but then we must ask whether the murder of one man and his wife is enough to bring so many of the civilized nations of the world into such an enormous and bloody conflict. Similar assassinations have occurred and no world conflict ensued. Why? Also, other serious conflicts had occurred in the years preceding the assassination at Sarajevo. Why did not the first and second Moroccan crises result in war? So the historian must look deeper to find the underlying causes. The immediate cause is a necessary condition, but it "is seldom a sufficient explanation of the result that follows without an understanding of its own remoter causes."[21]

[21] Louis Gottschalk, "Causes of Revolution," *American Journal of Sociology*, 50 (July 1944): 2.

For purposes of illustration let us accept Sidney B. Fay's interpretation of the underlying causes of World War I: the system of secret alliances, militarism, nationalism, economic imperialism, and the jingoistic newspaper press.[22] In the last quarter of the nineteenth century, and particularly from the time of the Franco-Prussian War, specific events and forces combined to create volatile and hostile attitudes among most of the large, and many of the small, nations of the world, until in 1914 war erupted on the European continent. The world might have been spared the inferno if these factors had been modified or eliminated. That is strictly an academic matter now, however, for they were not changed or eradicated. So Fay could generalize, after careful study, that the origins of the war lay within these factors. Some historians would wholly agree with him, while others would agree with him only in part. But, of course, even if we agree with Fay, this does not tell us that these are the *actual* causes, only that our evidence tends to support them as very *probable*. At best we shall never be able to do more than arrive at a close approximation of the actual causes, since ultimate truth is beyond the historian's ken.

The historian's range of responsibility ends at the point where he is able to detect discernible changes. In the instance of the origins of World War I, that point appears to be in the latter half of the nineteenth century, when a number of significant events took place, such as the unification of Germany and Italy, greatly increased imperialism, and a host of others. This is convenient for the historian in terms of the manageability of his subject. Causation, however, is really like a chain; hence we must ask, for example, why Germany was unified in 1871. This brings us face to face with other events and their causes: Bismarck's installation as the Prussian prime minister in 1862, the events which led William I to appoint him to the position, the events which set in motion the events which resulted in William's decision, and so on. Obviously, causation is even more than *a* chain of events; it consists of *many* chains of events.

We have spoken of causes rather than a cause. No significant event in history had a single cause; so we may

[22] Sidney B. Fay, *The Origins of the World War*, Vol. I (New York: The Macmillan Co., 1928), *passim*.

properly speak of multiple causation. The man who believes that all actions are divinely determined subscribes to the concept of monistic causation, namely, God's purpose. The historian can hardly accept that, however, since men cannot agree on what His purpose is. Perhaps the decline of the Roman Empire was caused by divine disfavor, but the historian *qua* historian can never know that, inasmuch as it cannot be determined by his method of inquiry. Thus in the case of Rome's decline, the historian looks not for a cosmic origin nor for a single cause but for several causes rooted in the human world. And the problem of finding the causes of the decline of a culture, a nation, or a civilization is about as difficult as any problem confronting the historian. Understandably, then, literally scores of reasons for Rome's decline have been advanced by historians. Still, the historian cannot simply ignore the problem; the Roman Empire did decline, and we want to know why it did. So the historian looks for causes in order to explain a real occurrence.

Assuming the historian is not content to rest his case on a single cause for a significant historical event such as, say, the Reformation, is he justified in arguing that *one* cause was more important than the others in producing the event? Thus should he contend that Martin Luther's action against the Church was the *main* cause of the Reformation and that economic, intellectual, social, and political causes, while important, played a lesser role? The answer to the question must be ambiguous because on the one hand the Reformation did begin when Luther took his stand, while on the other hand it is doubtful that the event would have occurred as it did if the other factors had not been present. The problem is that there is no sound basis for rendering such a decision, and if the historian chooses that course of action, he is "compelled, willy-nilly, to fall back upon guesses and vague impressions in assigning weights to causal factors." [23] To offer one cause as the principal agent in precipitating an event is a practice which most historians tend to avoid, even though they may go to greater lengths in discussing one event than they do in discussing others—in which case the amount of discourse may be warranted simply because the one factor requires more explanation than others.

[23] Ernest Nagel, "Some Issues in the Logic of Historical Analysis," *The Scientific Monthly*, 74 (March 1952): 169.

Some philosophers of history subscribe to the concept of "covering laws" in historical explanations. The idea was first developed by Carl G. Hempel, and it has since created considerable controversy among several philosophers and a few historians. Hempel argues that a set of events of a certain kind which are explained as "effects" is related to a "cause" by a general law of some type. For example, Hempel suggests that we consider

> the statement that the Dust Bowl farmers migrate to California "because" continual drought and sandstorms render their existence increasingly precarious, and because California seems to them to offer so much better living conditions.

Hempel contends that the basis for "[t]his explanation rests on some such universal hypothesis as that populations will tend to migrate to regions which offer better living conditions." Desirably, this hypothesis would be stated "in the form of a general law"; but, as Hempel acknowledges, it would be difficult to state an accurate general law of this sort. The best the historian can do is provide an *"explanation sketch,"* that is, "a more or less vague indication of the laws and initial conditions considered as relevant. . . ." And in order to turn the sketch into a complete explanation, the historian must "fill out" the sketch with "further empirical research." Although this type of approach falls short of "general 'deterministic' laws," Hempel maintains that it does suggest a "general regularity." [24]

In actual practice the historian may fall back "upon some form of covering laws, however loosely they may be formulated," as the historian Carl N. Degler notes.[25] Whenever he does use these general laws for explanation, the historian is probably more often than not unaware that he is relying upon them—though perhaps he *should* examine his assumptions more carefully in this regard. Certainly, the explanation of some historical events is dependent upon physical, biological,

[24] Carl G. Hempel, "The Function of General Laws in History," *Journal of Philosophy*, 39, 2 (January 15, 1942): 40–41.
[25] Carl N. Degler, "Do Historians Use Covering Laws?" in *Philosophy and History*, ed. Sidney Hook (New York: New York University Press, 1963), p. 211.

and psychological laws. Thus explanations regarding climatic elements, mortality, physical needs, and human behavior are assumed as universal laws by historians. And, harking back to Hempel's illustration of the migration of Dust Bowl farmers to California, we can see the broad application of such laws. The use of covering laws, however, is only one form of historical explanation, and it cannot be taken to be essential to every form of historical explanation.[26]

[26] For a detailed analysis and criticism of the covering law theory, see William Dray, *Laws and Explanation in History* (New York: Oxford University Press, 1957).

CHAPTER 5

Speculation in History

The human desire to understand the meaning of the past has led some philosophers and historians into the realm of speculation about the history of mankind. As a consequence, some writers have attempted to identify laws of history; others have sought to discover grand patterns of the genesis and decline of civilizations; and still others have endeavored to establish the determining forces which operate upon men and their societies. Most historians would argue that speculation is beyond the pale of their activities and that the limitations of their work make it impossible for them to isolate laws, patterns, or determining forces. Let us examine, therefore, the problems associated with speculative philosophies of history.

LAWS OF HISTORY

In the late nineteenth century a number of historians entertained the idea of a science of history which, as with any other science, could include the formulation of laws. Henry Thomas Buckle, an early representative of the scientific school of historians, chided historians in general for their failure to discover laws of history. Holding that history as a "great department of inquiry" was below the level of inquiry in "the different branches of natural science," he undertook to write a history of the civilization of England in which he hoped to demonstrate "the universality of order, of method, and of law." [1] If Buckle failed to identify any real laws of civilization, he was not the last historian to make a gallant effort to reduce the regularities in civilization to statements of unvarying uniformity. Toward the turn of the century Henry Adams, a noted American historian, and his brother Brooks Adams both essayed to identify a science of history and some of its laws. Though disappointed in his later life at the prospects of history's ever becoming a science, Henry Adams contended that historians must "not abandon the attempt." And, he continued, "Science itself would admit its own failure if it admitted that man, the most important of all its subjects, could not be brought within its range." [2] Adams wrote that statement in 1894, while he was President of the American Historical Association. At the same time Brooks Adams, quite obviously considerably more optimistic than his brother, published a work in which he formulated a "law of civilization and decay." In a spirit characteristic of the Social Darwinism of the age in which he wrote, Brooks Adams maintained that

> when a highly centralized society disintegrates, under the pressure of economic competition, it is because the energy of the race has been exhausted. Consequently, the survivors of such a race lack the power necessary for renewed concentration, and must probably remain inert, until supplied with fresh energetic material by the infusion of barbarian blood.[3]

Unfortunately, such a formulation is burdened with ambiguities and variables which are not characteristic of, say, a Boyle's law or a Newton's law of gravity. Hence Adams' law of civilization and decay turns out to be no more than Adams' hypothesis.

Seemingly undaunted by these previously unfruitful efforts to formulate laws of history, Edward P. Cheyney, in his presidential address to the American Historical Association in 1923, invited his fellow historians to devote a future meeting of

---

[1] Henry Thomas Buckle, *History of Civilization in England* (New York: D. Appleton and Company, 1884), 1:5.
[2] Henry Adams, *The Degradation of the Democratic Dogma* (New York: The Macmillan Company, 1919), p. 126.
[3] Brooks Adams, *The Law of Civilization and Decay* (New York: Macmillan & Co., 1895), p. viii.

the Association to the subject of laws of history. Not content merely to charge others with the task, Cheyney himself boldly "guessed" at six laws of history; in fact, he said that the laws which he identified were "natural laws which we must accept whether we want to or not. . . ." The laws of history, as Cheyney summarized them, were

> first, a law of continuity; second, a law of impermanence among nations; third, a law of the unity of the race, of interdependence among all its members; fourth, a law of democracy; fifth, a law of freedom; sixth, a law of moral progress.[4]

Cheyney carefully pointed out that these were his "guesses at some of them [i.e., historical laws]"; he did not claim to have identified all of them. And perhaps it is well that he limited his list to only six, for even those turn out, upon careful analysis, to fall short of being laws of history. His "laws" constitute on the one hand an expression of his hopes and, on the other, generalizations which merely characterize man in both time and society. Thus the fourth, fifth, and sixth laws are hardly applicable to recent totalitarian regimes; the third, from an anthropological and biological point of view, may well be valid, but it has no significance in terms of historical fulfillment; and the first two laws are simply descriptions of the human condition in general, that is, man living in time and in association with other men of certain kindred aims and interests.[5] In a very broad sense, the laws of continuity and impermanence among nations may perhaps be taken as laws of history, since all history is a story of both continuity and change. In a more restricted sense, however, they might better be seen as factors of human life without which we would have neither the word nor the concept *history*. Because we can in fact identify no unvarying uniformities, no regular patterns in history, we can never predict precisely the outcome of histori-

[4] Edward P. Cheyney, "Law in History," *American Historical Review*, 29 (January 1924): 245.
[5] See Henry Steele Commager, *The Nature and the Study of History* (Columbus, O.: Charles E. Merrill Books, 1965), pp. 84–85; and Warren B. Walsh, *Perspectives and Patterns: Discourses on History* (Syracuse: Syracuse University Press, 1962), pp. 25–55, for further criticism of Professor Cheyney's laws of history.

cal events. Unlike laws of science, so-called laws of history permit no degree of certainty, no assurance of invariance. Far from being undesirable, however, this lack of absolute certainty is in some ways a boon to mankind, since it allows us to be free to choose our course of action in life and leaves open the doors of challenge to mankind.

Yet to refute the idea of laws of history is not to reject the reality of some repetition and uniformity in history. Thus we *might* agree with Carr that "the group—call it a class, a nation, a continent, a civilization, what you will—which plays the leading role in the advance of civilization in one period is unlikely to play a similar role in the next period. . . ." [6] But to accept his suggestion that this is a law of history is to forego careful reflection on the nature of the statement. In the first place, how can it be a law when it is qualified by the uncertain term "unlikely"? Second, even though a pattern of group leadership may emerge from historical context, the number of instances and the variety of circumstances provide sufficient limitations to prevent us from calling it a law. And finally, precise prediction on the basis of the law simply is not possible. Perhaps it is a relatively sound generalization, and perhaps we would be willing to base our future actions on its validity, but it is not a law of history. Actually, Carr recognizes the limitations of prediction, for in the same work he asserts that the historian "cannot predict specific events, because the specific is unique and because the element of accident enters into it." [7] And so it is that historians by and large stick to the business of explaining particular events, occasionally drawing comparisons and suggesting analogies, but avoiding attempts to formulate historical laws.

METAHISTORICAL THEORIES

Even though the historian is concerned basically less with abstractions in historical inquiry than with reasonably definite

[6] Edward Hallett Carr, *What Is History?* (New York: Alfred A. Knopf, 1964), p. 154.
[7] Carr, *What Is History?* pp. 87–88. Other examples of "historical laws" may be found, for instance, in Edgar Zilsel, "Physics and the Problem of Historico-sociological Laws," *Philosophy of Science*, 8 (October 1941): 718–19. Zilsel admits, however, that "All these historical 'laws' have to be considered as preliminary and more or less probable assertions only."

and determinable facts and causes, he cannot avoid some speculation about patterns of development and influence within the larger context of history. Thoughts of this nature are really above or beyond history and so are properly called metahistory. Metahistory "approaches the poetic in its structure"[8] and usually relies quite heavily on metaphors and analogies from the natural processes, such as the growth-decay phenomenon.[9] For these reasons it tends to be popularly appealing. Metahistory is also different from regular history in that it is mainly derived deductively rather than inductively. Utilizing an approach similar to that used to put together a jigsaw puzzle, the metahistorian first establishes a pattern (broad generalizations or categories) and then selects the pieces (specifics) to fit it.

To illustrate some of these characteristics of metahistory, we can examine a brief excerpt from one of the works of the philosopher-metahistorian José Ortega y Gasset, who believes that the historian may discover "great historical rhythms," such as "the rhythm of sex":

> There is in fact a pendulum movement latent in history which swings from ages subjected to the dominant influence of respectability to ages that surrender to the yoke of the female principle. Many institutions, customs, ideas and myths, hitherto unexplained, are illuminated in an astonishing manner when the fact is taken into account that certain ages have been ruled and modelled by the supremacy of women.[10]

That this is universal history, above and beyond regular historical investigation, is quite obvious: It deals with a "movement" supposedly applicable from age to age; it is based on the analogy of sex or the "female principle"; and it is assumed as a pattern or "rhythm" from which specifics can be derived, for example, the "fact" of female rule.

[8] Northrop Frye, "New Directions from Old," in *Myth and Mythmaking*, ed. Henry Murray (New York: George Braziller, 1960), p. 117.
[9] For example, Oswald Spengler contends that "All modes of comprehending the world may, in the last analysis, be described as Morphology" (p. 100). The form of civilizations, like any organic life, is one of "youth, growth, maturity, decay" (p. 26). In *The Decline of the West*, trans. Charles Francis Atkinson (New York: Alfred A. Knopf, 1926), vol. I.
[10] Ortega y Gasset, *The Modern Theme* (New York, Harper & Row, 1961), p. 18.

Metahistory is not new; it is at least as old as history itself, if not older. Early speculations on the course of men and events are clearly identifiable in the works of the Egyptians, for example. Probably attributable to the regular inundation and recession of the Nile River and the phenomenon of the rising and setting of the sun, the Egyptians developed the notion of cycles, and they applied this concept to the birth-life-death-rebirth of natural events, including man. It remained for the Greeks, however, to systematize and elaborate the idea of cyclical history. Unlike the Egyptians, they developed, at least by the fifth century b.c., a sense of the historic vis-à-vis the mythic. Variously espoused, at least indirectly, by Plato (427–347 b.c.) and Lucretius (98–53 b.c.), the notion of cyclical history was rejuvenated under the pen of Giambattista Vico and Voltaire in the eighteenth century and Count Arthur de Gobineau and Sir W. M. Flinders Petrie in the nineteenth; at the hand of Oswald Spengler and Arnold J. Toynbee in the twentieth century, it gained new respectability—though mainly at the popular level and among some social theorists and not by the majority of academic historians.

Cyclical history is based on the metaphysic of a world or universe controlled by outside forces, and whether natural or preternatural, those forces impose an overall order on the events of mankind. That is not to say that chaos does not occur, for it does. Wars, famine, and anarchy happen, but they are not abnormal; they are merely part of the cycle: They are not interminable, for they are only points on the great orb of time. All cyclists do not agree in every respect, however. Lucretius, for example, assumed a natural base for his theory of the progression of atoms-into-worlds-into-atoms,[11] while Arnold J. Toynbee posited a spiritual base for his theory of the genesis, growth, breakdown, and disintegration of civilizations.[12] Nor are the metahistorians in accord on the idea of progress, some subscribing to total inevitability of events—hence mankind never moves forward beyond a certain point—and others holding that despite the pattern or cycle man can progress, even if only in small steps. The latter group, the majority, might be better described as spiralists (after Vico),

[11] Lucretius, *Of the Nature of Things*, trans. William Ellery Leonard (New York: E. P. Dutton & Co., 1921).
[12] Arnold J. Toynbee, *A Study of History*, Abridgement of Volumes VII–X by D. C. Somervell (New York: Oxford University Press, 1957).

contending that history repeats itself in large measure but not completely and that man moves forward in a spiral of progress. Toynbee may be included among the spiralists, for, his pessimism notwithstanding, he believes that man can alter the course of events: Like a vehicle civilization can move forward, but "it must be borne along on wheels that turn monotonously round and round." [13] In fact other cyclists imply the possibility of progressive spiralism through their gloomy declarations that civilization (particularly in the West) is on the decline. They believe, remarks Herbert J. Muller, that the apex of civilization lies behind them, and therefore "we have the curious spectacle of civilized man forever marching with his face turned backward—as no doubt the cave-man looked back to the good old days when men were free to roam instead of being stuck in a damn hole in the ground." [14] Despite their despair and despondency, most cyclists believe in the possibility of progress.

The cyclical concept of history, as previously suggested, postulates the repetition of history. A widely accepted view, the history-repeats-itself sentiment appeals to laymen and professionals alike. Just why it receives such energetic endorsement is a matter of conjecture, though the reason may be rooted in the enduring myth of the eternal return.[15] Be that as it may, the idea popularly persists, and the phrase "history repeats itself" is not at all uncommon. It finds expression, for example, in the form of a common caveat: "The United States is following the course of the Roman Empire." Uncritical comparisons of the events of modern civilization and societies with previous ones suggest the theory of occurrence-recurrence and are more often than not open to serious question. Since history deals with the unique, it cannot, strictly speaking, repeat itself. Similar events and circumstances may be compared, but the comparison is always limited by the fact that the times, the conditions, the people are never precisely the same.

Opposed to the cyclical theory is linear history which

[13] Arnold J. Toynbee, *Civilization on Trial* (New York: Oxford University Press, 1948), p. 15.
[14] Herbert J. Muller, *The Uses of the Past* (New York: Oxford University Press, 1957), p. 65.
[15] For a detailed discussion of this myth, see Mircea Eliade, *Cosmos and History: the Myth of the Eternal Return* (New York: Harper & Row, 1959).

holds that historical events are nonrepetitive and represent steps toward a particular goal or end. Logically enough, the idea of linear history originated with the Hebrews, who developed a sense of themselves as a peculiar people moving toward a divinely determined goal, which ultimately came to be the advent of a Messiah and the reign of peace. As history advanced toward the final goal, however, a great drama of tragedy would be enacted on the human stage, occasionally highlighted by extraordinary events, the intervention of Jehovah. Thus the Israelites would thwart divine purpose, suffer the ignominy of capture and immersion into a foreign culture, and later the remnant would have its great city razed and would itself be dispersed across the civilized continents of the world. But finally the people would be restored and move on toward their destined end. The linear theme, naturally enough, was seized upon by the Christians, who saw themselves as heirs to the divine purpose, moving along the cosmic continuum toward the great events, the Second Coming of Christ and Final Judgment. Hence, St. Augustine (354–430) declared that human history is part of the Divine Plan, and so the element of determinism in the form of predestination first intruded into the tent of historical causation.

Linear history and its corollary, determinism, did not remain exclusively in the hands of Christian historian-theologians, however—though it basically retained a religious orientation under Antoine Nicolas Condorcet (1743–1794), who wrote of historical progress toward the goal of a world of reason and brotherly love, and Auguste Comte (1798–1857), who saw man as striving toward the goal of science and rational religion. Assuming a spiritual but not a traditionally religious base, Georg W. F. Hegel (1770–1831) carried the linear theme into the realm of the dialectic of opposing forces (thesis-antithesis) resolving themselves into a synthesis and thus moving forward toward the absolute ideal. Under Karl Marx (1818–1883) the Hegelian dialectic was given a materialistic base. All history, Marx asserted, is economically determined, and all history of civilized men is a history of the struggles of class against class. History is moving toward the great synthesis of communism. In Marx's theory of the linear movement of history, man and events thus move toward a material goal, and precisely for this reason his theory is more vulnerable than the linear theories which espouse spiritual, extraterrestrial goals. In other words, given the class struggles and economic conflicts of the past, what in his dialectic assures us that a new thesis-antithesis will not recur?

During the twentieth century numerous other metahistorians have engaged themselves in looking for patterns of history, including Ortega y Gasset, Spengler, and Pitirim A. Sorokin; but perhaps one metahistorian deserves special attention, if for no other reason than the immense popular appeal of his work in recent years. Arnold J. Toynbee, historian, critic, and scholar, published his magnum opus, A Study of History,[16] in twelve volumes between 1934 and 1961. Toynbee's frame of reference, by his own admission, largely developed as a result of his classical education, both through formal schooling and under the powerful influence of several relatives who emphasized particularly the Greek classics and the Holy Scriptures. Hence his monumental study of the history of civilizations is replete with myths, metaphors, and analogies from the literature of ancient Greece and the Bible; his whole scheme is redolent of Hellenic life and thought and the language of the Holy Writ. To explain Toynbee's Study fully is too large an undertaking for this discussion. Thus our remarks are confined to a brief description and criticism of his theory.

Toynbee identified twenty-three civilized societies, of which "sixteen are affiliated to previous civilizations but six have emerged direct from primitive life," and one has no predecessor.[17] Once "dynamically progressive," all present-day primitive societies are now "static." Rejecting the factors of race and environment, Toynbee contends that mythology provides clues to the discovery that the viable societies had their geneses in their "response to a challenge in a situation of special difficulty. . . ."[18] Some civilizations have continued to grow while others have become arrested. The growth of a civilization "originates with creative individuals or small minorities of individuals," who withdraw from their present society—during which time they receive a type of enlighten-

---

[16] Toynbee, A Study of History. 12 Vols. (London: Oxford University Press, 1934–61).
[17] Quoted from Toynbee, A Study of History, abridgement of Volumes VII–X by D. C. Somervell, p. 357. Toynbee's number of civilizations varies from twenty-one to twenty-eight, depending on whether he is counting further divisions of two general civilizations and the "arrested civilizations."
[18] Toynbee, A Study of History, Somervell abridgement, p. 358.

ment—and later return to that society to enlighten it.[19] All civilizations "except our own" are either dead or have broken down, and some have been rocked with the rhythm of disintegration. Toynbee asserts, however, that to assume the disintegration of the West simply because other civilizations have perished is erroneous. Thus, he is not strictly a cyclist: The West may perish, and certain signs indicate it will; but its expiration is not inevitable. Particularly in the latter volumes of his *Study*, Toynbee plays up the importance of the "higher religions" and goes so far as to suggest that a synthesis of these four religions into a Religion may come to pass—and hopefully it will, states Toynbee, because civilization will thus be enhanced.

Toynbee's critics have been both numerous and vocal; but perhaps the most thorough of them all was the late Dutch historian Pieter Geyl. Foremost among Geyl's criticism is that despite Toynbee's touted claim to being open-minded in his investigation, *A Study of History* does not employ empirical methods: "He selects the instances which will support his theses, or he presents them in the way that suits him." [20] Or, to borrow from the mythology which Toynbee loves so well, he applies the methods of Procrustes to his evidence, stretching here and lopping off there to fit his schematic bed. Geyl also attacks Toynbee's laws of withdrawal-return and the verdict that for the last three centuries Western civilization has been in a state of decay. In the former instance, Geyl accuses Toynbee of treating the great personalities arbitrarily in order to make the facts conform to the pattern and, in the latter, of ignoring the progress of the United States as part of Western civilization. In short, Geyl avers, Toynbee's theory founders on the rocks of "apriorism," and he is acting not as a historian but as a prophet. Geyl elaborates his criticisms considerably, but they are too numerous to take up here. Other historians offer devastating criticisms too. For example, G. J. Renier reproves Toynbee for using myth to prove the validity of his theory,

---

[19] Toynbee, *A Study of History*, Somervell abridgement, p. 364.
[20] Geyl, *Debates with Historians* (Cleveland: Meridian Books, 1958), p. 116. Other criticisms can be found in Edward T. Gargan, ed., *The Intent of Toynbee's History* (Chicago: Loyola University Press, 1961); M. F. Ashley Montague, ed., *Toynbee and History: Critical Essays and Reviews* (Boston: P. Sargent, 1956); and Richard Pares, *The Historian's Business and Other Essays* (London; Oxford University Press, 1961).

noting that "Play with mythology leads us nowhere beyond mythology." [21] Likewise, W. H. Walsh censures him for writing a book which is replete with "personal opinions and prejudices," and he expresses a doubt that anyone will read *A Study of History* fifty years hence.[22]

What, then, of Toynbee and the metahistorians: Are we to ignore their works entirely? Probably not, for some value can be found in them. For one thing, Toynbee offers us a broad view of history, fracturing "the parochialism of professional historians by drawing attention to whole subjects of study which are commonly ignored." [23] Perhaps, as Walsh suggests, historians "could do with some of his largeness of mind." [24] And, as William H. McNeil says, "there are insights attainable by taking large views of the past which cannot be had from close inspection of the separated segments of history." [25] Moreover, recent metahistorians have introduced into historical study new themes and different ways of characterizing civilizations. Finally, their work is useful if for no other reason than that it stimulates debate and produces new hypotheses.

DETERMINISTIC INTERPRETATIONS

Were conflicts and changes in the past inevitable? Some historians are unequivocal in their belief that at least certain events were unavoidable, and others imply the inevitability of those events in their interpretation of the past. Taken in its extreme form, such a position suggests that determining forces are at work in societies and civilizations. And perhaps foremost among the determinists was Karl Marx, who felt that he had discovered that, at least up to the mid-nineteenth century, the dominating force in society was the struggle of social and economic classes. Other interpreters of the past have likewise sought to establish that the history of mankind has been

[21] G. J. Renier, *History: Its Purpose and Method* (New York: Harper & Row, 1965), p. 217.
[22] W. H. Walsh, *Philosophy of History* (New York: Harper & Row, 1960), p. 169.
[23] Walsh, *Philosophy of History*.
[24] Walsh, *Philosophy of History*.
[25] William H. McNeil, "Some Basic Assumptions of Toynbee's *A Study of History*," in Gargan, ed., *The Intent of Toynbee's History*, p. 30.

determined by the inevitable surge of progress, and still others have offered various views on the impelling agent which shapes the activities of men in society.

What are the basic assumptions of the determinists? First, we should note that they consider the power of a "force" to be the key to events of the past and of the future. The activity of men is therefore relegated to the role of serving as an instrument of the inevitable force. Or in other words, men do not exercise free will: They "choose" to act only within the boundaries of something larger than themselves, something which encompasses the operations of *all* men in societies. Second, the determinists assume the validity of a monistic interpretation of history—that is, only *one* force determines the process of history. All other "causal factors" are but outgrowths of that force. And finally, they claim that they have discovered the shaping force of history and that their discovery will be good for all time. Hence in a way the determinist places himself in the role of prophet: He has found the truth about the past, and he can thus foresee the future. Like the Queen in *Through the Looking Glass* when Alice inquired what the Queen remembered best, the determinists can reply, "Oh, things that happened the week after next."

Taken literally, the deterministic approach to history abnegates the responsibility of individuals for their actions, since they are simply *compelled* to act as they do. Moreover, it is to argue that forces alone fix the destiny of man. Actually, the Marxists eventually recognized the absurdity of this extreme position, and George V. Plekhanov later offered a modification: "Individuals can influence the fate of society," he stated.

In keeping with the deterministic interpretation, however, Plekhanov argued further that "Sometimes this influence [of individuals] is very considerable; but the possibility of exercising this influence, and its extent, are determined by the form of organization of society, by the relation of forces within it." [26]

To argue against the concept of forces as determining the operations of society, however, is not to deny the power and influences of forces upon men. The opposite extreme—that history is shaped alone by the actions of individuals—is

[26] George V. Plekhanov, *The Role of the Individual in History* (New York: International Publishers, 1940), p. 40.

equally vulnerable. "For men who work upon history," says Herbert Butterfield, "are themselves partly moulded by it in the first place, conditioned by it even at the moment when they imagine themselves most free, most masterly in their action upon it." [27] The truth of the matter is that history is an interaction between men and circumstances. Certainly, the two elements of this interaction are not always equal; but in every instance individuals play a role—sometimes, in Sidney Hook's words, as the "eventful man" and other times as the "event-making man." [28] In short, events are the result of the influence of men upon them, but men act as they have in turn been influenced by the conditions of their own time in history.

As we have previously observed, interpretations of man's past are modified and changed in keeping with man's views of the present and in accordance with the individual historian's frame of reference. It is futile to argue therefore that a single historical interpretation is valid for all time. To adopt such an interpretation as an immutable truth is to choose a dogmatic position. Moreover, to argue for a single cause in history is to ignore the reality of the historical process. Determinism offers a simple solution to the complex story of man's past. It is therefore untenable—perhaps partially correct but not wholly.[29] History must reflect the manifold hues of humanity if it is to capture the reality of the past.

[27] Herbert Butterfield, *History and Human Relations* (New York: The Macmillan Company, 1952), pp. 68–69.
[28] Sidney Hook, *The Hero in History* (Boston: Beacon Press, 1955), p. 154.
[29] For a thoroughgoing refutation of determinism, see Karl R. Popper, *The Open Society and Its Enemies*, 2 vols., 4th ed. (Princeton: Princeton University Press, 1963). Popper uses the term "historicism" in lieu of "determinism." See also Isaiah Berlin, *Historical Inevitability* (London: Oxford University Press, 1954).

CHAPTER 6

History and Related Studies

In some quarters history is associated with the humanistic studies, while in others it is linked with the social sciences. As we have already argued, the debate over whether history is an art or a science is largely futile, and to assign it exclusively to one or the other branch is to take a narrow view of the discipline of history. A broad branch of knowledge, history contributes to other disciplines and in turn profits from them. In this chapter we shall examine history's relationship to the auxiliary disciplines, to oral and folklore studies, and to the social sciences.

THE AUXILIARY DISCIPLINES

Traditionally, history has relied upon certain specialized sciences. Among these auxiliary studies probably the best known is archeology. Through the work of archeologists on the remains of early civilizations such as ancient Egypt, Sumeria, Mycenae, and Etruria, historians have been immeasurably aided in their study of the ancient past. Were it not for the discoveries of such early cities as Mohenjo-Daro and Harappa and of artifacts from the ancient civilizations along the Hwang Ho and Yangtze rivers of China, historians would find a tremendous gap in their knowledge of the activities of ancient peoples. In short, the exacting work of archeologists has provided the historian with essential knowledge of the art, architecture, religion, social life, government, commerce, and customs of many ancient civilizations. And before the historian can study changes in those civilizations, he must first acquaint himself with the knowledge archeology has already uncovered about those civilizations.

The historian naturally is concerned with the written records left by men of the past, and he can of course learn much about early societies through their symbols. In the first category, the contributions of epigraphy, paleography, and diplomatics are especially significant. The science of epigraphy is the study of inscriptions, and it is particularly useful to the historian of ancient civilizations because it helps to fill the gap in written sources. The study of handwriting, both ancient and medieval, is known as paleography. The study of styles of script and their transformation is extremely helpful to the historian in his effort to date and place written sources. Official documents, charters, treaties, registers, and deeds are very important to historians, especially those studying ancient and medieval times. The study of these official records is called diplomatics, and it is a science which has furthered research on the past by aiding the historian to sift out the spurious from the genuine document.

Other auxiliary sciences have likewise proved helpful to the historian. Among them are numismatics—the study of coins, medals, and medallions—and heraldry, or the study of escutcheons or shields which contain coats of arms. The former is particularly useful to ancient historians, and the latter, to medieval historians. In addition, the study of family descent or lineage, genealogy, is useful to historians, even to those who are concerned with the modern age. Genealogy, properly researched, requires the effort of specialists. When utilized by the historian, it is intended to show how lineage is important to the understanding of people and significant events. The study of linguistics is another discipline which illuminates certain types of historical research by aiding in decipherment of ancient script and by showing relationships among civilizations through comparison of languages. And finally, the science of chronology is an invaluable aid to the historian. The problems of dating and the complexity of conflicting calendars have been greatly simplified through the study of chronology. Because of this contribution the work of the historian has been made easier and more accurate.

ORAL AND FOLKLORE STUDIES

While the auxiliary disciplines by and large are used less now than a few decades ago, other related studies have become increasingly useful to the historian. It was not long ago that historians in general frowned upon historical inquiry which was not based upon the written document, and perhaps even today a few historians remain skeptical of oral sources. As the techniques of research in oral and folklore history have become more sophisticated and refined, these two disciplines have taken their rightful places as legitimate and useful fields of study.

In our earlier discussion of historical evidence, we spoke of oral sources, but we did not explore the techniques and contributions of oral history. Oral history is in fact the oldest kind of history, serving to pass on traditions before writing became a widespread skill. The ancient Greeks utilized oral history quite effectively, and both Herodotus and Thucydides, among other Greek historians, constructed much of their accounts from oral sources. Their work was limited, however, to fairly narrow segments of human activity. In recent years some historians have focused their attention upon the oral traditions of a society at large. Among the oral histories which have been published in recent years are those produced by Jan Vansina, Raymond K. Kent, and W. Lynwood Montell.

The Belgian historian Jan Vansina is interested primarily in African civilizations. Vansina says, "To me, history is the history of all the people in a culture. . . . In most cases, few of those people knew how to write, and therefore other methods of investigation must be developed to find out more about them." [1] And through his pioneering efforts in oral history, Vansina has succeeded in reconstructing the past of certain accomplished African civilizations. While the gap in our

[1] Jan Vansina, "How the Kingdom of the Great Makoko and Certain Clapperless Bells Became Topics for Research," in *The Historian's Workshop*, ed. L. P. Curtis, Jr. (New York: Alfred A. Knopf, 1970), p. 237.

knowledge of this portion of the world remains wide, it has been narrowed through the research of Vansina. His student Raymond K. Kent has likewise contributed to our knowledge through his studies of the early kingdoms of Madagascar. In one of his investigations, for example, Kent compared an early Malagasy community with communities on the western mainland of Africa. His studies led him into numerous fields of inquiry about those preliterate societies. He probed into linguistics, hair styles, divination, foodstuffs, cattle-markings, and other evidence "left" by these communities.[2] As it may now be obvious, the works of Vansina and Kent disregard any sharp distinctions between cultural anthropology and the type of cultural history in which they are engaged—and this they readily admit. In the United States W. Lynwood Montell has directed his attention to the history of an erstwhile Negro community in Coe Ridge, Kentucky.[3] Montell's pioneering effort in this field has opened new possibilities for reconstructing the past of a people who have not left us an abundance of written sources. Through personal interviews with survivors of the Coe Ridge community, by use of tape recorders, and through comparisons of "tales" extant about the community, Montell has demonstrated how historians can employ techniques other than those concerned with written records to reduce our ignorance of certain aspects of the past. The techniques themselves are hardly new; scholars in other disciplines are well acquainted with them. Today, however, oral history has gained its proper place in the study of man's past.

The strictures on oral history have also been applied to folklore. The study of folklore is hardly new, but only in recent years has it become accepted as a useful ally of historical inquiry. One of the historians who has devoted himself to serious study of the role of folklore in the history of American civilization is Richard M. Dorson, director of the Folklore Institute of Indiana University. As Dorson notes, the study of folklore traditions throws considerable light upon national myths, cultural heroes, and minority groups in the United

[2] Raymond K. Kent, "The Real Magnitude of a Small Historical Problem," in *The Historian's Workshop*, ed. L. P. Curtis, Jr. (New York: Alfred A. Knopf, 1970), pp. 77–100.
[3] W. Lynwood Montell, *The Saga of Coe Ridge: A Study in Oral History* (Knoxville: The University of Tennessee Press, 1970).

States. Thus the popular oral traditions "offer the chief available records for the beliefs and concerns and memories of large groups of obscured Americans. The historian can find history alive in the field as well as entombed in the library." [4] And the field of American studies has been enriched by the contributions of Dorson and several other historians who have a broad vision of the history of our culture.

THE SOCIAL SCIENCES AND HISTORY

History and the social sciences share a common subject: They are both concerned with man and his activities in a society. This fact alone should serve as a basis of mutual understanding and respect. Unfortunately, both historians and social scientists have not infrequently allowed themselves to cast aspersions upon the work of each other. The results have been on the one hand an inclination of historians to believe that social scientists are concerned only with worthless generalizations and a depersonalizing approach to the study of man and on the other hand a tendency for social scientists to derogate the work of historians as meaningless and irrelevant. And although the skeptics and scoffers remain with us on both sides of an imaginary fence, a much needed rapprochement between history and the social sciences seems to be taking place. Since this book is concerned with history rather than the social sciences, we shall endeavor to illustrate how history is benefiting from the social sciences and not the reverse. Before we do, however, it may be well to remind ourselves of some of the differences between the objectives of history and those of the social sciences, both imagined and real.

A persisting argument among many historians is that history is primarily descriptive while the social sciences are basically analytical. This distinction may not be as sharp as some historians believe. The historian does try to describe events through a narrative, but as we noted in a previous chapter, historical writing nowadays is concerned not only with what happened in the past but also with why events

---

[4] Richard M. Dorson, *American Folklore and the Historian* (Chicago: The University of Chicago Press, 1971), p. 144.

occurred. Thus the historian's work is usually a blend of a descriptive account and an analysis of the causes, or at least the antecedents, of the events in question. It is true, of course, that some historical studies are more description than analysis. Still, the social sciences are basically analytical in nature, and history is fundamentally descriptive in character.

History differs from the social sciences in that it is essentially a study of change over time, while social science is a study of man and his activities in a limited, and usually fairly current, situation. These restrictions are not absolute, of course, since historians sometimes devote their inquiries to narrow segments of time and social scientists sometimes focus upon the development of institutions over time. A difference of degree is once more the distinguishing feature between the two.[5] As a corollary of change over time, historical study is also interested in the continuity of the past with the present, and this involves the temporal element more fully than is typical for the social sciences.

The greatest difference between the social sciences and history, however, lies with the goals of their investigations. The social sciences, generally speaking, seek to abstract from their investigations generalizations regarding the behavior of men in social, economic, geographic, psychological, political, and religious situations. The resultant generalizations, though they are not laws of behavior, are useful in understanding man, and for some social scientists, they are potentially useful in learning to control man's behavior. The historian, on the other hand, is searching for unique, nonrecurring events in man's past. Thus he is concerned with the particular rather than with the general. Each of these functions tends to be exaggerated by those in the opposing camp, for as we have previously stressed, the historian cannot avoid drawing some generalizations from his study. His generalizations, however, tend to be applicable only to the particular time and events under study. Those of the social scientist are held to be applicable to the present and to the future. But contrary to the charge of some historians, generalizations from the social sciences are just that—generalizations. They are not held to be universal,

[5] See Werner J. Cahnman and Alvin Boskoff, "Sociology and History: Reunion and Rapprochement," in *Sociology and History*, ed. Cahnman and Boskoff (New York: The Free Press, 1964), pp. 3–4.

applicable for all time and in all situations in the future. In other words, social scientists in general do not claim to have discovered absolute, immutable laws.

The historian readily acknowledges the role of intuition in the methodology of his investigations. The social scientist, however, is prone to reject intuition as a fruitful mode of research. Even though it may be useful in the formulation of hypotheses, intuition has no place in the actual conduct of social research. That is not to favor or condemn intuition but only to say that while it is necessary to historical research, it runs counter to the methodological canons of research in the social sciences. The problem is that historians sometimes overplay the contribution of intuitive insight to their studies when more rigorous social science methods might be applied. At the same time, it must be recognized that many facets of the past simply will not yield to social science methods.

What is becoming apparent to an increasing number of historians is that the social sciences, properly applied, offer some new possibilities for probing the past. In spite of the misgivings of some historians,[6] new approaches to analytical history which employ methods, concepts, and theories from the social sciences promise to enhance our knowledge of man in the past—and hence our understanding of man in the present. The danger that some historians will fall victim to an idolatry of the new approaches and to a narrowness of view is probably unavoidable. But that should not negate the value of the new approaches,[7] and there is always the opposite danger, namely, that some historians will cling stubbornly to a point of view which rejects totally the contribution of the social sciences to their discipline. History can only become more valuable as historians apply whatever tools and ideas help to illuminate the past further. As A. S. Eisenstadt has phrased it:

A sense of the past requires something beyond retrospective imagination. It requires a view of the past as the outworking of human will and social tendencies. It re-

[6] For an example of the criticism of analytical history based on social science concepts, see J. H. Hexter's The History Primer (New York: Basic Books, 1971) and Doing History (Bloomington: Indiana University Press, 1971).
[7] The application of social science methods and ideas to history is not really new, for various historians have utilized them for many years. What is different, of course, is that they are being more systematically and rigorously applied to historical inquiries than they once were.

quires a deep insight into both individuals and society, insight that is informed and chastened by intelligences from all areas of knowledge, particularly from social science.[8]

Wherever historians may profit from crossing the imaginary lines of "disciplines," we feel that in the interest of providing us with a more enlightened view of man, they should take those steps. That they must proceed cautiously is understood; but that they should explore is, we believe, a fair expectation.

John Higham, an American historian of ideas, argues that "the special character of history inheres not in a definite and superior method of its own but rather in the convergence of all sorts of techniques and insights upon the explanation of human experience, in its full existential complexity, within the limits of a definite span of time." [9] Since the "techniques and insights" of the social sciences present possibilities for the understanding of our "human experience," let us examine a few of them. We shall discuss briefly the contributions to history—and the limitations—of psychology and psychoanalysis, theories and concepts, quantification, and comparative analysis.

PSYCHOLOGY AND PSYCHOANALYSIS

In 1957 William L. Langer, in his presidential address to the American Historical Association, appealed to his fellow historians to ponder the prospects of psychoanalysis as an aid to historical inquiry.[10] Whether because of Langer's invitation or for other reasons, the application of psychoanalysis to historical study has increased considerably during the last fifteen years. It is not as though historians had never engaged in psychological analysis of the subjects about whom they were

[8] A. S. Eisenstadt, "Research and Writing: Introductory Notes," in *The Craft of American History*, Vol. II, ed. Eisenstadt (New York: Harper & Row, 1966), p. 195.

[9] John Higham with Leonard Krieger and Felix Gilbert, *History: The Development of Historical Studies in the United States* (Englewood Cliffs, N.J.: Prentice-Hall, 1965), p. 144.

[10] William L. Langer, "The Next Assignment," *American Historical Review*, 63 (January 1958): 283–304.

writing, for historians have from the beginning found it necessary to probe the recesses of human motivation. And not infrequently historians have demonstrated a powerful, common-sense insight into the behavior of men. But a more sophisticated analysis was not possible until psychology and psychoanalysis themselves advanced beyond the seminal stages of development. Once they had progressed, it remained for historians to discover how those new tools could enrich the study of men of the past.

The traditional application of psychological principles to historical study suffered from the defect of what Bruce Mazlish has termed "surface" psychology, that is, the type of analysis which never penetrates the surface of "appearances" and "unexamined clichés about human nature and behavior." [11] Moreover, a conventional argument which has deterred progress in the application of psychological principles to historical study holds that we cannot judge past societies in terms of their behavior because, as David Hunt notes, some historians feel that the "autonomy and integrity" of each of these societies is unique.[12] A number of recent historical studies have demonstrated, however, that we *can* go beyond surface psychology and that we *can* gain a better understanding of the behavior of past societies and of men in those societies. "History is the story of human destiny," Robert Waelder reminds us. And because it is, we may better comprehend man "through the discovery of the unconscious psychic life that powerfully influences man's conduct while being withheld from his self-awareness." [13]

The study of human behavior in history, like the study of causation, is extremely complex, and simple explanations are apt to be not only misleading but also dangerous. Nevertheless, human behavior has remained fairly constant over the centuries. Hence the better we can fathom the basic aspects of human conduct, the more we may apprehend the actions of men in societies. Some of the deep-rooted traits of human

---

[11] Bruce Mazlish, in the "Introduction" to *Psychoanalysis and History*, ed. Mazlish (Englewood Cliffs, N.J.: Prentice-Hall, 1963), p. 3.

[12] David Hunt, *Parents and Children in History* (New York: Basic Books, 1970), p. 4.

[13] Robert Waelder, "Psychoanalysis and History: Application of Psychoanalysis to Historiography," in *The Psychoanalytic Interpretation of History*, ed. Benjamin B. Wolman (New York: Basic Books, 1971), p. 3.

conduct which account for the behavior of individuals and ultimately of societies have been summarized by the clinical psychologist Benjamin B. Wolman. They include the belligerent nature of man with its many results: "intraspecific murderous fights"; intragroup fighting which is destructive to unity of the human species; the role of the historical leader who captivates the loyalty of his own group and turns his aggressive propensities against others; the "fear of death" and the "lust for life" which have precipitated actions of both love and hate; the inclination to "escape into magic" as a defense mechanism; and "patterns of interaction" which take the form of "instrumentalism" (i.e., "using" other people), "mutuality" (which often emanates less from love or tolerance than from "avoidance of destruction"), or "vectorialism" (i.e., the "willingness of giving without asking anything in return").[14] *Homo sapiens* is a strange compound of interacting motivational forces, and psychology and psychoanalysis can contribute to the historian's study of this phenomenal animal and his behavior over the centuries.

As with any method or idea borrowed from one discipline to be applied to another, the use of psychology and psychoanalysis in history is limited. An inherent danger is that the historian will become so captivated with the approach that he will come ultimately to accept it as *the* method of historical inquiry. That is not a fault of the method, however, but a problem of human perspective. One of the most serious limitations, though, is the difficulty a historian faces getting the training which qualifies him to apply psychological principles properly. Superficial grounding in the discipline of psychology may well result in a worse study than might have been produced without any training at all. Happily, more historians are "tooling" themselves to the task, and others are engaging in cooperative studies with men who have been trained as clinical psychologists.

Aside from these problems, there are others. Since theory is very important in psychology and because most psychoanalytic studies develop from clinical situations, historians must exercise caution in applying the principles of these disciplines to the study of the past. And once applied, the forthcoming

[14] Benjamin B. Wolman, "Sense and Nonsense in History," in *The Psychoanalytic Interpretation of History*, pp. 87–107.

generalizations must be recognized as limited in their inferential quality. Thus, the pathological problems of one or two abolitionists may not be automatically generalized as typical of all abolitionists.[15] A corollary to this problem is the usual paucity of data for an individual of the past. Rarely is the psychohistorian privileged enough to find sources on the childhood of his subject, or if studying a broader problem, such as parents and children in seventeenth century France, the historian finds that the sources inform him "about only a limited segment" of the society—and that is usually the literate group.[16] Moreover, in the psychological study of individuals, the historian must recognize that each individual develops in stages, and he cannot conclude that Martin Luther, for example, was motivated by the same psychological needs in his mature years as he was as a young man. And finally, it is recognized that psychoanalysis is a clinical relationship between the patient and the psychoanalyst. Judgments from written sources on the "patient" are therefore limited. The extant sources are in effect preselected and not comprehensive. That fact, unfortunately, was not recognized by Sigmund Freud in his collaborative study with William C. Bullitt on Woodrow Wilson.[17] Freud accepted uncritically the biased data collected by Bullitt, and the result was a totally useless psychohistorical study of the twenty-seventh President of the United States.

In spite of these limitations, however, a number of invaluable psychohistorical studies have been published in recent years. Probably the first real breakthrough in the application of depth psychology to a historical individual was made by Erik H. Erikson, a psychoanalyst by training and an insightful practitioner of clinical psychology. Erikson's *Young Man Luther*[18] represents an important achievement in the application of psychoanalysis to historical study. Interestingly enough, the book was not reviewed in any of the leading historical journals, but it is now frequently cited as a seminal

---

[15] On this point see Martin Duberman, "The Abolitionists and Psychology," *The Journal of Negro History*, 47 (July 1962): 183–91.

[16] Hunt, *Parents and Children*, pp. 6–7.

[17] Sigmund Freud and William C. Bullitt, *Woodrow Wilson: A Psychological Study* (New York: Avon Book Division, 1968).

[18] Erik H. Erikson, *Young Man Luther* (New York: W. W. Norton & Company, 1958).

CARL A. RUDISILL LIBRARY
LENOIR RHYNE COLLEGE

work in the field of psychohistory. The concept of *identity crisis* in adolescence developed by Erikson has been very useful, for example, to others who have conducted studies on historical personages. Erikson interprets Martin Luther's rebellion against Rome as an assertion of his ego independence and as a reaction to his own father's treatment of him in his childhood and adolescence. Erikson documents his analysis as thoroughly as possible, and even though some historians refute his theory, it does represent an approach which historians ignore at their own peril.

The number of studies of this nature is increasing very rapidly, and the best we can do here is cite some of the more interesting analyses of important historical figures. In recent years Erikson has moved away from his study of adolescence and young manhood to the investigation of men in their mature years. His study of Gandhi is an analysis of the psychological forces which impelled the Mahatma into his leadership of the militant nonviolence movement in India.[19] Victor E. Wolfenstein has employed depth psychology in his study of Lenin, Trotsky, and Gandhi. Focusing upon the revolutionary personality of those three men, Wolfenstein has probed the questions of "why a man becomes a revolutionist," "why a revolutionist does or does not become a leader," and how the revolutionist effects a "transition to power." [20] Gustav Bychowski has examined the paranoid personality of Joseph Stalin, and Robert Waite has investigated the psychological roots of Adolf Hitler's anti-Semitism.[21] Peter Loewenberg has studied the adolescence of the Nazi *Reichsfuehrer S.S.* Heinrich Himmler.[22] Other studies could be cited, but the point here is only to demonstrate the contribution of psychology to the study of historical individuals. That these studies are controversial goes without saying; that they have opened a new dimension, however, is obvious.

Not all psychohistory is concerned with particular individuals. It is likewise being applied to the study of groups, and

[19] Erik H. Erikson, *Gandhi's Truth* (New York: W. W. Norton & Co., 1969).
[20] Victor E. Wolfenstein, *The Revolutionary Personality: Lenin, Trotsky, Gandhi* (Princeton: Princeton University Press, 1967), *passim*.
[21] In Wolman, ed., *The Psychoanalytic Interpretation of History*, pp. 115–49 and 192–230.
[22] Peter Loewenberg, "The Unsuccessful Adolescence of Heinrich Himmler," *American Historical Review*, 76 (June 1971): 612–41.

this approach seems to offer some fruitful explanations of collective behavior. David Hunt, for example, has examined the psychology of family life in early modern France.[23] Loewenberg has explored

> what happened to the members of this generation [of German youth who reached maturity circa 1929] in their decisive period of character development—particularly in early childhood [i.e., during and immediately after World War I]—and . . . their common experiences in childhood, in psychosexual development, and in political socialization that led to similar fixations and distortions of adult character.[24]

In other words, Loewenberg shifts attention away from the leader to the followers to find out why they behaved as they did. And Robert Jay Lifton has researched the psychological impact of the atomic bomb upon some survivors of Hiroshima, finding, for example, that the survivors experienced "*a vast breakdown of faith in the larger human matrix supporting each individual life, and therefore a loss of faith (or trust) in the structure of existence.*"[25] Set in the context of other historical disasters, Lifton's finding presents some important ideas on human beings and their reactions to death as a psychological phenomenon.

As Lifton notes elsewhere, "psychohistory may turn out to be nothing more than a minor intellectual curiosity . . . or it could develop into a significant body of thought whose evolving ideas will be as compelling as they are difficult to establish."[26] Historian critics of the psychohistorical approach are not wanting.[27] Their criticisms should not be ignored. But acceptance of different methods of historical inquiry has never come rapidly. That has undoubtedly saved historians from the embarrassment of embracing ephemeral fancies, though it has sometimes deterred them from broadening their vision of the variety of ways they can study the past.

[23] Hunt, *Parents and Children in History.*
[24] Peter Loewenberg, "The Psychohistorical Origins of the Nazi Youth Cohort," *American Historical Review*, 76 (December 1971): 1458.
[25] Robert Jay Lifton, *History and Human Survival* (New York: Random House, 1970), p. 153; italics in original.
[26] Robert J. Lifton, "On Psychohistory," in *The State of American History*, ed. Herbert J. Bass (Chicago: Quadrangle Books, 1970), pp. 295–96.
[27] See, for example, Jacques Barzun, "History: The Muse and Her Doctors," *American Historical Review*, 77 (February 1972): 36–64.

SOCIAL SCIENCE THEORIES AND CONCEPTS

Anthropology, economics, geography, political science, and sociology have developed useful theories and valuable concepts as they have expanded our understanding of man in his social setting. Some of these theories and concepts have been applied to historical study, and some historians have emerged as strong advocates of social science knowledge for the study of the past. As we have previously stressed, only a few radicals wish to renounce the traditional goals of historical research. Instead the proponents of an associated endeavor between history and the social sciences recognize that the question is "not whether to use social science knowledge, but what to use." [28]

Historians generally have been opposed to the application of theories and models to their investigations because they fear the danger of allowing themselves to be *guided* into selecting only those data which substantiate the theory or model. That is not an unreasonable position to hold in the interest of finding the truth. On the other hand, as the historian Roy F. Nichols has maintained, "historians are prone to make their thought processes too simple," [29] and for that reason some historical studies are devoid of any adequate explanatory scheme. Applicable social science theories may in fact provide "meaning and organization to otherwise diffuse data. . . . In manipulating the empirical findings the model may be modified or destroyed, but almost inevitably the process will have called attention to previously unnoticed characteristics of the evidence." [30] If theories and models are taken as points of departure for questions about the data and if they aid the historian to make his focus more precise, they may provide useful insights into otherwise meaningless facts about the past.

A number of social science concepts have been utilized by historians, and here we will cite two examples. Thomas C.

[28] Robert F. Berkhofer, Jr., *A Behavioral Approach to Historical Analysis* (New York: The Free Press, 1969), p. 5.
[29] Roy F. Nichols, *A Historian's Progress* (New York: Alfred A. Knopf, 1968), p. 137.
[30] Thomas C. Cochran, *The Inner Revolution: Essays on the Social Sciences in History* (New York: Harper & Row, 1964), p. 30.

Cochran, for instance, has applied the concept of "social role" to railroad leaders of the latter half of the nineteenth century. These role characteristics "provide an explanation for various attitudes and a scheme for their logical arrangement . . ." and thus eliminate the problem of trying to determine the motivation of the individual railroad leaders.[31] The concept of social mobility has proven to be very useful in studying certain segments of past society. Thus Oscar and Mary Handlin have traced social mobility in the United States from the founding of the nation to the present century,[32] and Stephan Thernstrom has examined social mobility in a nineteenth century city in the United States.[33]

QUANTITATIVE STUDIES

Many historians who consider their discipline humanistic recoil at the thought of applying quantitative techniques to the study of the past. Fearful of a dehumanizing effect, they depreciate the efforts of "quantitative historians" to utilize statistics as a tool of historical research. Yet, as Lee Benson apprises us, historians show no aversion to "counting" in such terms as "typical," "representative," "significant," "widespread," "growing," and "intense"; and to this list David H. Fischer has added other "impressionistic" terms employed by historians (e.g., "few," "some," "most," "many," "singular," and "normal").[34] The obvious problem is the imprecision of such quantitative expressions. It is often impossible, of course, to be exact in historical accounts, and historians are not vulnerable because of that fact. Where precision and more rigorous analysis are possible through quantification, however, historians must recognize the contribution of this new technique. If, as William O. Aydelotte suggests, quantification is "a

[31] Cochran, The Inner Revolution, p. 30.
[32] Oscar and Mary Handlin, The Dimensions of Liberty (Cambridge: Harvard University Press, 1961), chapter 7.
[33] Stephan Thernstrom, Poverty and Progress: Social Mobility in a Nineteenth Century City (Cambridge: Harvard University Press, 1964).
[34] Lee Benson, "Research Problems in American Political Historiography," in Common Frontiers of the Social Sciences, ed. Mirra Komarovsky (Glencoe, Ill.: The Free Press, 1957), p. 117; David Hackett Fischer, Historians' Fallacies (New York: Harper & Row, 1970), p. 124.

powerful tool in historical analysis" which helps "to render the darkness [of the past] less opaque," [35] then historians must come to accept it as another useful vehicle for probing the past.

Like so many other aids to historical research, quantitative techniques are not new. Frederick Jackson Turner, for example, applied statistical methods to his study of the American frontier. As generally used by historians, however, statistics has been applied in descriptive fashion, and that continues to be an appropriate method in some historical writing today. The utilization of inferential statistics has only recently become recognized as having a legitimate, if limited, place in historical inquiry. Thus the concepts of probability, measures of central tendency, and tests of statistical significance are now being employed by some historians.[36]

Quantitative methods applied to historical research are no different from other social science methods: They possess certain advantages and suffer certain limitations. Among the former are their ability to render increased precision to the treatment of numerical data, their capacity to yield a more complete analysis of certain historical evidence, and their efficiency in imparting greater insights into the actions of large groups (e.g., voting patterns, social mobility, demographic factors, and conduct of legislative bodies). The foremost limitation of quantitative methods is their inapplicability to a considerable amount of historical evidence. The tendency to jump on the bandwagon of quantitative history is no less real than the inclination of some individuals to accept any other method as the key to historical truth. Aside from that obstacle, however, the quantitative approach contains other shortcomings. It must be recognized that classificatory schemes are frequently necessary to apply statistical procedures, and that operation requires the forcing of data into categories. At best, quantification is simply "a convenient arrangement of the

[35] William O. Aydelotte, *Quantification in History* (Reading, Mass.: Addison-Wesley Publishing Company, 1971), p. 61.
[36] It is beyond the scope of this book to explicate these concepts. For additional information, see, for example, Charles M. Dollar and Richard J. Jensen, *Historian's Guide to Statistics* (New York: Holt, Rinehart and Winston, 1971). This volume contains a comprehensive bibliography on quantitative historical research.

evidence,"[37] and for that reason it is not superior to some other arrangement. Moreover, statistical techniques require the use of samples, and thus certitude about such results can never be guaranteed—though we should add that this is equally true of the traditional sampling of manuscript sources.[38] Finally, the findings of a quantitative study no more speak for themselves than do the facts in conventional historical research; they must also be interpreted if they are to convey any meaning.

The computer has been a boon to quantitative history, making it possible to complete calculations in a reasonable amount of time which otherwise would have taken an individual a lifetime to accomplish. Gerald S. Hawkins was able to unlock the mysteries of Stonehenge, for example, by employing the aid of a computer to determine the alignment of that magnificent monument with the solar body.[39] Other uses of the computer have not been as elaborate, but they have nonetheless proven that the computer can be an important ally of the historian who is interested in examining certain statistical data of the past. The same caution regarding the appropriate use of this device is necessary, just as it was for the other approaches to historical study we have mentioned. The computer cannot determine what the historian ought to study, but it can be used to find answers to important problems which are not otherwise amenable to conventional methods of research.[40]

One effective use of quantification is content analysis. This method may be described as the counting of the frequency of appearance of words, phrases, and symbols in a given body of literature. The purpose of content analysis is not merely to count, however, but to explore attitudes and thought. Based on the assumption that the frequent recurrence of certain expres-

[37] Aydelotte, *Quantification in History*, p. 52.
[38] Ideally, of course, the historian will exhaust all sources pertinent to his topic. In actual practice, however, he often falls short of his goal for such reasons as (1) restrictions on release of certain government documents, (2) the overwhelming number of sources available on some topics, and (3) the paucity of sources on some topics. Hence, he is compelled to use a "sample"—though he generally prefers not to use that term.
[39] Gerald S. Hawkins, *Stonehenge Decoded* (Garden City, N.Y.: Doubleday & Co., 1965).
[40] See, for example, the comments of Stephan Thernstrom, "The Historian and the Computer," in *Computers in Humanistic Research*, ed. Edmund A. Bowles (Englewood Cliffs, N.J.: Prentice-Hall, 1967).

sions is indicative of inward feelings, content analysis often provides clues which may not be verified through impressionistic analysis. As an example we can cite Richard L. Merritt's study of the emergence of American nationalism. The question raised by Merritt was when did the American colonial press begin to reflect a "sense of group identification," that is, when did the symbolic shift "from the British political community to a strictly American political community" become most pronounced? Merritt categorized the symbolic expressions of self-reference into those which identified the subject as being British and those which stressed an American orientation. Then, through sampling the newspapers between 1735 and 1775, he tabulated the number of self-referent symbols in each category. By plotting the average number of symbols per year on a frequency polygon, he was able to study the overall trend in the usage of self-referent symbols. Merritt discovered that for the period 1735 to 1775 the use of these symbols fluctuated in cycles but the general trend was toward increased identification as Americans. In other words, the process of becoming "American" was "gradual and fitful, with a few periods of extremely rapid advances . . . interspersed with other periods of more or less mild relapses," and it was in the early 1760's and just prior to the Revolution that the process reached its greatest points of intensity.[41] Thus, Merritt has demonstrated the usefulness of one of the simpler forms of content analysis. More elaborate varieties of content analysis are also possible.

Studies in correlation and more sophisticated statistical tests which take into consideration the interplay of several variables have made it possible for historians to examine a mass of numerical data with a view to any relationships which exist among them. The research of Aydelotte on the 815 members of the British House of Commons between 1841 and 1847 permitted him to learn more about "the social and economic composition of the house and the political behavior of the various groups in it. . . ."[42] Similar studies of the composition of the Congress of the United States have enlarged our understanding of the actions of that body as a whole

[41] Richard L. Merritt, "The Emergence of American Nationalism: A Quantitative Approach," in *Sociology and History*, ed. Seymour Martin Lipset and Richard Hofstadter (New York: Basic Books, 1968), pp. 138–58.
[42] Aydelotte, *Quantification in History*, p. 136.

during given periods. In a study of the United States Senate from 1861 to 1863, for example, Allan G. Bogue applied statistical techniques to analyze blocs and alignments on key issues considered by that body.[43] And Bernard Silberman statistically analyzed the nature of recruitment and advancement of civil bureaucrats in Japan from 1868 to 1899 as compared with the post-1899 period.[44]

The studies employing statistical tests of significance are also applicable to larger groups. Thus Richard P. McCormick statistically tested the standard historical hypothesis that "the [Andrew] Jackson elections involved a 'mighty democratic uprising' " and concluded that the actual voting data do not support that interpretation.[45] Sheldon Hackney employed a statistical method to study violence in the South.[46] And historical demography has thrown new light on populations of the past. Quantitative techniques have been applied quite successfully, for example, to studies of change in medieval population and to movements of population in nineteenth century France.[47]

Quantitative research in history, then, opens new avenues to the past. That it is not the only road has already been stressed. But it may be well to remind ourselves that history is still basically a humanistic study, and quantification is useful to historical research only insofar as it helps us to understand human beings in the past. The lure of certainty and exactness inherent in quantified studies may draw the historian into a cave of deception if he does not remain alert to its limitations.

[43] Allan G. Bogue, "Bloc and Party in the United States Senate: 1861–1863," in *Quantification in American History*, ed. Robert P. Swierenga (New York: Atheneum, 1970), pp. 131–48.
[44] Bernard Silberman, "National Development and the Evolution of the Legal-Rational Bureaucracy: The Prefectural Governor in Japan, 1868–1945," in *The Uses of History*, ed. Hayden V. White (Detroit: Wayne State University Press, 1968), pp. 247–77.
[45] Richard P. McCormick, "New Perspectives on Jacksonian Politics," *American Historical Review*, 65 (January 1960): 288–301.
[46] Sheldon Hackney, "Southern Violence," *American Historical Review*, 74 (February 1969): 906–25.
[47] See, for example, Josiah C. Russell, *Late Ancient and Medieval Population* (Philadelphia: American Philosophical Society, 1958); Guillaume de Bertier de Sauvigny, "Population Movements and Political Changes in Nineteenth Century France," in *Quantitative History*, ed. Don Karl Rowney and James Q. Graham, Jr. (Homewood, Ill.: The Dorsey Press, 1969), pp. 308–16; and, for a general treatment, see T. H. Hollingsworth, *Historical Demography* (Ithaca: Cornell University Press, 1969).

COMPARATIVE STUDIES

"Historical comparisons," says C. Vann Woodward, "are
notoriously dangerous and misleading, and historians as a rule
are reluctant to make them." [48] But, as Woodward concedes,
such comparisons are unavoidable, and for that reason historians should not shun them but should lend their expertise to a
field which has been growing in importance in recent years. In
the next chapter we will discuss the use of analogies in history,
but here we are concerned more with an in-depth analysis of a
single institution as it developed in two or more societies. The
purpose of the analogies is to compare and contrast the ways
in which that institution evolved in each of the societies. While
the approach is akin to social science analysis, it differs in its
aims. For the social scientist the aim of comparative study is
"to produce theories of cultural and social change or of
political and economic development," but for the historian the
goal is to examine events in their temporal setting without
regard to developing a theory from them.[49] By the very nature
of comparative history, the historian is compelled to observe
the general factors peculiar to the institution under study, but
his purpose is not primarily to formulate laws from his limited
comparisons.

If for no other reason, comparative studies are useful
because they provide a broader perspective of the past than
can be gained by focusing only upon the development of
institutions in one society. A principal danger of specialization
is that it will promote historical parochialism. Thus a comparison of the colonial experience, slavery, civil war, imperialism,
or economic depression in the United States with similar
historical experiences in other countries may enlarge our
understanding of the relationships between our country and
others. As Woodward suggests, comparative studies serve to
challenge "invidious claims of national priority or excel-
lence . . . ," and they provide us with a more reasonable basis
for disproving "the validity of commonly accepted parallels or
comparisons. . . ." [50] The comparative approach to historical

[48] C. Vann Woodward, ed., *The Comparative Approach to American History*
(New York: Basic Books, 1968), p. x.
[49] Berkhofer, *A Behavioral Approach to Historical Analysis*, pp. 264–65.
[50] Woodward, *The Comparative Approach to American History*, p. 348.

analysis is another way of merging the interests of social science and history.

As we indicated at the outset of this chapter, history has broken the bonds of a narrow approach to studying man's past. The related studies which we have mentioned have aided historians to broaden their horizons. Each approach is necessarily limited, and it would be folly to believe that one method is superior to all others. It would be no less unwise, however, to cling doggedly to the conviction that only traditional approaches to historical inquiry are valid. Our knowledge has advanced too far to ignore the value of many approaches to the study of man, but our sometimes irrational nature often precipitates premature decisions which cause us either to reject a new approach outright or to endow it with unexcelled qualities.

CHAPTER 7

The Uses of History

Opinions on the usefulness of history range across a continuum to both extremes. Perhaps we have all seen the school pupil or the college student who states flatly that the study of history is a waste of time because it is totally irrelevant to present needs. From that extreme we can move to the opposite end of the continuum to find the metahistorian who swears with the strength of his soul that history is the fount of all wisdom and guidance. As with all dogmatic assertions, neither of these immoderate positions is really satisfactory, for somewhere in between lies the truth. History does serve some useful purposes, but it is not an infallible teacher. Let us therefore examine both what history can do and what it cannot do.

LESSONS, ANALOGIES, AND PREDICTION

"Those who cannot remember the past are condemned to repeat it," declared the philosopher George Santayana.[1] Taking "history" as synonymous with "the past" in Santayana's

[1] George Santayana, *The Life of Reason* (London: Constable and Company, 1905), p. 284.

statement, who can deny the value of historical study? The assumption underlying Santayana's dictum is, of course, that history does contain lessons. But we must raise the question of whether that is in fact the case.

How often have we heard the expressions "History has shown that . . ." or "History teaches us that . . ."! Implied in these facile statements is the belief that we know what the lessons of history are. That, unfortunately, too often expresses only our wishes and not reality. "The lessons of history," observes Carl G. Gustavson, "are not as easy to discern as some people would have us believe. Any statement in which the prefatory 'History teaches us that . . .' is used as a springboard should be very carefully scrutinized; the accompanying assertion may be quite valid and acceptable, but the odds are against it." [2] A typical example of the belief that the lessons of history are clear may be found in the recent statement of a newspaper journalist. Indicting the Secretary of Defense for timidity in handling the seizure of the United States vessel *Pueblo* by the North Koreans in 1968, the writer asserts that

> The lesson of history is that victory goes to the bold and daring. If the free world fails to use its scientific and technological know-how to stop the armed hordes of communism, it may be bled to death by the modern guerrilla war version of the old oriental torture death of a thousand cuts.[3]

How nice it would be if the lessons of history were so simple and clear-cut. Unhappily, the writer conveniently forgets that Hitler was bold and daring but hardly achieved any real victory; Japan boldly and daringly attacked a major power and instead of victory reaped disaster for its efforts—the story could go on with repeated examples refuting the writer's "lesson of history."

Although historians have been more reluctant than philosophers, prophets, and others to draw the lessons of history for us, even a few of them have endeavored to tell us what history

[2] Carl G. Gustavson, *A Preface to History* (New York: McGraw-Hill, 1955), p. 5.
[3] Thurman Sensing, in his column "Sensing the News," *Athens* (Ga.) *Banner-Herald*, February 5, 1968, p. 4.

teaches. Among them was Theodore Roosevelt, a historian in his own right and president of the American Historical Association in 1912. Speaking of the demise of Holland as an influential nation, Roosevelt pronounced that a lesson of history is: "To be opulent and unarmed is to secure ease in the present at the almost certain cost of disaster in the future." [4] One cannot but wonder, though, to what extent Roosevelt's lesson of history was influenced by the events of the time in which he formulated it.

On the other hand, it may be foolish to argue that we cannot learn something from history. Whether or not we *do* is another matter, but that we *can* is something else. Certainly, the reflective historian is in a position to suggest some *possible* lessons in the form of generalizations about our past. Samuel Eliot Morison, the doyen of American historians, states that "the historian who knows, or thinks he knows, an unmistakable lesson of the past, has the right and the duty to point it out, even though it counteract his own beliefs or social theories." [5] It is indeed a risky business, but that is not an adequate reason to forego it altogether. If we understand the tentative quality of the lesson, then we are not in danger of reading more into it than is there. Hence we may profit from such a limited lesson or generalization as that drawn by Dexter Perkins from his long-time study of foreign affairs. In reference to communist revolutions Perkins believes he has discovered a useful lesson: "Not social discontent alone, but social discontent which has undermined the authority of the army and destroyed its morale, is the situation which brings about a Communist takeover." [6]

What should now be obvious in our argument concerning lessons of history is that the lessons are circumscribed by time and the historian's own limited ability. The broader and more widely applicable the lesson reputes to be, the greater the danger that evidence will refute it. There is an added danger too. It is possible that a so-called lesson will be taken so much to heart by the people of a nation that they will become rigidly

[4] Theodore Roosevelt, *Biological Analogies in History* (Oxford: The Clarendon Press, 1910), p. 27.
[5] Samuel Eliot Morison, "Faith of a Historian," *American Historical Review*, 56 (January 1951): 265.
[6] Dexter Perkins, *Yield of the Years* (Boston: Little, Brown and Company, 1969), p. 137.

bound to their image of the past. In the 1890's Alfred T. Mahan, for example, drew what he felt were practical lessons about the influence of sea power upon the history of nations. Some national leaders took Mahan so seriously that his "lessons" played a critical role in the armaments race prior to World War I.

The past can in fact become onerous, Santayana notwithstanding. When man's image of his nation's past is not tempered by a critical view of history, it can lead to all kinds of unmitigated evil. As Herbert Butterfield so perceptively remarks, "Historical memories, especially in Eastern Europe—and also in Ireland—have engendered much of the national animosity of modern times. . . . One must wonder sometimes whether it would not have been better if men could have . . . thrown off the terrible burden of the past, so that they might face the future without encumbrances." [7]

If historians are reluctant to point out lessons of history, they are less reserved about noting parallels, that is, about comparing events of a later period of time with those of an earlier era. Historical analogy is a legitimate use of history, though any analogy must not be extended beyond the limits which circumscribe it. Thus while it would be a mistake to assume too much applicability of historical analogies, we can at least expect them to provide us with insights about similarity of situations and perhaps some future *possibilities*.

Even though the historian is unlikely to believe in the inevitability of the outcomes of similar events, he is at least aware of the possibility that certain consequences will issue from events which are comparable to other events of the past. To explore and explain cause-effect relationships is part of his business, and these in turn necessitate some comparisons. Stringfellow Barr, for example, found some similarities between modern America and ancient Rome. The two states are alike, he concludes, in that each has a legend of beginning with a ship, the Aeneas and the Mayflower, and each ship bore an Elect, refugees who "founded a new City"; each became a young republic, "increased and multiplied, and its land hunger grew insatiably"; each "brought in slaves," from Africa in the

[7] Herbert Butterfield, *History and Human Relations* (New York: The Macmillan Company, 1952), pp. 166–67. See also J. H. Plumb, *The Death of the Past* (Boston: Houghton Mifflin Company, 1970) for an optimistic point of view on this topic.

case of America and as prisoners of war in the case of Rome; each developed a "desire for money"; and each moved to take vast "stretches of land," which invited the twin characteristics of "activism and voluntarism." Then, Barr further argues, while the two states are separated by "great and obvious differences," the "American Century" may lead to "where the Roman Century of Augustus led," with the development of a military-industrial complex and our swift rise to world power which may corrupt us with an unwonted "faith in the efficacy of power." [8] Many questions leap to mind concerning Barr's comparison, such as "isolating just the one strain about the use of force";[9] but it is an analogy which deserves our consideration.

Analogies between past and present events need not be confined to comparisons of one nation or civilization with another, however. Similarities and parallels may be found between one era and another within the same country. Thus C. Vann Woodward observes the correspondence of conditions in the United States between circa 1930 and the mid-1950's and those of the South in the 1830's. Recognizing that the "dangers inherent in any such comparison between historical epochs are numerous and forbidding," Woodward proceeds with proper caution to "venture a comparison, not between the two institutions [of modern capitalism and slavery as a system of labor], but between the public attitudes toward them and the transformations that took place in those attitudes." The 1930's in the United States were a time of intense criticism of the capitalist system: "No corner nor aspect nor relationship of American capitalism was overlooked, and no shibboleth of free enterprise went unchallenged." This attitude was accepted on the whole as a salutary sign of the strength of the society. By the mid-forties, however, a transformation occurred, and the "floodstream of criticism dwindled to a trickle and very nearly ceased altogether." The nation was then beset with accusations, counteraccusations, charges of disloyalty, and McCar-

---

[8] Stringfellow Barr, "Consulting the Romans: An Analogy Between Ancient Rome and Present-Day America." An Occasional Paper. (Santa Barbara, Calif.: The Center for the Study of Democratic Institutions, 1967). This paper is based on his larger work, *The Mask of Jove* (Philadelphia: J. B. Lippincott Company, 1966).

[9] Barr, "Consulting the Romans," p. 19. This is a question raised by William Gorman in a discussion of Barr's paper.

thyism or witch hunting of the first magnitude, and institutions which had been the object of criticism became the object of "rapturous praise."

This transformation, notes Woodward, was reminiscent of the events in the South in the 1830's, where, prior to that decade, "a vigorous school of antislavery" flourished. The critics of slavery, as with the critics of capitalism, "included men of influence and standing." But antislavery thought reached its apex in the debates over emancipation in the Virginia legislature of 1831–32, and from that point the movement "withered away to almost nothing in a very brief period during the middle thirties." In fact, by 1837 not a single antislavery society existed in the South, and as in the 1940's and 1950's, loyalty to institutions became a matter of conformity, with fervid attention given to scrutinizing the past records of men of public life. While several reasons explain the two transformations, Woodward observes that "both of these revolutions in public attitudes were reactions to contests for power in which the two societies found themselves involved." And what is the upshot of this comparison if not to draw some potential lessons? Woodward suggests that we may learn from this that

> economic systems, whatever their age, their respectability, or their apparent stability, are transitory and that any nation which elects to stand or fall upon one ephemeral institution has already determined its fate.

And in a broader sense this comparison implies that

> an overwhelming conviction in the righteousness of a cause is no guarantee of its ultimate triumph, and . . . the policy which takes into account the possibility of defeat is more realistic than one that assumes the inevitability of victory.[10]

Perhaps the most popular analogy of the last decade has been that comparing North Vietnam's aggression against South Vietnam with Hitler's aggression against Czechoslovakia, or the Munich analogy. The analogy has been offered by

[10] C. Vann Woodward, *The Burden of Southern History*, rev. ed. (Baton Rouge: Louisiana State University Press, 1968), pp. 187–211.

officials of the United States government, including President Lyndon B. Johnson. The proponents of the analogy argue that the dissenters against United States involvement in Vietnam are like the appeasers of Nazi Germany at Munich in 1938. To have failed to stand against the aggression of North Vietnam would have been similar to the moral error committed at Munich, for appeasement only allows the aggressor to proceed with his policy of seizing more and more territory (often referred to as the Domino Theory). The validity of the analogy has been attacked by several historians. A brief but effective indictment of the analogy has been made by George O. Kent. "This analogy," says Kent, "seems mistaken on several counts." And he summarizes the mistakes as follows:

> Britain and France were motivated by their fear of another world war and by the conviction of their own military inferiority. This, however, does not apply to the United States in the late 1960's. (If military weakness leads to appeasement, it would seem as Arnold Toynbee pointed out in *Life* Magazine of December 8, 1967, that China is appeasing the United States to an unprecedented extent.) There is also the military strategic factor. Germany in the 1930's was a highly industrialized state, actively rearming and pursuing a policy of thinly veiled aggression. (The re-occupation of the Rhineland and the annexation of Austria were the most obvious signs.) It seems, furthermore, that the strategic importance of the Sudeten areas to Britain and France in the 1930's was infinitely greater than that of South Vietnam to the United States today.[11]

Thus it is that analogies in history are sometimes fallacious. And Arthur Schlesinger, Jr., goes a step further by suggesting that the Munich analogy in the case of American policy in Vietnam is not only invalid but also an instance wherein people have "wrenched [a historical generalization] illegitimately out of the past and imposed [it] mechanically upon the future. Santayana's aphorism must be reversed: too often it is those who *can* remember the past who are condemned to repeat it. . . ."[12] The Munich analogy has for too many people

[11] George O. Kent, "Clio the Tyrant: Historical Analogies and the Meaning of History," *The Historian*, 32 (November 1969): 100–101.
[12] Arthur Schlesinger, Jr., "On the Inscrutability of History," *Encounter*, 37 (November 1966): p. 14. For other criticisms of this analogy, see Arno J.

become the guiding star for all future action in foreign affairs. However limited the analogy, however short of being a law, fruitful comparisons are one use of history. Though pointing up analogies is not the sole function of the historian, perhaps many historians have overreacted to the work of metahistorians and consequently neglected to study, observe, and duly note analogies or parallels in history. Their comparisons will be stated as generalizations, but if we are not guided by valid historical generalizations, then we will be guided by myths.

The limitations of historical lessons and analogies necessarily reduce the possibility of forecasting future historical events. To predict the future on the basis of what happened in the past is somewhat like shooting an arrow at a distant target in a large field at twilight. Thus about the best the historian can do is locate the general direction of the target and aim in that direction. The target will at best be barely perceptible, and a number of factors may intervene so that the target moves or the arrow is thrown off course by a sudden gust of wind. Fortuitous circumstances are ever-present in the life of man, and man's reaction to events is never so constant that we can state with lawlike precision that he will behave in the same way at all times.

Anticipation of the possible outcome of a future event may be as close as history can ever bring us to the realm of prediction. "If, for instance, it is true that Prussia collapsed rapidly under military defeat in 1806 and 1918, one of the *possibilities* to anticipate should be the rapid collapse of Prussia after another military defeat." [13] The argument here is, of course, not that the collapse of Prussia upon another military defeat is inevitable, only that it *may* be anticipated. The nature of history will never permit us to view the future with the certitude we often crave. "But," states Arthur Bestor,

to expect that history will enable a man to arm himself with foresight is to cherish a rational hope. If foresight be

---

Mayer, "Vietnam Analogy: Greece, Not Munich," *The Nation* (March 25, 1968), pp. 407–10; and David Hackett Fischer, *Historians' Fallacies*, pp. 248–50.

[13] Louis R. Gottschalk, Clyde Kluckhohn, and Robert Angell, *The Use of Personal Documents in History, Anthropology, and Sociology*, Bulletin No. 53 (New York: Social Science Research Council, 1945), p. 70.

defined as the ability to make informed guesses about the characteristics of future situations and thus to encounter them forewarned, then history, by fostering foresight, is making no inconsiderable contribution to the intelligent conduct of human affairs.[14]

To hope for more is to expect too much of history. But it is at least preferable to uninformed opinion and wild guess.

While historians are disinclined to peer into the future to guess at what may occur, they are not averse to glancing backward to speculate on how it could have been if certain things had happened differently. Some philosophers of history refer to this action as "retrodiction." At first consideration it may seem futile to speculate upon the "might-have-beens of the past," for the past is the past and therefore cannot be changed. "But the finality [of the past] means that historical events are irreversible, not that they are all necessary . . .‚" Sidney Hook reminds us.[15] Such conjectures are valid, of course, only as long as what is considered were actual possibilities at the time of the event. If they were possible, then the historian may contribute to our understanding by indicating the alternatives which were open at the time. In some instances mere luck or chance was the determining factor and therefore not under the control of men. In other cases, however, decisions were made by men, groups, or nations, and for that reason the "if . . . then" relationship points up what was a possible course of action that was either rejected or overlooked.

A few examples of "hypothetical history" should suffice to illustrate this point. Both of the following examples deal with World War II—a momentous event of our time and for that reason worthy of conjecture about alternative actions. In the first instance, William L. Shirer raises a "might-have-been" regarding the Munich crisis:

Germany was in no position to go to war on October 1, 1938, against Czechoslovakia and France and Britain, not

---

[14] Arthur Bestor, "History as Verifiable Knowledge: The Logic of Historical Inquiry and Explanation," in *Research Methods in Librarianship: Historical and Bibliographical Methods in Library Research*, Monograph No. 10, ed. Rolland E. Stevens (Urbana: University of Illinois Graduate School of Library Science, 1971), p. 124.

[15] Sidney Hook, *The Hero in History* (Boston: Beacon Press, 1955), p. 134. See pp. 119–50 for a full discussion on the topic of "ifs" in history.

to mention Russia. *Had* she done so, she would have been quickly and easily defeated, and that would have been the end of Hitler and the Third Reich. *If* a European war had been averted at the last moment by the intercession of the German Army, Hitler *might* have been overthrown by Halder and Witzleben and their confederates carrying out their plan to arrest him as soon as he had given the final order for the attack on Czechoslovakia.[16]

The second example deals with the Potsdam Declaration and the surrender of Japan:

> The Allies thus had here, in late July 1945, the very document which Japan finally accepted in mid-August. Had Prince Konoye, as the fully empowered personal representative of the Emperor of Japan, been permitted to travel to Moscow (or anywhere else, for that matter) and had he there been handed the text of this proclamation prior to its release to the world at large, he conceivably could have resolved speedily the very issues which government leaders in Tokyo spent the next three weeks in debating without result. *Had* the Allies given the prince a week of grace in which to obtain his government's support for acceptance, the war *might* have ended toward the latter part of July or the very beginning of August without the atomic bomb and without Soviet participation in the conflict.[17]

Surely, no one can assert positively that either of these events *would* have ended differently, but it is entirely possible that they *could* have. And such knowledge may afford us a better grasp of *why* events took the turn they did.[18] At any rate, reflection about such alternative courses of action may help us to sharpen our mental processes and increase our ability to cope with decision-making situations.

[16] William L. Shirer, *The Rise and Fall of the Third Reich* (New York: Simon and Schuster, 1960), p. 426; italics added. Copyright © 1959, 1960, by William L. Shirer. Reprinted by permission of Simon and Schuster, Inc.
[17] Robert J. C. Butow, *Japan's Decision to Surrender* (Stanford: Stanford University Press, 1954), p. 133; italics added.
[18] For a brief discussion of the application of "counterfactual conditionals" to broader problems, see J. D. Gould, "Hypothetical History," *Economic History Review*, 22 (August 1969): 195–207.

KNOWLEDGE, EXPERIENCE, AND APPRECIATION

As human beings we are forced to make decisions every day of our lives, and we act on the basis of those decisions. More often than not, these decisions are routine and of no great import, though occasionally we are compelled to make momentous decisions and to act in ways which may affect us deeply. The basis for such personal decisions is to be found in our beliefs, experience, and knowledge—or in a combination of all three. If we were suddenly deprived of all our beliefs, experience, and knowledge, that is, if our memory failed us completely, we would be forced to begin at the most elemental stage of man's existence to work out basic solutions to our immediate needs. And it would be a long time before we could through trial and error build up a system of beliefs, useful experience, and new knowledge which would save us from mistakes and gradually make life more bearable. Happily for us no such traumatic experience is likely to occur. What we may often fail to appreciate, however, is the value of the past to our lives.

A person can function on the basis of a very limited system of beliefs, a narrow background of experience, and a constricted amount of knowledge—at least where his decisions affect him primarily only in a personal way. As literacy spreads and as civilization becomes more complex, however, man is less and less left to himself. Consequently, he encounters life on a larger scale, and his actions have a greater bearing upon the society of which he is a part. Thus, the more he understands the world in which he lives, the greater the likelihood he will not be the victim of his own ignorance. And to understand the world and the present, one must have some knowledge of the past. Understanding the past, however, is more than possessing an unexamined mental image (or a myth, if you will) of what has gone before. When the past becomes history, as we defined it at the outset, then man is in a position to make more carefully reasoned decisions and to act in a rational way. That he will not necessarily do so is granted, but that he will be able to do so is justification enough for studying his past.

To argue for a knowledge of the past is not to defend the mere acquisition of historical facts. As Frederic Harrison noted some seventy years ago: "Facts are infinite, and it is not the millionth part of them that is worth knowing. What some people call the pure love of truth often means only a pure love of intellectual fussiness. A statement may be true, and yet wholly worthless." [19] History, as we have previously argued, is more than a compilation of facts. Its life depends on facts, of course, but its end is not the mere memorization of those facts. By a knowledge of the past we mean that one understands something about the processes of social change, possesses some insight into the multitude of factors which have shaped our present and how these have shaped the present of other societies in different ways, and, above all, sees the wisdom of having a critical attitude toward what men say about the past. It is a broad knowledge which can help us to see beyond the narrow confines of our own immediate and personal world, to grasp the concept of the great community of man from the time *homo sapiens* appeared until the present, which is ever becoming the past. To help us see ourselves in perspective is a task of history. And having properly seen ourselves in "time and space," Commager reminds us, we can moderate "our instinctive and pervasive parochialism" and subdue our intolerance "with different faiths, different loyalties, different cultures, different ideas and ideals." [20]

History can help us shake off the shackles of excessive ethnocentrism and the debilitating bias of cultural and racial purity; it aids us to become "coterminous with humanity." [21] History helps to illuminate the human condition. Far from making us "unpatriotic," history helps us to know why we hold particular loyalties; it promotes in us the greatest kind of loyalty—a commitment to freedom of critical inquiry.

As creatures of our own immediate surroundings, we are naturally prone to believe that the light of culture shines brightest in our own circle. Our ideas, our beliefs, and our customs seem to us to be sanctified; those of others seem to suffer the defects of inferiority, or at the least they are viewed as unenlightened. As the philosopher Morris R. Cohen has so

[19] Frederic Harrison, *The Meaning of History* (New York: The Macmillan Company, 1902), pp. 10–11.
[20] Henry Steele Commager, *The Nature and the Study of History* (Columbus, O.: Charles E. Merrill Books, 1965), p. 92.
[21] A. L. Rowse, *The Use of History*, rev. ed. (New York: The Macmillan Company, 1963), p. 26.

meaningfully stated it: "History is necessary to control the exaggerated idea of our own originality and of the uniqueness of our own age and problems. To live from day to day without a wider vista is to fail to see all that is involved in the issues of the day." [22] Surely, we cannot claim that the study of history alone can accomplish this goal: The study of literature, philosophical and religious systems, cultural anthropology, and a whole host of other activities of man in differing societies and at various times in his past—all are important to enlarging our perspective. History is one vital dimension of our reality, however, and it can aid us to appreciate our humanity.

Most of us recognize the value of experience, and we usually laud experience as a great asset in any man because it renders him more capable of making proper value judgments. It is not only the length of experience which we prize, however, but also its variety. As individuals we can *personally* experience only so much—and naturally some individuals profit more than others from their experience. Thus history can expose us not only to more experience and a greater variety of experience but also to the experience of men in past ages. "History," Ernest Scott informs us, "clarifies, criticizes, compares, co-ordinates experience, and makes it available for all." [23] If we are but willing, we can further expand our intellectual and humanistic horizons by partaking of the fruit of our historical experience.

HISTORY AND IDENTIFICATION

Not the least of the values of history is its existential function: It provides us with a sense of being. Without history we would not know who we are, either individually or collectively. True enough, we often identify ourselves by fantasies and myths, but the value of good critical history is that it helps us to acquire a more realistic identity. History viewed thus "is no mere complex of settled events, no museum of dead objects. History is a living thing, it is with us and in us every moment of

[22] Morris R. Cohen, *The Meaning of Human History*, 2nd ed. (LaSalle, Ill.: The Open Court Publishing Company, 1961), p. 277.
[23] Ernest Scott, *History and Historical Problems* (London: Oxford University Press, 1925), p. 6.

our lives." [24] Through history we become conscious that we are links which connect the past, present, and future. We are particular men and women, existing in a particular historical time—continuants in one sense but shapers of the future in another sense. Thus we do not serve history by obeisance to the past, but history serves us by telling us who we are and by enlarging our prospects. For this reason, "history has to be periodically rewritten," as Barzun notes, so that we become capable of dealing "not with a crisis once every ten years, but for dealing with life itself, every day. . . ." [25]

Over the long span of his existence in civilized communities, man has endeavored to memorialize himself. This attempt to transcend his temporal life has taken a variety of forms, but one of the most persistent has been the recounting of his activities, sometimes on clay tablets or papyrus and at other times simply by oral story telling. Man did not begin to develop a sense of genuine historical consciousness, however, until he broke the bonds of cyclical recurrence and substituted a linear conception of purposeful, goal-oriented history. From the time of the Hebrews man began gradually to envisage a past which is a continuum with the present and the future. This notion has made it possible for man to transcend his own moment in time. "There is pleasure," says Paul Weiss, "in knowing that we are not alone, that we are part of a single totality, that we have in a sense lived a long time." [26] History can nourish this desire for memorialization, and it can do so within the confines of man's finite being. Religion permits us to transcend the mundane if we wish, but history can help to satisfy our craving for continuation as human beings. That in itself is no mean contribution.

History affords a source of pleasurable reading for some people, and thus we can extend its dimension as a source of identification to include its humanizing function. Certainly all history does not qualify as good literature, and surely all

[24] Erich Kahler, *The Meaning of History* (New York: George Braziller, 1964), p. 24.
[25] Jacques Barzun, "History, Popular and Unpopular," in *The Interpretation of History*, ed. Joseph R. Strayer (Princeton: Princeton University Press, 1943; reprint ed., New York: Peter Smith, 1950), p. 52.
[26] Paul Weiss, *History: Written and Lived* (Carbondale: Southern Illinois University Press, 1962), p. 42. For a more elaborate treatment of this idea, see John T. Marcus, *Heaven, Hell, and History* (New York: The Macmillan Company, 1967).

125

people do not enjoy reading even that history which is skillfully written. But some histories are masterpieces of literature, and many people derive personal pleasure from immersing themselves in such works. It may be true that the Gibbons and the Macaulays of historical writing are no more to be found among our modern-day historians, but the picture is not as bleak as some historians claim. The works of such historians as Samuel Eliot Morison, Garrett Mattingly, and C. V. Wedgwood, for example, are masterfully written, and they have proved themselves to be sources of great delight for a large number of people. It may well be, in fact, that it is not so much the lack of good historical writing which has stifled public interest in the reading of history as it is our failure to impart to students the excitement and joy which history has to offer. The excessive emphasis upon memorization of facts, the dullness of so many history lectures, and the stress upon history textbooks in our schools and colleges hardly serve to whet interest in reading history as a pleasurable activity. But the fault lies more in our approach than it does in historical writing itself.

THE ABUSE OF HISTORY

It is easy to claim too much for history, and the tendency to overstate its values has in no small measure reduced its credibility. Perhaps the single greatest abuse of history is committed by those who try to make it a repository of moral examples and caveats. The ascription of this function to history is typified in the statement of Lord Bolingbroke that "history is philosophy teaching by examples." The concept of history as instruction for good citizenship was further elaborated by Bolingbroke in the following statement: "An application to any study, that tends neither directly nor indirectly to make us better men and better citizens, is at best but a specious and ingenious sort of idleness . . . the study of history seems to me, of all other, the most proper to train us up to private and public virtue." [27] And so it is that the function of

[27] Henry Saint-John, Lord Viscount Bolingbroke, *Letters on the Study and Use of History* (Paris: Theophilus Barrois, Jr., 1808), pp. 11–12. The statement was not original with Lord Bolingbroke; it was made by Dionysius of Halicarnassus who seems to have borrowed the idea from Thucydides.

history in the school curriculum is frequently viewed solely as civic education. This is an unfortunate misuse of history, for while history may make us wiser citizens, it should not be used to entrench partisan and parochial impressions.

In the same vein history is abused by those who would select from it those elements which support their particular cause. Needless to say, the practice of "using" the past to sanctify change toward some revolutionary end, no matter how worthy, is to adapt it to authoritarian purposes. And, likewise, the "use" of the past to justify traditional institutions is a corruption of history. From our study of history we may see possibilities, potentialities, and alternatives, it is true. But we cannot use it as a source of ironclad authority.

A search for the *practical* use of history invariably ends in disappointment. That should not be taken to suggest that history is useless, however. Wisdom does not emanate solely from a study of utilitarian knowledge. History, properly understood and appreciated, is educative, and for that reason it is useful.

PART II

Approaches to Instruction in History

CHAPTER 8

A Rationale for the Teaching of History

Recently, on an eighth grade United States history examination, the following question appeared: "What are five things that have helped make America the greatest nation on earth?" That question typifies the most flagrant abuse of history possible, namely, history as nationalistic propaganda. On another recent test—this one for a tenth grade world history class—students were asked: "Which king, Louis XIII or Louis XIV, came to power when he was five years old, and which one began his reign when he was nine years of age?" That question exemplifies the most distorted notion of history possible, namely, history as trivial facts. Yet questions of this nature are not at all uncommon to the history class. What they reflect, unfortunately, is a basic misunderstanding of the nature of historical study. Over and beyond that, however, such questions indicate something about the teacher's viewpoint on the purposes for including history in the school curriculum, that is, to propagandize pupils and to stuff their memories with facts. Moreover, implicit in these ends of history teaching is the idea that the most effective mode of instruction is indoctrination and that memorization is the only proper form of learning. But we may question the wisdom of these points of view and thereby improve our own understanding of the aims of instruction in history. In the process, we can set forth a rationale which may be helpful to those who are committed to the teaching of history.

CLARIFYING ENDS

The conception of history as education for patriotism became the primary reason for including history in the school curriculum in nineteenth century America,[1] and it continues to flourish today as a basic justification for the teaching of history. Now we cannot deny that patriotism is both a necessary and a desirable virtue. Taken in an extreme form, however, it becomes blind obedience which ignores the faults of one's own country and postulates the inferiority of all others. When patriotism passes over into chauvinism, it not only robs the individual of seeing the variety of forms of life in other nations but also isolates him into a dangerously perverse sense of national self-righteousness. History warped to achieve such ends ceases to be history; it has been transformed into myth. Granted that inculcation of loyalty to one's own country is a worthy aim, the teacher is not justified in twisting history into a tool for that end. This is not to suggest that the study of history is to result in disloyalty but only that the abuse of history for nationalistic purposes is antithetical to the spirit of free inquiry on which history is founded.

Actually, it is that spirit of free inquiry which in the long run contributes most to effective citizenship by aiding the student to develop the knowledge, intellectual skills, and value system necessary to independent thinking and the exercising of rational judgment. History is not the only subject which can furnish the student with such mental ability, but it is the specific subject which allows us to view man and his societies in the past and thereby provide a base for balanced judgments about man's behavior. In a totalitarian society history is used as an instrument of the state, and the substance of study is dictated by authority. In an open society history serves to liberate us from the tyranny of mandated truth, enabling us to understand how our society has evolved into its present form

[1] See George H. Callcott, *History in the United States, 1800–1860* (Baltimore: The Johns Hopkins Press, 1970), pp. 180–89.

and why other societies have developed their own peculiar institutions. The ultimate decision on the worth of a particular form of society is a moral judgment. Although it may aid us to see the variety of choices, history cannot make the final decision on matters of principle. To encumber history with responsibility for the dispensation of chauvinistic attitudes is to impair its value as a source of questing for the truth.

We are no better off when history is disguised as a repository of facts. That instruction in history is frequently viewed as the transmission of facts for their own sake is too painfully real to ignore. It is not a vice of recent vintage, for, as Charles Langlois and Charles Seignobos have indicated, in nineteenth century French secondary schools the teacher, "[a]rmed with a note-book in which he had written down the list of facts to be taught . . . read it out to the pupils. . . ." [2] In a day when books were less accessible than at present, that instructional method was not totally without justification. But that far too many teachers still feel bound to act in the fashion of an executive dictating memoranda to his secretary is distressing, especially in light of the abundance of books available to students today. And if our definition of history is correct—that is, a critical interpretation and ordering of the evidence on man's past interaction with other men in society—then facts alone do not constitute history. Moreover, if history is seen as a mental attitude toward the evidence, the facts are no more than the clay from which history is molded. Lying about in the mind as so much substance waiting to be shaped into some kind of form, the facts only clutter the memory.

Why teachers fall victim to the facts-as-history theory is difficult to analyze. In large measure, it is probably a result of misunderstanding the nature of historical inquiry. It may also stem from pedagogical simplicity, for, after all, the easiest examination to construct and grade is the factual test. More enigmatically, the conception of history as purely factual substance may arise from our desire for the concrete and unchanging. Reinterpretations and revisions of standard theses in history run counter to a basic human craving for certitude. In part, the problem is compounded by the difficulty

[2] Charles V. Langlois and Charles Seignobos, *Introduction to the Study of History*, trans. G. G. Berry (London: Duckworth & Co., 1898; reprint ed., New York: Barnes & Noble, 1966), p. 326.

of keeping abreast of changing interpretations. But if the historical attitude had been apprehended during the course of the teacher's initial education in history, he could not become ensnared in the trap of teaching history as mere factual knowledge, even if he remained ignorant of recent interpretations.

The history-as-fact theory is also vulnerable on another count. Only limited reflection is necessary to expose the impossibility of teaching *all* the facts of history (and it becomes incredibly so in the instance of a course on Western civilization, not to mention a course on *world* history)! What the teacher is compelled to do, of course, is fall back upon a selection of facts. Instantly, then, we must raise the question of the criteria to be employed in choosing facts to be taught or, in other words, of deciding which facts are most important. An answer to that question will vary with each individual. And how absurd it can become is reflected in the statement of one historian-educator that it is important to know "that Thomas Jefferson and John Adams died on the same day, July 4, 1826." [3] A cursory examination of some teachers' tests will suffice to convince one that there is no agreement on what facts should be taught, and the most trivial test items often carry as much value as the more significant ones. This is not to deny that certain facts are more significant than others but only to argue that facts taught as ends in themselves do not qualify as history.

The teacher has not necessarily progressed a step further if he views the end of teaching history to be memorization of generalizations and interpretations. True enough, he has introduced other facets of historical study, but in reality he has merely substituted longer statements of synthesized facts for particular facts. His view of history remains the same—only now it is a storehouse of statements rather than a repository of facts. The danger of this position is that students will accept the generalizations and interpretations solely because they are supposed to represent authoritative pronouncements. That is no less contrary to the spirit of historical inquiry than the other errors we have already mentioned.

[3] Mark M. Krug, *History and the Social Sciences* (Waltham, Mass.: Blaisdell Publishing Company, 1967), p. 135. Krug's argument is somewhat muddled on this point, but the statement appears to be congruous with the context of the paragraph in which it appears.

When history is taken as a *mass* of facts and generalizations, the end result of teaching it is apt to be *massive* frustration, both for the teacher and even more so for the student. Names, dates, and other facts often merge in the minds of students in complete confusion. Nowhere has the futility of that idea been more effectively expressed than in Charles Dickens' *Hard Times.* "Now, what I want is, Facts," stated Mr. Gradgrind, the stern schoolmaster. "Facts alone are wanted in life," he continued. And upon the failure of Sissy Jupe to repeat the definition of a horse, he cried that she was "possessed of no facts, in reference to one of the commonest of animals." Turning to the boy Bitzer, he called for and got the answer he sought. "Quadruped. Gramnivorous," replied Bitzer. "Forty teeth, namely twenty-four grinders, four eye-teeth, and twelve incisive. Sheds coat in the spring; in marshy countries, sheds hoofs, too. Hoofs hard, but requiring to be shod with iron. Age known by marks in mouth," concluded the young boy. Satisfied, Mr. Gradgrind stated to Sissy that now "You know what a horse is." The incident would seem amusing today if it no longer represented the reality of life in an uncomfortably large number of history classrooms. The facts to be cited are different, of course, but the same rote regurgitation passes as a substitute for understanding. And before the college instructor of history can smile with a satisfied belief that it occurs only in the elementary and secondary schools, let him look around himself to see if the situation is not also applicable to many college survey courses in history.

These traditional misunderstandings of the ends of instruction in history have been recently joined by a different kind of abuse, which is that history should be taught for the purpose of rectifying the sins of society. The social engineers of this school, drinking from the cup of the radical historians, are fired by an idealism, sometimes bordering on dogmatism, which would utilize history to lay out their blueprint for the perfect society. Their transgressions against history, no matter how noble their aims, are no less deplorable than those of teachers who would sully history by making it a source of nationalistic propaganda. This is not to argue that we can or should hide the defects of our society, and in fact the study of history will inevitably expose some of those flaws. Nor is it to argue against the right of the teacher to stand on his ideological convictions. It is only to reason that history used to attain political goals is both wrong and a threat to freedom of inquiry.

Until teachers of history abandon all of these ends of instruction in history and until they envision more worthy goals for the subject, we shall remain attached to a losing proposition. In fact, while the older generation may continue to impose the requirement of history upon the young, the prospects for history as a meaningful study will continue to diminish—unless it can experience a renewal. This is not to deny that many teachers are successfully engaged in communicating a sense of the past to their students. It is only to say that the failure of a considerable number of teachers to recognize more significant ends for history in the schools than those described above is a contribution to the demise of history as an invaluable subject for study. When history is seen as enlightenment of man's past and hence as the roots of our present, when it is viewed as insight into man's behavior through the ages, and when it is understood as a means of clearing away the cobwebs of fable about the past—then instruction in history can be justified. The fundamental goal of instruction in history is to make us wiser and more tolerant human beings. As we have already stated, the study of history alone is insufficient to attain that goal, but at the same time it can help us toward that end in ways which other subjects cannot. If the history teacher sets this broad view before him as though it were emblazoned on a giant billboard, he should be able to impart the humanistic qualities of history to his students. When history is viewed as a broad landscape of life itself, the teacher is prepared to enlarge the experience of his students, and he is ready to search for the means which will aid his students to develop a broadly humanistic outlook on life.

SELECTING MEANS

"History is essentially method, not matter. It is a method of studying mankind," maintained the late Carlton J. H. Hayes.[4]

[4] Carlton J. H. Hayes, "History," in *A Quarter Century of Learning, 1904–1929* (New York: Columbia University Press, 1931), p. 9.

Properly understood, then, history should not be taught as though it were matter to be memorized: It is as much a process as it is a product. But the problem of equating information with understanding is an old one, and Lord Bolingbroke recognized it more than two centuries ago:

> Much pains are taken and time bestowed, to teach us what to think; but little or none of either, to instruct us how to think. The magazine of the memory is stored and stuffed betimes; but the conduct of the understanding is all along neglected. . . .[5]

It was that same problem of confusing memorization with discernment which, in Aldous Huxley's *Brave New World*, discouraged the fictional experimenters who tried to teach children through "hypnopaedia," or drilling a youngster's mind with facts while he was asleep. In the account, a young boy named Tommy hears repeated over and over the statement, "The Nile is the longest river in Africa and the second in length of all the rivers of the globe." But the next morning he is queried, "Tommy . . . do you know which is the longest river in Africa?" He persists in saying that he does not know the answer, and when the cue "The Nile is the . . ." is provided, Tommy can simply intone, "The-Nile-is-the-longest-river-in-Africa-and-the-second-in-length-of-all-the-rivers-of-the-globe. . . ." The conclusion of the unhappy experiment was: "You can't learn a science unless you know what it's all about." [6] And that is the message of substituting facts for understanding in the history class today! Even if the student is fortunately endowed with strong powers of memory, we have no guarantee that he will exhibit the powers of understanding simply because he can commit large quantities of fact to memory.

As Sir Herbert Butterfield has stated, "the best kind of history-teacher is not the one who tells us most clearly what to believe—not the one who seeks merely to transfer a body of knowledge from his head into the heads of his pupils." [7] The

[5] Henry Saint-John, Lord Viscount Bolingbroke, *Letters on the Study and Use of History* (Paris: Theophilus Barrois, Jr., 1808), p. 349.
[6] Aldous Huxley, *Brave New World* (New York: Harper & Row, 1960), pp. 28–29.
[7] Herbert Butterfield, *History and Human Relations* (New York: The Macmillan Company, 1952), pp. 168–69.

137

best kind of history teacher is the one who recognizes that the most useful means of teaching history is through the development of a historical attitude. Labelled by various names—"historical habit," "historic sense," "historical thinking," and "historical-mindedness"—the idea of a historical attitude is simply an open-mindedness about evidence, an appreciation of the limitations of historical study, a critical view of interpretations about the past, and a deep sense of commitment to find the truth, wherever it may lead. Memorization is essential mainly as it aids the student to muster evidence and to locate sources; it is the ability to think about the evidence, to try to make sense of it, and to employ the canons of historical inquiry which equip the student to deal effectively with the past—and consequently with the present.

As a beginning, the teacher can make the student aware of basic questions which serve as a guide to studying the past. These questions provide a frame of reference for the pursuit of historical knowledge, and they can help guard against a tendency to select trivial and meaningless facts. The first question is this: What is the social structure of the society, nation, or civilization? This will lead into such subquestions as these: Is the society divided into classes or castes? What, if any, are the forms of social mobility? What is the role of the male, of the female? What marital arrangements prevail? What roles are prescribed for children? The second basic question is this: What are the religious, mythological, and ideological beliefs of the society? Subquestions in this category include these: What are the major principles which govern individual and collective behavior in the society? What forms of worship and celebration are followed, and what deeds are expected or required of the adherents? What are the origins of the beliefs, and what links do the ideas have with other religions, myths, and ideologies? Connected with this question on beliefs is another basic one: What is the nature of the intellectual activities of the society? More specifically: What types of books are written and read? What roles do the arts play? What is the nature of the educational system? What is the role of science and technology?

Following these fundamental questions is a fourth: What is the economic structure of the society? This question can likewise be subdivided into more specific questions: To what extent is the society agrarian, industrial? What modes of transportation are employed? What is the role of government in the economy, and for whose benefit do its policies seem to be designed? What goods are imported and exported? In what ways is the economic tied to the social order? In conjunction with this basic question, a query into the geographical features of the land in which the society thrives is necessary: What natural resources are available? What effects do the resources of the land have upon the economic structure of the society?

A question on the political organization of the society is also essential, and it can be separated into more specific questions: How did the political structure evolve as it did? Who exercises decision-making powers? Who controls executive, legislative, and judicial functions? What is the relationship of the political organization to the social, economic, and religious structures of the society? What role does tradition play in the operations of the political structure? Tied to this question is another fundamental one: What have been the relationships of the country to other nations? More specifically, what, if any, traditional and ideological conflicts exist between that state and others? How has the state resolved its difficulties with other countries?

These questions can be used as guides to analyzing any society, civilization, or nation.[8] But they must always be tied to a fundamental historical question: What changes did the state undergo over time? It is this question which qualifies the study as history. Other basic questions may be framed by the teacher, and certainly other subquestions in each of the categories can be formulated. The most important point to bear in mind is that the study of the past can be no better than the questions which are asked of it, and it is as important for students to learn to ask questions as it is for them to find answers. To seek knowledge without knowing what one is looking for is likely to end too frequently in ascribing the same weight to unimportant information as to more significant knowledge.

To raise questions and to seek answers is only the beginning of knowledge in history, however. It is equally important that the student develop some basic skills of

[8] Similar questions are posed in Gabriel Jackson, *Historian's Quest* (New York: Alfred A. Knopf, 1969), pp. 28–35; and a framework based on the themes of historical study may be found in Carl Gustavson, *A Preface to History* (New York: McGraw-Hill, 1955), *passim.*

historical inquiry. Thus he must learn the rudiments of historical methodology, not as a professionally trained historian, but certainly as a serious inquirer into the past. If he does not understand the necessity for sifting through the evidence, if he does not comprehend the tentativeness of historical data, if he does not grasp the crucial nature of personal detachment and objectivity and how hard these are to achieve, and if he does not fathom the inevitability of interpretation in history—then the student must always rely upon the authority of the textbook and the teacher. This is not to deny the value of authority but only to argue against equating the study of history with the memorization of an inherited repository of "truth." The true historic sense is as much a matter of attitude as it is an absorption of the facts and generalizations which historians have uncovered. In subsequent chapters we will outline some approaches to instruction in history which are designed to aid in the development of the historical attitude.

The stress upon questions and the emphasis upon skills of inquiry in studying the past may seem to throw out narrative history altogether, or at least to relegate it to a position much lower than that of analytical history. Such is not our intention, but the matter deserves to be clarified. Good narrative history is exciting, and it can reward the reader with an immeasurable inner satisfaction. To read a moving account of a story well told is an experience which every student should enjoy, and no survey course in history is complete if it fails to expose students to the pleasures of well-written narrative history. It is worth noting, however, that certain mistaken notions about narrative history in the school curriculum have tended to undermine its value. First, the history textbook has been equated with good narrative history. This is, unfortunately, not the case. A history textbook, at least the kind most frequently used in secondary schools and in college survey courses, is more often than not a broad synthesis of secondary works. It must cover topics only superficially and in broad generalizations, and it simply cannot capture the mood and spirit of a narrative account of a more limited topic or of the unfolding experience of the life of an individual as treated in a biography. Thus, the ordinary history textbook, no matter how well written, is not a substitute for good narrative history.

Another erroneous impression about narrative history is that it is the only effective means of teaching history. This attitude automatically equates the verbal retelling of the story of man's past with effective teaching. It may be done well, and some teachers are masters of the lecture approach. The failure of teachers in far too many instances to recognize that they are presenting a dull account of history, however, is in no small measure a reason why students harbor such a dislike for the subject. The lecture can play a valuable role in the teaching of history, and in some instances it may be the most effective means of teaching certain aspects of the course on history. That it is too often deadly and soporific, however, should give cause for reconsideration. We will return to this subject later.

A third mistake about narrative history as the best form for the schools is made by those teachers who hold adamantly to the belief that students are incapable of coping with analytical history. To be sure, the analytical study of history is not easier than the study of narrative history, and certainly the ability of students will determine the levels of reading materials and the sophistication of analysis they can manage. But it is a mistake to believe that narrative history accomplishes more than analytical history. The present sad state of history teaching is sufficient to refute that belief. What we must realize is that history takes many forms and that an understanding of the processes of reconstructing the past is as necessary as the substantive content. When teachers grasp this concept of history, they liberate themselves from the restrictive bonds of history as only a body of content. The *story* and the *telling* are still there, of course; but they cease to be the end-all of historical study. It is not a matter of having one's cake and eating it too: Narration and analysis are viable facets of history, and both can augment the experience of students who are exposed to them.

CHOOSING CONTENT

The typical secondary school courses in history are intended to be broad surveys: the United States from its origins to the present and world history from the earliest civilization to the space age. Every teacher knows the frustration of covering such spans of time in the space of a nine-month school year. As a consequence of these unrealistic expectations, teachers are compelled to "cover" the courses in such a way that topics are treated very superficially, and they are forced to deal with the content in highly generalized and abstract terms. That is the situation for teachers who abide by the regulation that calls for coverage of the history of the United States or of the world. More often than not, however, teachers simply do not complete the course. Thus the United States survey is frequently truncated somewhere between the end of World Wars I and II, while the world history course is not uncommonly ended anywhere between the Congress of Vienna and World War I. One may argue that teachers in the latter group have at least covered certain topics in some depth, but the most unfortunate shortcoming of their approach is the failure to expose students to the most recent era, which not only is important in its own right but is also the area in which students generally have the greatest amount of interest— though, as we shall discuss later, the importance of a broadened understanding of man works against the adoption of a curriculum which includes only recent history.

The problem of covering the content of the survey courses in history is compounded by the fact that more substance is added with each passing year. Thus, if the teacher clings to the belief that everything in United States history from the European Commercial Revolution to the most recent presidential election must be covered or that in world history everything from Zinjanthropus to the most recent probe into space has to be accounted for, content must be compressed even more tightly. The effort becomes incredibly more frustrating, for both teacher and student. The superficiality of treatment inevitably increases, and the student's memory is taxed even more heavily. Neither of these outcomes represents sound pedagogy.

An alternative approach is to generalize more, that is, to abstract content to the point that everything can be covered. This approach is also of highly questionable pedagogical value. It violates the nature of historical inquiry because it begins at the end—that is, it takes abstract conclusions as the starting point. To teach and to study history in this fashion is to ". . . start up in the clouds, at the very top of the highest skyscraper." [9] At the risk of repetition, it must be pointed out

[9] Butterfield, *History and Human Relations*, p. 168. See also, George E. McCully, "History Begins at Home," *Saturday Review* (May 16, 1970), p. 75.

that the study of history must be more than merely the memorization of what is contained in history textbooks; it must include an understanding of how generalizations and conclusions about the past are derived. The student who can repeat historical abstractions without knowledge of their limitations has not begun to comprehend the nature of history: His "skyscraper" is built on an infirm foundation.

Surely enough, all history teachers wish for more time, and pity the unfortunate history student in the final few weeks of a school year when the teacher announces his intention to "speed up" to finish the textbook, or at least to "get through chapter 27." More time will not be forthcoming, and it is debatable that more time for the history course is even deserved. The other social studies can make valid claims for more time too, and since history already has the lion's share, only the most parochial history teacher can be short-sighted enough to believe sincerely that history ought to replace the other studies of man as a social animal. And even if more time were granted, who can assure us that the same problem would not continue? What is necessary is a reasoned view that history can never be covered fully anyway and that the teacher must *select* content. How the content is to be selected will depend once again upon the teacher's understanding of the nature of historical inquiry.

Although the content of the secondary school history course may be chosen in several different ways, it must be organized on the basis of its chronological order. Naturally, the study of events in the broad context of a survey course can never be rigidly bound to a strict day-by-day recounting, since "flashbacks" are necessary and because some topics (e.g., international relations) do not lend themselves to such a "chopped-up" version. Nevertheless, what especially distinguishes history from other social studies is its temporal reckoning, and the study of the past must be taken in at least a broad time sequence, allowing students to comprehend both the continuity and change which characterize a given series of events.

As long as we are bound to the idea of survey history courses for the secondary schools, we must reconcile ourselves to an approach which will allow for some breadth of coverage and at the same time permit the teacher to develop the historical attitude. One way to accomplish these twin goals is to set the stage for historical study with some initial lessons devoted to the nature of historical inquiry and then to blend coverage with some in-depth study of historical problems. A certain amount of lecturing and textbook reading will suffice to set the stage for the in-depth studies and to bridge the gap between these more focused inquiries. The in-depth studies (also called "postholing") can be centered around certain themes in the story of man's past or around some of the significant issues in man's history as a "civilized" being, or they can focus upon a particular historical concept. An automatic prescription for selecting the themes, the issues, or the concepts cannot be offered; that will be left to the individual teacher, depending upon his interests and areas of preparation in history and, to a limited extent, upon the interests of students.

An in-depth focus depends, of course, upon the accessibility of materials and sources other than the standard textbook and the ubiquitous encyclopedia. It requires some primary source materials as well as interpretive books. Although this requirement can pose difficulties for teachers in some school systems, it is no longer the formidable obstacle it once was. The availability of appropriate new materials especially designed for secondary school history courses and the abundant supply of paperbound volumes have eased the problem of source materials. But even where these hurdles may remain, a great deal of imagination and the utilization of mimeographic duplication machinery can go a long way toward aiding the teacher to attain the goal of employing in-depth studies in his history courses. No matter how trite the expression, it is important for teachers to believe that where there is a will, there is a way! In subsequent chapters we will examine some in-depth lessons, the likes of which teachers can imitate if only they possess the determination and if they are not totally isolated from books, magazines, and newspapers— a rarity indeed in the modern United States, unless self-imposed.

The significant issues approach to in-depth studies has the built-in quality of forcing students to cope with the problems of historical inquiry. One such issue could be the following: Was the Industrial Revolution in England beneficial for or detrimental to the working man and to society in general? This problem will call for an examination of primary evidence and an evaluation of interpretations by various historians.[10] Obviously, the teacher could "give" his students an answer to that question within the space of a few moments, and then he could move on to cover more material. A study of the issue by students, however, will make it possible for them to engage in some probing of their own and thereby develop important intellectual skills as well as learn some content.

We cannot deny the limitations of the significant issues approach, and they should be noted here along with responses on how they can be checked. First, the danger of dichotomization into an either-or interpretation is ever-present. Under proper guidance and by recognizing that the issue has merits in both camps, the student can be made to see that a simple schism of issues is rarely possible in history. Second, a tendency of students to overlook the tentative nature of their conclusions is inherent in the study of a limited amount of data. That can be overcome, however, if the teacher continues to stress a cardinal principle of historical inquiry, namely, that judgments are no more sound than the evidence on which they are based. And, we may suggest, the problem is certainly no greater than the opposite tendency, that is, to accept the authority of the teacher or of the printed word on the basis of even more limited study by the students. Third, the issues approach may lead to the impression that history consists only of problems. Lectures and readings which express the continuity of history can be interspersed to offset that notion, however. And, in fact, we have not advocated a total expenditure of time on the in-depth studies at the loss of a broad survey. Finally, the issues approach, with its emphasis on the tentative nature of truth about the past, may result in excessive skepticism concerning truth. Salted with an understanding that we must base our lives, our decisions, and our actions on whatever truth we can approximate for the moment, however, this problem need not lead to a disregard for all interpretations of the past. Properly understood, it should keep us from falling victim to the error of dogmatism and the fallacy of revealed truth in history.

[10] See, for example, an arrangement of the issue in Bernard Feder, *Viewpoints in World History* (New York: American Book Company, 1968), pp. 225–48; and, for a more advanced approach, see Brian Tierney, Donald Kagan, and L. Pierce Williams, eds., *Great Issues in Western Civilization*, 2nd ed. (New York: Random House, 1972), pp. 269–331.

Another way to present in-depth studies is to organize and select content on the basis of important themes in the history of a given period of time. As an example, we may take the suggestions of D. C. Watt for the study of twentieth century history. Watt offers the following possible themes: (1) "the intermingling of nationalist and ideological considerations in the history of the period after 1919," in which the conflicting views of international politics are stressed on the one hand as a "world-wide, or at least Europe-wide, struggle between the forces of populist democracy, social democracy and socialism . . . against the forces of social reaction, élitist conservatism, aristocracy, plutocracy and fascism" and on the other hand as "only nation-states in pursuit of traditional national interests clashing over the control of Europe"; (2) "the development of a common European culture, a common social, political and intellectual consciousness"; (3) "the rise of the super-powers each with its amalgam of ideology, revolutionary tradition, revulsion from and attraction to Europe . . ."; (4) "the decline of Imperial Europe and the growth of nationalism, decoloniza- tion and anticolonialism, [and] the rhetoric of independence and the reality of economic aid . . ."; and (5) "the transforma- tion of world politics from the conference of great powers of the 1890s and 1900s to the United Nations of today, with the impact of two world wars." [11] This approach has the advantage of broad perspective, allowing students to study a historical period from an international angle, and it can wrench the student from a narrow view of his own little corner of the world. Obviously, the procedure suffers from some of the same shortcomings as the significant issues approach, and it has the added disadvantage of requiring more sophistication on the part of students. It can be used to great advantage, however, if the teacher scales it down to the ability level of his pupils.

A final way in which the in-depth focus can be accom- plished is via attention to important historical concepts, usually treated on a comparative basis. The concept of revolu- tion will serve as a case in point. Thus the teacher may organize and select materials appropriate to the English Revolution (1688), the American Revolution (1776), the French Revolution (1789), and the Russian Revolution (1917). Stu- dents can be expected to cope with the problems of definition,

[11] D. C. Watt, "Twentieth-century History," in New Movements in the Study and Teaching of History, ed. Martin Ballard (Bloomington: Indiana University Press, 1970), pp. 72–74.

analysis of aims, methods, and outcomes, and comparison and contrast of revolutions. Using the model of Crane Brinton's *The Anatomy of Revolution*, students can be guided into the testing of Brinton's generalizations ("tentative uniformities") about revolutions, and they can broaden their study to include economic and sociological models as well as the standard historical design. Moreover, they may test the applicability of the model to present situations—that is, if they remain mindful of the limitations of historical analogies and prediction. The concept of revolution can be expanded to include other types as well—for example, intellectual, scientific, technological, and industrial revolutions.

The conceptual approach includes some of the limitations of the other in-depth studies, but it presents a special difficulty of its own. The very nature of the approach requires that the student cut across time periods, and this can result in a confusion of the unique sequential character of each event. Since history deals with particular events, generalized statements of comparisons are very risky. Thus only under the skillful guidance of the teacher can the student avoid the pitfall of incorrectly comparing animals which are of the same genus but of a different species. Moreover, the teacher must be careful to convey an understanding that concepts are mental inventions and not concrete constructs. Otherwise students are in danger of closing their minds to the fluid nature of the defining characteristics of concepts and thereby of forgetting that conceptualization is itself subject to change over time. Still, the conceptual approach has much to offer when it is handled well.

All three of the in-depth approaches have been attacked on the grounds that students do not possess a sufficient background of factual knowledge to deal with them. The critics argue in effect that until students have had an adequate number of survey history courses, they are not mentally equipped to tackle these special approaches. A grain of truth in this assertion, however, does not qualify it for sanctification as the *full* truth. Certainly, students must possess some historical knowledge before they can cope with issues, themes, and concepts in history. But that does not mean that they must have committed large stores of historical information to memory in advance of such studies. If we wait for that happy moment to arrive, we shall never advance beyond the same plateau where we have been stuck for so long. In fact, the necessary knowledge can be sought in conjunction with the activity of searching for answers; thus it is not *always* necessary to spoon feed students with "background" information. History viewed as a process as well as a product will help to eliminate the mental myopia of requiring students to know *all* the facts first. The important point is not how much factual knowledge students can absorb but rather how well they understand that facts are important to support or refute hypotheses about the past. The low esteem in which history is held by so many students today is largely a result of the too common notion that the possession of historical facts is an end in itself. When historical facts come to be viewed as *evidence* and not as a *goal*, the teacher and the student have begun to acquire the historical attitude.

In the last decade, history in the schools (and the survey courses in college as well) has come under heavy fire on the grounds that it is totally irrelevant to the needs of young people. The sad fact about that charge is that it contains a germ of truth. We cannot escape the indictment if we remain slavishly devoted to the idea that all historical facts are of equal worth and that instruction in history is synonymous with the memorization of all those facts—large and small alike. All history is not irrelevant, however. Even ancient history is relevant if we view it as helping us to understand ourselves better in the present. Any study of the past can be useful if it enlightens us about the nature of man in civilized communities, if it aids us to find the roots of our identity. Thus the problem is not just that we give too little emphasis to the immediate past but that we often lose sight of the educative value of historical study. Relevancy is not a substitute word for personal interest. An education which liberates us from the bonds of ignorance includes a study of what man has done before now, how he has behaved over the ages. To insist on including only very recent history in the school curriculum is to forego the advantage of a broad perspective on man and societies.

UNDERSTANDING LEARNING PROCESSES

The emphasis upon developing the historical attitude is important not only because it is consistent with the nature of historical inquiry but also because it accords with our knowledge of the processes of learning. It is beyond the scope of this volume to summarize research on cognitive learning and to provide a full-scale discussion of learning theory. What we can do, however, is to single out a few of the important principles of learning which are pertinent to the teaching of history. These principles have been synthesized by the cognitive psychologist Jerome S. Bruner, and they represent a composite of extended research on learning.[12]

Because learning is an active rather than a passive process, it is important to involve students as directly as possible in history lessons. Aside from the occasional lecture necessary to provide basic background information, to bridge the gap between one topic, issue, or theme, and to arouse interest in a new area of study, the teacher should design his instructional procedures so that he can maximize student participation. This is particularly important inasmuch as the most effective form of learning requires students to engage in the use of intellectual skills such as intuition, analysis, and hypothesizing. These skills are called into play in order to understand the basic structure of the subject with which they are dealing. As Bruner explains it: "Mastery of the fundamental ideas of a field involves not only the grasping of general principles, but also the development of an attitude toward learning and inquiry, toward guessing and hunches, toward the possibility of solving problems on one's own." [13] Certainly history does not possess a structure in the same sense that mathematics and the sciences do, but as we have previously attempted to demonstrate, it does have a discipline of inquiry that must be understood if one is to perceive history as a process of probing the past. Hence good learning in history requires more than taking notes and repeating information back to the teacher in class recitations and on examinations.

Again, we must emphasize that the acquisition of historical knowledge is a necessary but not sufficient goal of instruction in history. "An unconnected set of facts has a pitiably short half-life in memory," Bruner reminds us. "Organizing

[12] Jerome S. Bruner, *The Process of Education* (Cambridge: Harvard University Press, 1962). For a detailed discussion of the research on which many of the ideas in *The Process of Education* are based, see Jerome S. Bruner, Jacqueline J. Goodnow, and George Austin, *A Study of Thinking* (New York: John Wiley and Sons, 1956).
[13] Bruner, *The Process of Education*, pp. 20 and 55–68.

facts in terms of principles and ideas from which they may be inferred is the only known way of reducing the quick rate of loss of human memory." [14]

To tie up the whole bag of history teaching with only facts and generalizations is to believe that learning is synonymous with memorizing. But few are the history teachers who would deny that they are interested in developing historical thinking among their students. And to accomplish that goal, we must recognize that learning in history requires the use of appropriate mental skills as well as the absorption of historical information. Surely our desire is to prepare students to function effectively in the world of tomorrow, and if we attain that end, it will be because we understand that learning consists of knowing how to transfer and transform knowledge as the need presents itself. Since our world is not static, we must not allow our understanding of history to become thus either.

[14] Bruner, *The Process of Education*, pp. 31–32.

CHAPTER 9

Instructional Plans and Materials

If variety is the spice of life, it is also the spice of instruction in history. But variation is not an end in itself: Its value lies in its potential for sustaining life and vigor in the teaching of history. Some teachers will naturally find certain approaches more suitable than others to their own personality and style. To fail to try different approaches and to write them off as useless, however, is to entertain the belief that one has at last found the Holy Grail of Instruction. If the teacher happens to be a master of one technique, he may indeed succeed very well in employing his single pedagogical procedure. That teacher is atypical, however, for most teachers are unable to maintain a single routine which is equally stimulating to their own intellectual interest and challenging to their students as well. And in addition, history itself is a variegated study, and to allow it to be presented prosaically is to vitiate its multifarious character.

The choice of specific instructional procedures will vary, of course, with the nature of the material to be presented, the ability level of a class of students, and, above all, with the teacher's aims for a lesson. If we accept the premise that instruction in history is aimed to impart significant knowledge, develop some particular intellectual skills, and promote selected appreciations, then our choice of teaching approaches must be calculated to accomplish those aims.

DESIGNING HISTORY LESSONS

A history lesson can be no more effective than its design. The failure to plan units of study and daily lessons is the cause of much haphazard and ineffective instruction in history. As long as the history teacher views his goal as coverage of the textbook, he is likely to cling to the notion that the only plan he needs is one which sets forth the number of chapters he is to include in a unit of study and the number of pages he is to take up on a given day. Whenever the teacher realizes other aims for teaching history, however, he must surely recognize the importance of reflecting in advance of his lessons on what he hopes to accomplish. Without a plan the teacher is like a carpenter who essays to construct a house without a blueprint. And to plan a unit of instruction and a series of lessons, the teacher must begin with the question: "What am I trying to do?"

Instructional objectives for history fall into two broad categories: cognitive and affective. The former may be divided into two parts: knowledge and intellectual skills. The latter deals with appreciations, attitudes, and values. A useful scheme for classifying cognitive instructional objectives has been devised by Benjamin S. Bloom and others. The Bloom classification system can be immensely helpful to the history teacher as a guide to the types and levels of instructional objectives which can be formulated for both units of study and daily lessons. Arranged in a hierarchy, the broad categories include the following: (1) knowledge, (2) comprehension, (3) application, (4) analysis, (5) synthesis, and (6) evaluation.[1] Each of these categories is subdivided into more specific classifications.

Usually no more than two, or perhaps three, categories will be used in the planning of each lesson, and some of them will be used rarely during any unit. All units, however, should make some use of the six categories. Thus, it may be useful here to provide examples under each category. The examples are stated as goals for students to achieve, although they are expressed in terms meaningful to the teacher and not in

[1] Copyright © 1956 by David McKay Co., Inc. From Benjamin S. Bloom et al., *Taxonomy of Educational Objectives, Handbook I: Cognitive Domain* (New York: David McKay Company, 1956).

ordinary student language. The objectives are ends to be attained, and they do not specify means or procedures to be employed by the teacher in helping students reach those goals. To facilitate understanding, all examples are related to a series of lessons on Nazi Germany.[2]

I. KNOWLEDGE
   A. *Terminology:* Students will be able to define fascism, National Socialism, totalitarianism, appeasement, genocide, and *Blitzkrieg.*
   B. *Specific Facts:* Students will be able to cite dates of the Nazi regime and of World War II, principal personalities of the Nazi party and government, major countries engaged in World War II, and a few important sources of information related to the Nazi era.
   C. *Conventions:* Students will be able to demonstrate familiarity with standard map symbols representing the political and physical situation in Europe during the reign of Hitler.
   D. *Trends and Sequences:* Students will be able to relate the sequence of major events in Germany from 1923 through 1945.
   E. *Classifications and Categories:* Students will be able to recognize the various categories (such as social, economic, ideological, political, and diplomatic) by which the origins of National Socialism can be analyzed.
   F. *Criteria:* Students will be able to recognize the criteria by which selected primary sources on the Nazi era can be judged for validity.
   G. *Methodology:* Students will be able to state the fundamental steps of historical inquiry appropriate to the study of a problem on the Nazi era.
   H. *Principles and Generalizations:* Students will be able to recall selected major generalizations about the era of National Socialism.
   I. *Theories and Structures:* Students will be able to outline the Fuehrer Principle.

Obviously, these examples of knowledge objectives are in some cases very broadly stated, and in others, fairly specific.

[2] The examples are to be taken as representative, not comprehensive. An extensive listing is not necessary, since the purpose is merely to illustrate types of objectives which go under each classification. A modified version of the *Taxonomy* has been employed here in the interest of simplification.

153

Moreover, they are only partially complete. But perhaps they will help us to understand better the broad range of possibilities in imparting certain basic knowledge to students in the history class. As it should be apparent, however, all of these objectives call only for memorization. Thus, we have no assurance that the student who can cite schemes of classification, criteria for judgment of sources, and the fundamental steps of historical inquiry will be able to apply any of those schemes, criteria, and steps to appropriate cases. To get students to think critically about the readings on Nazi Germany, then, we must move into the area of objectives for development of intellectual skills:

II. COMPREHENSION
   A. *Translation:* Students will be able to translate the symbolic forms of selected political cartoons and tables of economic data on the Nazi regime into verbal form.
   B. *Interpretation:* Students will be able to relate information from selected documents (or primary sources) in a cause-and-effect explanation of the impact of Nazi party ideology on German governmental policy.
   C. *Extrapolation:* Students will be able to interpolate missing data on selected tables of social, political, and economic data on the period in Germany from 1923 through 1945.
III. APPLICATION: Students will be able to transfer from previous lessons the basic principles of historical inquiry to the study of a selected problem on the Nazi regime. [This can be accomplished through the assignment of a written criticism of a selected interpretation of the rise of Nazism, for example.]
IV. ANALYSIS
   A. *Elements:* Students will be able to identify some unstated assumptions in the interpretations of two or three historians on Hitler's role in creating Nazi Germany.
   B. *Relationships:* Students will be able to check the evidence offered by a historian of Nazi Germany against his thesis.
   C. *Organizational Principles:* Students will be able to identify the bias of selected historical passages on the Nazi era.

V. SYNTHESIS
   A. *Production of a Unique Communication:* Students will be able to compose a creative account of the impact of the Nazi regime upon German culture.
   B. *Production of a Plan or Proposed Set of Operations:* Students will be able to devise a plan for testing a hypothesis on the character of the German people in the period 1923 through 1945.
   C. *Derivation of a Set of Abstract Relations:* Students will be able to formulate a hypothesis on the role of churches in the development of the fascist regime in Germany.
VI. EVALUATION
   A. *Judgments in Terms of Internal Evidence:* Students will be able to detect the logical fallacies of Nazi racist arguments.
   B. *Judgments in Terms of External Criteria:* Students will be able to appraise the values of the Nazis against a formulated standard for Western civilization and in light of alternatives open to Germans at the time.

Quite clearly, the intellectual abilities required to attain the foregoing objectives increase in difficulty in ascending order. And, just as clearly, some students will find it demanding to function at the highest levels. That is insufficient reason, however, to dismiss the higher level objectives as inappropriate. They may be very effectively utilized for above-average students, and in simplified form they can be made appropriate to average and below-average students. In fact, there is no reason why history teachers should not strive to engage all of their students in tasks which require some use of all the cognitive skills. When lessons are carefully planned and skillfully executed, teachers can succeed in developing some critical thought among the average and below-average students in their classes.[3]

Some educators would argue that instructional objectives must be stated in terms of expected "behavioral" outcomes. Hence they would contend that the objectives listed above are too vague and nonspecific. Their argument is valid if we accept

[3] See Norris M. Sanders, *Classroom Questions: What Kinds?* (New York: Harper & Row, 1966), for an excellent translation of the *Taxonomy* into practical usage.

the point of view that learning in history consists of specified quantities, that is, that students will be able to perform a *number* of listed operations. The danger of this argument is that it may turn history into a mechanical subject, and it may tend to diminish the humanistic quality of the discipline. Perhaps the advocates of "behavioral objectives" have over-reacted to the failure of too many teachers to specify any clear objectives, and certainly their efforts to improve the quality of testing and measurement of student achievement through specification of desired performance is laudable. But we must steer a course between extremely broad, vaguely formulated objectives and highly specific, rigidly enumerated aims if we are to maintain a suitable approach to instruction in history.

Many teachers have reacted negatively to the position that objectives must be stated in written form. A written statement of objectives is not absolutely mandatory for the effective teaching of history, of course, but the unhappy fact is that in most cases where objectives are not specified in writing, the history teacher possesses no clear sense of what he is trying to accomplish. Just as the carpenter must often refer to his blueprint, so the teacher must check himself on his aims—and that necessitates a written plan for the great majority of teachers. By committing himself to a written statement of objectives, the history teacher forces himself to reflect care-fully upon *what* he hopes to accomplish, *how* he hopes to accomplish those ends, and *how* he will determine that he and his students have arrived at the desired destination. This does not necessarily entail the designing of an elaborate plan, but it does call for at least a skeletal outline of (1) knowledge objectives, (2) intellectual-skills objectives, and (3) attitude and appreciation objectives. And, it should be added, a written plan is only a *guide;* it is not the law of the Medes and Persians. The sensitive teacher will wisely deviate from the plan when spontaneous opportunities arise during the course of a lesson.

Thus far, we have discussed only the cognitive objectives for the teaching of history. Most history teachers will agree that certain attitude and appreciation (or *affective*) objectives are also appropriate to instruction in history. This draws us into murky waters, of course, for we are dealing now with personal beliefs. The history teacher obviously has no right to modify or alter certain personal values held by his students. But he has an unquestionable responsibility to expose his students to the varying value systems subscribed to by men and societies over the ages. And there is nothing wrong with attempting to reduce prejudice and bias, to increase tolerance and understanding, and to inculcate a sense of the dignity and worth of all individuals. If the history teacher views his task as enlarging the vision of his students through history, he has grasped the humanistic quality of history. One of the chief values of understanding the nature of history and how historians work is that it helps the history teacher gain a better perspective of his subject. Thus he will also include instructional objectives which are intended to develop desirable attitudes toward historical evidence, generalizations, analogies, and other facets of historical inquiry. And he will aim to aid his students to gain an appreciation of the value of historical study.

Perhaps the most basic consideration in developing desirable attitudes within the context of historical study is that of helping students to be willing to receive new information and to entertain seriously the historical issues and questions put to them. In brief, this means a willingness first to *listen* and second to *respond* with the attitude: "I want to see all sides of the question and weigh them carefully before I state my own position." That is an idealized situation, of course, but in general it is fundamental to the historical attitude. Corollary to this is the necessity for the teacher to value the spirit of free, but disciplined, inquiry. In fact, if the teacher is to achieve any success in getting students to operate at the levels of analysis, synthesis, and evaluation, he must impart to his students the importance of questioning, suspending judgment, and understanding one's personal frame of reference. In a sense, then, the categories of cognitive and affective objectives are interrelated. Unfortunately, these two domains have been dichotomized as though one could deal with them separately.[4] Only when the teacher sees their relationship is he ready to integrate both facets into a humanistic approach to the teaching of history.

Values, attitudes, appreciations, and beliefs change slowly, and the history teacher will do well to remain con-

---

[4] This is the case, for example, in the scheme designed by Bloom *et al.* in their *Taxonomy of Educational Objectives.* The first handbook of the *Taxonomy* deals with the "Cognitive Domain," and the second, with the "Affective Domain."

stantly aware that any objectives related to those areas must be of a long-range nature. Moreover, he must realize that influences outside his own classroom constantly counteract his own efforts to reduce dogmatism and authoritarianism. About the best the history teacher can hope for is to provide information, improve skills of critical thinking, and set an example as an honest seeker of truth. These alone are insufficient to effect desirable attitude changes, but they are all prerequisites. We can only strive to help our students liberate themselves from the tyranny of a predetermined view of the past by assisting them to take an open-minded approach to inquiring about the past—which is, after all, in perfect harmony with the spirit of the historical quest. Thus freed from prejudgment of the past, students are more likely to be liberated from a predetermined view of the present and of the future.

To the three categories of objectives we have just discussed—namely, knowledge, intellectual skills, and attitudes, appreciations, and values—some social studies educators would add a fourth, that is, aims of community participation or social action. We would argue, however, that such aims are outside the responsibility of the history teacher. While the aims of social action may be noble, to introduce them into the study of history is to entertain the belief that history can be utilized for ideological purposes. Certainly, we cannot refute the argument that social action is valuable, but we must remind ourselves of the dangers of dogmatism inherent in the position that history is a source of authoritarian pronouncement. Social action, we believe, is a matter for personal commitment; and if a student finds that a study of history has enlarged his perspective on man and society, thereby providing him with a base for active participation in community affairs, then we will do well to applaud his commitment. But if the history teacher aims to choose social activities for his students, he is subscribing to the belief that he knows what action is best for society, and that, to say the least, is hardly in keeping with the spirit of free inquiry.

UTILIZING THE TEXTBOOK

The history textbook can serve as a very useful tool for teaching and learning, but it can also be badly abused as an instrument of pedagogy. The following statement, made over seventy years ago, has an unfortunate ring of reality about it even today:

> In many schools the so-called teaching of history is literally a mere hearing of recitations. I have heard of a person, by courtesy called a teacher, who habitually kept his finger upon the line in the textbook before him, and limited his instruction to the work of correcting the trifling variations of the pupil from the phraseology of the text.[5]

Instead of serving as an aid, a guide, and a source of reference, the history textbook is often allowed to become a catechism. This is reflected all too frequently in the examination question which is lifted directly from the textbook and for which students are called upon to supply verbatim a missing word or phrase. Such misuse of the textbook not only produces a profound distaste for history but also undermines the spirit of historical inquiry.

The textbook itself is an imperfect instrument of instruction, as most authors of history textbooks will agree. Certainly the history textbook of today is in many ways superior to its counterpart of a few years ago, but the typical history survey textbook will probably never fully meet the expectations which some teachers hold for it. In the first place, it must encompass a broad span of time in such a way that the book remains usable for its audience. To make it so, the textbook writer is forced to compress descriptions and explanations into broad generalizations, and as we have previously noted, students are thereby introduced to the study of history at a high level of abstraction. Theoretically, of course, survey textbooks could be expanded to a point that would allow students to comprehend the treatment of evidence and the development of interpretations, but then the book would be so forbidding as to be useless. Moreover, limitations of time would vitiate the effort expended in enlarging the textbooks, for, after all, only two semesters are usually allotted for the study of the history survey course.

Textbooks for history survey courses cover a multitude of

---

[5] C. K. Adams, "On Methods of Teaching History," in *Methods of Teaching and Studying History*, ed. G. Stanley Hall (Boston: D. C. Heath, 1902), p. 209.

topics on which no historian can be an authority. Hence, a single author of a textbook is hard put to provide superior treatment of the entire range of topics—and that is especially true of a textbook on world history. Thus, the multiauthored text would tend to be superior because each specialist can lend his talents to writing about the topics he knows best. On the other hand, problems of unison and style are presented by such a publication, and rarely does the multiauthored textbook adequately meet those difficulties.

Proponents of the multiauthored textbook argue that the problem of bias is better offset in that type of survey book, and they contend that if such a work is not accessible to students, the least the teacher can do is make available several one-author texts. The argument for having students read more than one point of view would seem to be valid were it not for the fact that the typical survey textbook cannot be faulted for presenting a one-sided account. The problem is that authors of history survey textbooks usually strive to achieve too strong a degree of impartiality and neutrality of presentation. Those textbooks do have their share of biased statements, as we shall shortly discuss, but on significant issues they tend to gloss over controversial matters and historiographical questions with such a general phrase as "Historians disagree on the causes of the Civil War." That statement would be entirely appropriate as an introduction to a study of the disagreement, but followed only by a highly synthesized presentation of the causes of the Civil War, it is inane and worthless.

A textbook spiced with imagination and a strong point of view may be preferable to a too highly neutral account because it can stimulate and provoke critical reflection. True enough, the teacher must utilize such a textbook as a motivational device rather than as a repository of information, but through skillful guidance he can capitalize upon it as a source of hypotheses for debate, discussion, and investigation. It is difficult indeed to arouse the interest of students in some history textbooks which read like Leo Tolstoy's parody of a school history in the nineteenth century:

Louis XIV was a very proud and self-confident man; he had such and such mistresses and such and such ministers and he ruled France badly. His descendants were weak men and they too ruled France badly. And they had such and such favorites and such and such mistresses. Moreover, certain men wrote some books at that time. . . .[6]

Happily, most history textbooks are no longer quite as prosaic as that described by Tolstoy, but a few have risen to only a slightly higher level of quality.

The scholarly pursuit of the past produces a flood of new knowledge and changing interpretations or revisions. And for that reason history textbooks are ever becoming dated. Although textbook authors revise their works every five to ten years, they all must struggle to keep their heads above the waters of revision which, constantly ebbing and flowing, cover topics from the ancient world to the contemporary period. That problem is further compounded by the fact that the period of use of history textbooks is inordinately long, the result of which is the extended use of outdated books in the classroom. Additionally, the busy classroom teacher is pressed to find time to remain abreast of the latest scholarly changes.[7] Aside from these difficulties, however, some textbook writers have persisted in presenting standard and long-accepted interpretations which ignore important reinterpretations. Three critics found, for example, that thirty-five years after J. F. Jameson published his *The American Revolution Considered as a Social Movement*, several leading high school history textbooks failed to deal with the revolution in terms of Jameson's thesis. On the subject of the "internal aspects of the American Revolution," many textbooks either omitted any reference to the matter or simply treated it "as a minor and fortuitous element of an external war." These textbooks "imply that there is not even an intermediate approach to the question," and hence, students are presented with "a unilateral version." [8] Similar omissions occur elsewhere with respect to other significant theses developed by recent historians.

[6] Leo Tolstoy, *War and Peace*, trans. Louise and Aylmer Maude (New York: Simon and Schuster, Inc., 1942), 2: 1315. © Oxford University Press. Quoted by permission of Oxford University Press.
[7] The American Historical Association publishes a series of pamphlets titled "Discussions on Teaching" which provide current interpretations and bibliographies. These were formerly published in different form by the Service Center for Teachers of History.
[8] Harold J. Noah, Carl E. Prince, and C. Russell Riggs, "History in High-School Textbooks: A Note," *The School Review*, 70 (Winter 1962): 416.

The lot of the author of school histories is not easy, of course, for he is beset on every side by pressure groups to produce an account which is compatible with the accepted version of each group. Henry Bragdon, coauthor of a popular United States history textbook, describes, for instance, the attack of a newspaper columnist upon his treatment of George Washington. Quoting only fragments from the paragraph on Washington, the columnist distorted the meaning of Bragdon's description to make it appear that Washington had been vilified.[9] Such attacks are not uncommon, and the history of attempted censorship of school textbooks is an old and sordid story. Only a few years ago a junior high school textbook, titled *Land of the Free* and written by three reputable historians, John Hope Franklin, John W. Caughey, and Ernest May, became the victim of a vicious attack by ultraconservative groups in California.[10] And as late as 1971 a state board of education withdrew an American history textbook from its list of approved school books. A spokesman for the majority faction of the board charged that the book tends "to create disruption and dissension in our society" and that the book gives more coverage to the conflict in Vietnam than to the American Revolution.[11] Thus the safest history textbook in the United States is the one which embellishes the story in favor of obstreperous, superpatriotic pressure groups or which bows to an innocuous neutrality. It is to the credit of textbook writers and publishers that they have refused to bend to efforts at outright censorship, but unfortunately the "market" has sometimes compelled them to produce textbooks which avoid controversy.

Actually, of course, bias inevitably intrudes into history textbooks. In some instances it is readily apparent, while in others it is subtle and harder to detect. In either case, the teacher can use it to advantage by designing lessons which include exercises in the discernment of bias. As an example, the teacher could select the following passage from an elementary state history textbook:

Many nights you [a plantation owner's child] have gone with your mother to the "quarters" where she cared for

[9] Henry Wilkinson Bragdon, "Dilemmas of a Textbook Writer," *Social Education*, 33 (March 1969): 294–95.
[10] Harry N. Scheiber, "The California Textbook Fight," *Atlantic Monthly*, November 1967, pp. 38–47.
[11] *Atlanta Constitution*, December 17, 1971, p. B19.

some sick person. She is the best friend the Negroes have, and they know it . . .

As you ride up beside the Negroes in the field they stop working long enough to look up, tip their hats and say, "Good morning, Master John." You like the friendly way they speak and smile; they show bright rows of white teeth . . .

"How's it coming, Sam?" your father asks one of the old Negroes. "Fine, Marse Tom, jes' fine. We got mes more cotton than we can pick." Then Sam chuckles to himself and goes back to picking fast as he can.[12]

The teacher can take this egregious excerpt as a starting point for a discussion of whether it presents a valid and representative picture, that is, whether it is historically accurate. Then students can be asked to formulate a hypothesis which is then to be tested against the evidence, in which case both primary and secondary sources can be brought into play. The problem of capturing the spirit of the black man will also arise as the students pursue the evidence. And here slave songs can be introduced as one form of supportive evidence; for example, the following slave song will serve as a useful source:

Freedom Land

Git along there, Jeff Davis,
Git along there, General Lee.
I'm going up to that freedom land,
Got me two pigs, got 'em here in my hand.

The Bible says it's wrong to steal and lie,
So I ask my dear Lord to close both his eyes.
While I dance me a jig and dance me a jog,
'Cause I got me a pig and I got me a hog,

Ain't no one gonna take 'em from me.
Git along there, Jeff Davis,
Git along there, General Lee.

Didn't want no posse come chasin' after me,
So I took all the livestock and set 'em free.
Oh, master be so mad that he's liable to bust,
'Cause he's gotta catch 'em while I'm kicking up dust.

[12] Quoted in Kenneth Reich, "Alabama Text Stirs Some Parents," *Atlanta Journal and Constitution*, March 29, 1970, p. D2. See also, Melton McLaurin, "State Textbooks: Distorted Image of Negroes Presented in Some Histories," *South Today*, 2 (October 1970): 8, for a report on the treatment of blacks in state history textbooks.

If you pigs are wondering how you got your names,
Well, you and those two rascals are one and the same.
And if you don't stop acting like your two name-
sakes,
I'll have roast pork in the morning and some tasty ham
steaks.

I'm an old man, but I'd like to bet,
That I'm one old man that master won't forget.
The look on his face will be something to see,
When he finds his pigs are gone, and I am free.

I'm goin' up to that freedom land,
Got me two pigs, got 'em here in my hand.
The Bible says it's wrong to steal and to lie,
So I ask my dear Lord to close both his eyes.[13]

With a lesson of this sort, the history teacher can capitalize upon a textbook which would otherwise be a useless piece of badly biased writing.

Instances of bias as revealed in history textbooks can also be utilized effectively in the study of other minority groups. Often bias is indicated more by glaring omission than by obvious commission, as, for example, in the following account of the American Indian:

War paint and tomahawk, colorful feather headdresses, and blankets of many patterns made up the costume of the American Indian. In western cowboy stories and television plays, the Indian often plays the part of the villain and sometimes the part of the hero.

The North American Indians' civilization was very simple. The Mayas of Central America, the Aztecs of Mexico, and the Incas of Peru were more advanced peoples and their civilizations were superior to those farther north.[14]

This passage is intended to serve as a complete account of the

[13] Quoted in Donald C. Lord, "The Slave Song as a Historical Source," *Social Education*, 35 (November 1971): 767. Reprinted with permission of the National Council for the Social Studies and Donald C. Lord.
[14] Gerald Leinwand, *The Pageant of World History* (Boston: Allyn and Bacon, 1966), p. 254. This textbook and several others are examined in Michael B. Kane, *Minorities in Textbooks* (Chicago: Quadrangle Books, 1970), which, although it stretches a point here and there, is a very useful book for history teachers.

North American Indian in a world history textbook. What becomes immediately obvious is its romanticized treatment of the North American Indian and, in the second sentence, its condescending tone. The history teacher can launch a lesson from this brief excerpt by raising such questions as these: Did all Indians wear the costumes described in the account? Were such costumes used on all occasions? Were American Indian tribes as similar in dress as indicated? How accurate are cowboy stories, television plays, and moving pictures in their treatment of the Indian? What comparisons can be made between and among the Indians of Central and South America and those in North America? What evidence can be offered to support your argument? What difficulties does the historian encounter in reconstructing the past of the Indian? Were the United States Plains Indians uncivilized? What is a civilization, and does it differ from a culture? Were the acts of the Plains Indians barbaric, and if so, does our action against them constitute barbarism? And, of course, numerous other questions can be raised, depending upon the depth of probing desired. The teacher can thus utilize to advantage a textbook which is otherwise a good book but which, like most survey works, overextends its generalizations at certain points. What is required of the teacher is careful reflection, insight, imagination, and a willingness to search for other sources which can be made accessible to his students.

Among the forms of bias in history textbooks, none is as persistent as nationalistic partiality. This has been very effectively demonstrated in several works.[15] For our purpose here, however, we will illustrate only how nationalist bias operates in Anglo-American textbooks. Ray Allen Billington and other historians, acting as a Committee on National Bias in Anglo-American History Textbooks, made a thorough study of history textbooks in England and the United States. They were able to identify six forms of national bias in the books they examined. The first form is "deliberate falsification." Recognizing that intentional distortion can rarely be demonstrated,

---

[15] For example, see E. H. Dance, *History the Betrayer: A Study in Bias* (London: Hutchinson & Co., 1960); David C. Gordon, *Self-Determination and History in the Third World* (Princeton: Princeton University Press, 1971), pp. 83–89; and D. C. Gordon, "History and Identity in Arab Text-Books: Four Cases," paper presented at the annual meeting of the American Historical Association, 1970.

the committee was nevertheless able to state that "some authors have strayed so far from objectivity, and always in the direction of national glorification, that they must be charged with falsification, even though this is not deliberate." As an example, they cite the repetition of "discredited myths" and the enshrinement of "outworn folktales"; one author, in fact, has titled a chapter on the American Revolution "The Colonies Unite to Resist British Oppression," which is, of course, now recognized by scholars as an invalid point of view.

"Bias by inertia" is a second form recognized by the committee. It fails to take notice of scholarly revisions and includes such outdated interpretations as that of George III ". . . as a power-hungry monarch, buying votes and manipulating ministers to achieve absolutism. . . ." A third form of bias is "unconscious falsification," which is "traced to a subconscious assumption of group superiority. . . ." British textbooks avow, for example, "that the regular army 'could be relied upon to beat the irregular levies of the rebels whenever they fought on anything like equal terms.' " "Bias by omission" appears as a fourth type of nationalistic distortion. In British textbooks, for instance, "The War of 1812 is virtually excluded from their pages, or dismissed in a sentence or two," and regarding World War I, ". . . the contributions of the Allies are minimized, and those of the United States almost forgotten." A fifth form of bias obtrudes in the "use of language." United States history textbooks find it difficult, for example, to "resist referring to the 'blunders' of British ministers, or the 'stupidity' and 'tyranny' of their measures, . . ." and British writers are prone to paint "Britain's victories as 'brilliant.' . . ." Finally, "bias through cumulative implication" occurs in both American and British textbooks, which have implied, for example, "that either America or Britain won a disproportionate share of battles in the Revolution or War of 1812 or that one or the other achieved victory by its own herculean efforts without awarding credit to allies who bore a major share of the burdens." [16]

The history teacher could employ the six forms of nationalist bias as a model for analysis of the American Revolution as recorded in the class textbook. Students would be expected to

[16] Ray Allen Billington et al., The Historian's Contribution to Anglo-American Misunderstanding (New York: Hobbs, Dorman & Company, 1966), pp. 92–100.

search for the forms of bias indicated. This will also require some familiarization with selected basic documents and interpretations. A very useful source in this regard is the chapter on the causes of the American Revolution in *Viewpoints: USA*,[17] which is designed specifically to engage secondary school students in utilization of the historical method. The reading of the textbook in this case takes on added significance: Students are not only acquiring information about the Revolution but also developing critical intellectual skills and gaining an appreciation for the complexity of important historical events.

The study of the nationalist point of view in history textbooks can also be effected through a comparative analysis. One of the most revealing insights into historical interpretation is achieved by seeing ourselves as others see us. The teacher can thus design a lesson which requires students to compare and contrast an interpretation in the class textbook with that of a textbook from another country. A brief example should suffice to show the advantages of this approach. The following account of the siege of the Alamo is taken from a United States history textbook:

> In February, 1836, he [Santa Anna] began a siege of the Alamo mission station in San Antonio, where the Texas commander William B. Travis and his 187 men were garrisoned. Serving under Travis were the famous frontiersmen James Bowie, supposed inventor of a stout hunting knife, and Davy Crockett. On March 6 the Mexicans finally overwhelmed the tiny American garrison through sheer force of numbers, and not one of the defenders of the Alamo lived to tell the story. Nevertheless, the Texans' heroic stand at the Battle of the Alamo gave Houston a chance to strengthen his forces to continue to fight.[18]

The next account of the same battle is from a Mexican textbook:

> On February 17, 1836, Santa Anna [crossed] . . . the Nueces River and advanced with his army on San Antonio

[17] Bernard Feder, *Viewpoints: USA* (New York: American Book Company, 1967).
[18] Jack Allen and John L. Betts, *History: U.S.A.* (New York: American Book Company, 1967), p. 237.

Bejar, which he occupied on February 23, as the rebels, some 180 men, retreated to the fort at Alamo. Santa Anna asked for its surrender from the head of the fort, [William] Barret Travis, but Travis answered with gunfire. The fort was encircled by trenches, dug under constant enemy fire, except at the north. On March 5, an assault in four columns, with a force of little over a thousand men, was ordered at night to surprise the enemy. The enthusiastic yells of one battalion sounded an alarm for the Texans, who put up a desperate defense that cost the Mexicans 70 dead and 300 wounded. But at last the fort was taken; all of its defenders were shot.[19]

This interesting juxtaposition invites a number of questions for students: Were the Texans actually "rebels"? Why does the United States account mention "famous frontiersmen," while the Mexican account refers to them simply as "rebels"? What opposing acts of bravery are suggested in each account? Was the action of the men of the Alamo a "heroic stand," or was it a "desperate defense"? Did the Alamo in fact possess any strategic value? What casualties are mentioned in each account? Since there were no survivors on the Texans' side, what problems are posed in reconstructing the event? What sources would be useful in recreating the event? How is the event treated in United States movies and popular books? Other questions may be raised, of course, and a number of inquiry assignments can be centered around the two accounts. Once again, the teacher who uses foresight and imagination can turn a standard textbook account into a meaningful and exciting history lesson.

EMPLOYING PRESS MATERIALS

Newspapers and popular magazines offer a fruitful source for instruction in history, and the history teacher should search for appropriate items which can serve as sources of hypothe-

---

[19] From Alfonso Toro, *Compendio de Historia de México: La Revolución de Independencia y México Independiente*, 18th ed. (Mexico City: Editorial Patria, S.A., 1966), as quoted and translated in *As Others See Us*, ed. Donald W. Robinson (Boston: Houghton Mifflin Company, 1969), p. 74. Quoted by permission of Editorial Patria, S.A.

ses and generalizations to be tested by his students. Editorials, syndicated columns, interviews, and letters to the editor are often loaded with potential for provocative discussion. The use of press materials has the advantage of permitting students to tie relevant issues to their historic roots. Moreover, it can aid the teacher to develop critical intellectual skills among his students. And since it is likely that newspapers and magazines will serve as the most basic reading materials for the students when they become adults, we will do well to teach students to apply the historical attitude to the reading of press materials.

A few years ago Premier Nikita Khrushchev of the Soviet Union uttered the following statement in reference to the United States: "We will bury you." The phrase was generally taken in the United States as a belligerent threat, and many people cried that the statement could mean only that the Soviet Union intended to annihilate the United States in a nuclear war. Let us read a letter from Premier Khrushchev to the editor of the *Saturday Review*, however, and hear his side of the story:

> . . . I often see references to the fact that I once said about the United States: "We will bury you." This quotation is used by people to prove that we in the Soviet Union intend to murder the United States and all its citizens. The way this quotation is used is an example of the difficulty of taking an expression from one language and giving it literal meaning in another. When I was in the United States, I watched an American television program. It was a dramatic sketch. Two good friends were talking. One of them said something slightly impolite and the other told him to drop dead. I could hardly believe my ears and I told my interpreter he must have made a serious mistake. Then he told me not to take it literally. It's just a casual expression. Many people in the United States go around telling even their best friends to drop dead; it's just a figure of speech. No one thinks anything of it.
>
> In the Soviet Union we have an expression that is sometimes used when two men happen to disagree. One of them, feeling certain he will ultimately be proved to be right, will say to the other that he will attend the other's funeral.
>
> When I said that Communism will bury capitalism, I meant that ultimately capitalism will cease to exist in its pure form and that we socialists will be around when it

happens. But I don't believe we can do it by force. As I said, I don't believe war is the proper means for proving the superiority of either of our systems. All war can prove is how stupid we are and that we prefer suicide to everything life has to offer. . . .[20]

Tied to a lesson on the Cold War, this statement can be used as a focal point for the discussion of the nature of the conflict. The teacher can raise such questions as the following: When did Premier Khrushchev make the original statement, and when did he offer his explanation? What are some problems faced by the historian in dealing with language? Do you believe Mr. Khrushchev's explanation is satisfactory? Why? What sources should you consult to see the problem in larger context? What evidence can you produce to support or refute the hypothesis that the Soviet Union intends to use force to overthrow capitalism? These and similar questions offer a stimulating approach to an analysis of the excerpt.

Broad generalizations about the past often appear in newspapers, as, for example, the following analysis of the effects of physical features upon influential individuals in history:

Napoleon was . . . a short man, goaded by his ulcer, plus a desire to prove that despite his lack of height, he was more than 100 per cent he-man.

Same was true of "shorty" Hitler and Mussolini. Hirohito was also a small man!

F. D. Roosevelt likewise was so handicapped by polio that he was usually a wheelchair patient.

H. L. Mencken apparently psychoanalyzed the resulting FDR egotism even while Roosevelt was just starting his second term in 1937. For Holmes Alexander quotes Mencken as warning:

"If there's a war before 1940, that ——— will join it.

"If there isn't, he'll start one of his own.

"Roosevelt's got to have a reason for breaking the third term tradition, because he'll never be an ex-President. He'll die in office like a king."

Could Mencken's diagnosis have explained why Roo-

---

[20] Quoted in Norman Cousins, "The Improbable Triumvirate: Khrushchev, Kennedy, and Pope John," *Saturday Review*, October 30, 1971, p. 35. Copyright 1971, Saturday Review, Inc. By permission of *Saturday Review* and Norman Cousins.

sevelt deliberately forced the Japanese into attacking
Pearl Harbor . . . ?[21]

Not denying the value of a psychoanalytical approach to the
study of historical personages, we can raise several questions
about this highly generalized statement: What evidence does
the writer offer to support his generalizations? Can you find a
nonsequitur (i.e., a conclusion which does not logically follow)
in his argument? Did Emperor Hirohito and President Roosevelt play the same role in their countries as did Napoleon,
Hitler, and Mussolini? What sources are cited by the writer?
What sources should be consulted? Can you test the hypothesis that a physical handicap leads some rulers and statesmen
to take aggressive action against other countries? How tentative must your conclusion be?

Columns of letters to the editor of a newspaper likewise
often contain broad general conclusions about the past, usually intended to draw a parallel with "undesirable" conditions
in our own country. The following letter is an example:

The Editors: All students of world history are familiar
with the approach of events leading to the decline and fall
of the Roman Empire. These events stand out in sequence.
They can be listed thus:

1. The increase in divorce decrees which spells out doom
   for home life.
2. Ever-increasing tax programs which beget extrava-
   gance and waste of public funds.
3. The wild craze of pleasure which evades depth and
   seriousness of thought.
4. The massing of armaments which feeds suspicion and
   forebodes destruction.
5. The turning away from their God which breeds a
   hardened heart and bad behavior.

Can you find a parallel in contemporary history? If
you've found it, do you like it? If you don't like it, try to
correct it.

If everyone helps it can be corrected. If we pass the
buck, disaster is in the wind.[22]

[21] George W. Crane, "The Worry Clinic," *Athens* (Ga.) *Banner-Herald*, November 1, 1970, p. 27.
[22] *Atlanta Journal and Constitution*, September 25, 1966, p. 30.

171

Questions which can be raised about this letter include these: What is the writer's purpose? What assumptions does he make about the decline of Rome and about the nature of history? What is his source of information? Does he quote directly from his source, or does he paraphrase? If the latter, how accurately does he represent the conclusions of the author of the source? What difficulties are encountered in drawing analogies between the United States and Rome?

These are only a few examples of press materials which the teacher can employ in the history classroom. Over the years he can build up a file of them, and, by alerting his students to the type of material he wants, the teacher can enlist their aid in searching for such materials. The newspaper can also be used as an invaluable source for the pursuit of local history—a topic which will be emphasized in Chapter 10.

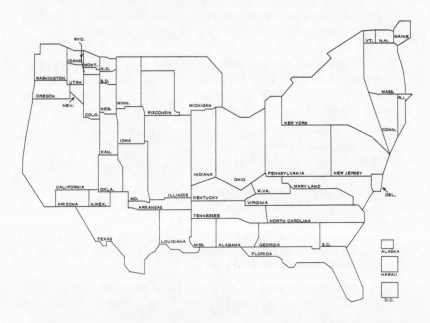

FIGURE 1.   *United States Proportionate to Population, April 1970.*

Chart E-500, Division of Research and Statistics, Ohio Bureau of Employment Services, Columbus, Ohio. Data from the United States Bureau of the Census. Reproduced by permission of the Division of Research and Statistics, Ohio Bureau of Employment Services.

APPLYING ILLUSTRATIVE MATERIALS

Illustrations, charts, graphs, and social and political cartoons provide another useful source for the teaching of history. When they are used to provoke thought, discussion, and hypotheses, these materials add a dimension to history lessons. Aside from the standard maps, for example, the teacher can present a different conception of the territorial and population sizes of the countries of the world, as illustrated in Figure 1. These cartograms are maps "scaled in proportion to some areal quality (phenomenon) in contrast to the normal geographic area." [23]

A particularly challenging exercise can be built around this kind of map transformation or distortion of space. Students can be assigned the task of producing similar cartograms for selected eras of the past. This can be made easy by supplying them with the necessary data, or it can be made more difficult by requiring them to search for the data. Then students will be asked to follow up from the cartograms which they have constructed by elaborating upon the changes reflected over the given period of time. Reflections of historical consequence and comments of a speculative or extrapolative nature can follow, and in the process students can gain a different perspective and insight into the transformation of population in historical context.

Social and political cartoons offer a wonderful opportunity to develop skills of translation and interpretation, and they are particularly useful with students who are handicapped by reading disabilities. The works of Thomas Nast present some of the most graphic criticisms of the American political scene ever produced.[24] The contemporary cartoons of Herbert Block (Herblock) are also extremely useful for the most recent period in United States history, as, for example, in the era of Senator Joseph McCarthy and the attempted purge of "communists" from the government.[25] The key to successful utilization of

[23] Phillip C. Muehrcke, "Trends in Cartography," in *Focus on Geography*, Fortieth Yearbook of the National Council for the Social Studies, ed. Phillip Bacon (Washington, D.C.: The Council, 1970), p. 205.

[24] See, for example, Roger Butterfield, *The American Past* (New York: Simon and Schuster, 1947), for a number of cartoons by Nast and others; and Morton Keller, *The Art and Politics of Thomas Nast* (New York: Oxford University Press, 1968).

[25] These have been compiled under the following titles: *The Herblock Book* (Boston: Beacon Press, 1952); *Herblock's Here and Now* (New York: Simon

FIGURE 2. *Driving the Stake.*

From *Israel and the Jews in the Soviet Mirror*, ed. Moshe Decter (New York: Conference on the Status of Soviet Jews, 1967), p. 26. The original appears in *Bakinski Rabochi*, June 21, 1967. Reproduced by permission of the Conference on the Status of Soviet Jews.

cartoons lies not in merely presenting them to a class for their viewing but rather in constructing a sort of "discovery" lesson around them. As an example we can take the cartoon in Figure 2.

This cartoon can be reproduced on a spirit duplicator or a transparency for the overhead projector. Students can be asked initially two basic questions: What countries appear to be represented in the cartoon, and what clues do you find to

and Schuster, 1955); and *The Herblock Gallery* (New York: Simon and Schuster, 1968).

support your contention? Then, a question on the source of the cartoon can be raised, after which students will be assigned the task of finding written evidence to support their hypotheses. Following this assignment students can be requested to locate American cartoons which depict an opposing point of view, and a discussion of the accuracy and influence of political cartoons can ensue. The wealth of such cartoons is abundant, and their potential for instruction in history by symbolic representation is enormous. In addition, exercises designed to make students create their own political cartoons on some event in history will result in considerable creative endeavor by some students.

If we view history as a colorful painting of the past which shows the many sides of men and women living and acting within their societies and struggling with the phenomena of their multidimensioned cultural and natural environment, we should see the necessity for selecting aims and choosing instructional materials which reveal the viable nature of history. And if we see the importance of developing the historical attitude, we must discriminate among those aims and materials and choose those which best foster that attitude. Thus, the history teacher must employ his imagination if he is to treat the study of a conventional subject in unconventional ways. Hopefully, some of the suggestions we have made in this chapter will provide a glimpse into the wealth of ideas which lies beyond the door of convention, waiting for the teacher who is willing to grasp a share of it.

CHAPTER 10

Approaches to Instruction in History

What history teacher has not faced this question from a student: "Why do we have to study all this stuff?" Although the question may be phrased differently, its essence is always the same, namely, that the study of history is boring, without value, and a waste of time. We may react in a number of ways, such as by attempting to explain why the study of history is important, by ignoring the question, or by replying with an indignant response about the student's temerity. The question is more than an indication of rude behavior, however, because it reflects a failure on our part to demonstrate that history is a worthy subject for study and that it can be exciting and meaningful to students. No one can deny, of course, that we will never succeed in convincing *every* student of the importance of history. When the question reflects—as it too often does—the general attitude of students toward the study of the past, however, it is probably an indication of inadequate instruction. And, as the noted historian Charles G. Sellers comments, unless we undergo a "rejuvenation of historical learning," history may be on the way out of schools.[1] This holds as much for the college survey courses in history as it does for the schools. It is therefore incumbent upon us as

[1] Charles G. Sellers, "Is History on the Way Out of the Schools and Do Historians Care?" *Social Education*, 33 (May 1969): 509.

teachers of history—that is, if we really care—to initiate a renewal of interest in the study of history. The task is difficult, and the challenge is stupendous; the solutions are neither easy nor automatic.

REFLECTING ON INSTRUCTIONAL PROCEDURES

The lecture has been, and probably still is, the predominant method of teaching history. Perhaps it is because the lecture is the prevailing approach that many teachers feel it is the most appropriate method. At one time, of course, the paucity of books made it necessary to use the lecture, but since that is no longer the case in the United States, we should question its place in the teaching of history. Research studies indicate that if the goal of instruction is to impart information, the lecture is as effective as any other approach. In fact, if that is the only goal of instruction in history, it is wasteful to keep class size below three hundred or five hundred or whatever number can be accommodated in a large auditorium. In other words, the limitation of the physical facility is the principal consideration. Moreover, lecture via closed circuit television can be utilized to effect further economy, and although students prefer a "live" teacher to a "TV" instructor, they can acquire as much information through the latter medium as they can through the former.

When instruction in history aims to develop intellectual skills and the historical attitude, however, the lecture is less effective. Student participation and involvement are crucial to the attainment of these goals, and the lecture, including the so-called "informal lecture," not only restricts student participation but also by its very nature structures the lesson so that maximum involvement is impossible. Also the typical history lecture covers material which is readily available in the textbook, and for that reason students often feel it is unnecessary to read the textbook, since they can take enough notes in class to pass an examination. To thwart this bit of clever maneuvering, the history teacher devoted to lecturing will include textbook-based questions on his examinations. But generally speaking, the lecture which does no more than reiterate the textbook is largely a waste of time, except perhaps as it may reinforce a limited amount of learning. Where this is done in college survey courses, the student usually has a choice: He can read the textbook and not attend class, or he can attend class, take notes on the lecture, and avoid reading the textbook. The same would be true of secondary school pupils if they had the option. To argue that students miss something by absenting themselves from the lectures is not borne out: The fact is that they can still pass the examinations without lecture attendance if only they read the textbook or secure the notes from a classmate. To base a portion of the final grade upon attendance is to admit in part that the lecture method is not doing the job well, and there is certainly no justification in compelling students to attend simply because the teacher wishes to salve his wounded pride.

This is not an argument for the abolition of the lecture approach to the teaching of history but merely a plea for restricting its use. The lecture can play an important role in instruction. Since the acquisition of knowledge is *one* of the goals of instruction in history, the lecture can be used effectively to provide basic background information for the study of a new topic, and it can be employed as a means of synthesizing and covering large segments of information between topics. This is particularly important in the survey-type course when the in-depth focus, the conceptual approach, or the thematic organization is used. In addition, the well-planned and effectively delivered lecture can stimulate interest and thought. Properly understood and effectively presented, then, the lecture can continue to serve its place in the teaching of history. Used as the chief medium of communication and viewed by students as a human computer spewing forth facts to be memorized, the lecturer will only contribute to the withering away of the spirit of historical inquiry.

One way to involve students is through the discussion method. It offers no magic formula for success, however, and the teacher must plan carefully and exert considerable energy to make the discussion method work well. If a discussion is to be more than a "bull session" and if it is to be more than a forum for pooling the ignorance of students, it has to be based upon carefully selected themes, ideas, concepts, or topics. And naturally, it cannot succeed if students have not read the necessary material. That is, of course, the greatest problem!

Some students will not read, and others cannot—at least, they are unable to read beyond an elementary level.

We gain nothing, however, by wasting our time with lamentations; we must do the best we can with what we have. This means that topics and reading materials must be carefully selected and graded; that constant encouragement is necessary; that materials of an illustrative and low-verbal nature must be located; and above all, that history must be viewed as something other than a repository of information to be memorized. In addition, the teacher must strive always to induce students to become involved, tugging and prodding but never humiliating his students. A sense of balance, checking against domination by a few and encouraging the reluctant, is crucial to successful discussion sessions. Even the most reticent student can become involved if he feels his opinions are valued, and in an atmosphere of inquiry and free expression, the spirit of learning can be fostered. This does not mean that anything goes or that students will not be pinned down. frequently to support their arguments; it means only that the worth of the individual is maintained within a framework of intellectual inquiry.

The assignment of special projects and term papers is another technique employed by history teachers. Both of these can be useful endeavors if they lead to historical thinking. Unfortunately, they are often viewed by students as "busy" work which bears little relation to the study of history. The student who constructs a model of an eighteenth century American fort is usually absorbed with craftsmanship and not the more significant matter of how the fort fits into the context of American life at the time. There can be little justification for having the student spend untold hours gluing matchsticks together when he is dealing with antiquarianism and not history. Likewise, the term paper which results in large-scale copying from an encyclopedia on the topic of women's fashions of dress in the ancient world, while it may be fascinating to the students, is not history. The shortcoming of such projects and papers usually lies in the failure of the student to isolate a problem, formulate a working hypothesis, muster his evidence, and follow through to a valid historical conclusion. The idea of projects and papers is sound enough if the task is clearly related to the development of the historical attitude, and that can only be accomplished by tackling a reasonably small, workable problem and by applying the canons of historical method to its solution.

For many years teachers of history have been told that they can enliven their classes through the utilization of audio-visual media (now called "instructional media"). And it is true, of course, that audio-visual materials can add a different and exciting dimension to the study of history. But again, as with other approaches to instruction, audio-visual materials must be carefully chosen and meaningfully presented. Films, records, slides, and other media are no different from history textbooks: They vary in quality, and they do not automatically improve instruction or attain the most desirable objectives. They are *materials* of instruction, not *methods*. Visual aids can be extremely helpful, of course, when they provide an insight that cannot be expressed in an effective verbal sense. Thus, it is inexcusable that a history teacher should attempt to describe the art and architecture of a period when a film or set of slides would do the job more vividly and effectively. Nor does it make much sense to ignore the potential impact of a documentary film when we are trying to convey the horrors of the atomic bombing of Hiroshima and Nagasaki or of the Nazi concentration camps. But audio-visual media can do more than illustrate; they can also provide provocative hypotheses or ideas to be discussed and tested. We are required to recall our aims for teaching history and to remember that mere coverage of material is insufficient if we are to find a useful place for audio-visual aids. A good example of this can be found in a filmstrip on medieval and Renaissance art and architecture.[2] Arranged in pairs, the filmstrip depicts one frame of medieval art and one of Renaissance art. Students are asked to identify characteristics of each, and at the end they summarize them for each of the two eras. Thus they have "discovered" on their own some of the transformations in Western art. The teacher could have lectured five minutes on the topic and thereby "saved" time. But if we believe that student involvement is important, that development of the historical attitude is one of our goals, and that critical thinking skills are crucial, then we should search for such tools as this.

Other instructional techniques such as debates, role

[2] For a further description of this filmstrip and other similar aids, see Mitchell P. Lichtenberg and Edwin Fenton, "Using AV Materials *Inductively* in the Social Studies," *Audiovisual Instruction* 2 (May 1966): 330–32.

playing, and simulation games offer opportunities for variety and attainment of certain types of objectives. They must be used purposefully, of course, if their use is to be justified. Strictly speaking, the past happened as it did, and nothing can change that. Unlike debate, role playing, and simulation in the other social studies where the emphasis is upon decision making and where the alternatives are still open—as in the case of a legislative game dealing with, say, social welfare or civil rights—history does not afford opportunities to "re-do" the past. Nevertheless these techniques, even though limited, may be used to help capture the "feel" of things as they were at a given time by allowing students to re-enact a historical episode. Students are thus thrust into a situation where they must understand the mood of the time and the alternatives which were open to the people of that era. They can also pursue the "if . . . then" speculation in which, for example, they may try their hand at "reconstructing" what might have happened if Lincoln had not been assassinated or if the opposition of General Beck and the German Army High Command had been effective against Hitler in 1938.[3] Still, they must be brought back to the hard reality that events occurred as they did and that that is why we have history. These adventuresome exercises can open the door to active involvement, and for that reason they deserve serious consideration by teachers of history.

Field trips offer the greatest opportunity for students to see traces of the past, and visits to museums extend the advantage of witnessing symbols of our heritage. Again, these experiences will be only as valuable as the purpose behind them, that is, in proportion to the amount of preparation and follow-up planned by the teacher. Unfortunately, every school does not have ready access to such museums. What every school does have, however, is immediate access to the traces of local history, and this is often overlooked by the teacher. One of the best ways to create interest in history is to bring it home to the local community, and one of the most fruitful opportunities for developing elemental research skills lies in the pursuit of the history of some aspect of the local area.[4]

[3] For an elaboration of this idea, see Wayne Dumas, "Speculative Reconstruction of History," *Social Education*, 33 (January 1969): 54–55.
[4] For a discussion of the large range of possibilities in the history of a town, see "Main Street" in Lucy Maynard Salmon, *Historical Material* (New York: Oxford University Press, 1933), pp. 161–82.

Tracing the history of a small defunct mill town, or of a local river, or of a local business which has long been in operation, or of the transfer of some local property, or of an old cemetery—all of these provide ready-made historical problems which necessitate the use of evidence such as local newspapers, county records, testimony from "old-timers," tombstones, and so on. And the teacher can even set up a simulated situation by burying "evidence" and arranging for students to engage in an archeological "dig" which students will follow through to a written reconstruction of the history of a fictitious community.

Hopefully, our reflections upon instructional methods appropriate to history have shown that we are not so much in need of new methods as we are in need of deeper insight into the potential of the existing ones and an enhanced imagination about how to revivify the study of the past. The emphasis has been placed upon greater involvement of students and less narration from the teacher. This is intended not to diminish the role of the teacher but to modify his function from that principally of the teller or narrator to that of precipitator of intellectual inquiry, director of thought-provoking activities, and motivator of interest in the study of the past. The argument, then, is that instruction in history should focus upon the student as inquirer rather than as passive recipient of knowledge. Again, at the risk of repetition, we must note that while the memorization of certain knowledge is still expected, it is the use of knowledge which becomes the focal point of learning. A variety of teaching techniques will be maintained under this arrangement, but they will be selected on the basis of their potential contribution to inquiry-oriented learning. At this point, then, we should examine more fully the idea of inquiry procedures in the study and teaching of history.

CONSIDERING INQUIRY PROCEDURES

"The simple-minded student . . . says it is a great comfort to have everything in black and white, so that he can carry it all home. But no scrap-book of facts can give wisdom, any more than a tank of water can form a running spring. It is, perhaps, of as much consequence to teach a young person *how* to study history as to teach him history itself."[5] This plea by a nineteenth century American historian was largely ignored by teachers of history for half a century. Within the last decade, however, a number of historians and educators have launched an effort to rejuvenate historical study in the schools in keeping with that historian's idea. Stressing the importance of understanding historical processes, such historians as Edwin Fenton and Richard H. Brown not only called for a reconsideration of aims in the teaching of history but also initiated projects designed to reorganize and revise the history curriculum. Their efforts have precipitated a reformation in the teaching of history, though as with most curriculum reforms, change has been slow in reaching many schools. The new emphasis has come to be called the discovery or inquiry method.

As with so many movements in education, the discovery or inquiry method is not really new, having roots in the ideas of John Dewey and others. But that is less important than the fact that the method has been refurbished and that now more and more teachers are coming to recognize its value. What precisely is the discovery or inquiry method? Perhaps it can best be described as an instructional approach which shifts the responsibility from the teacher as dispenser of knowledge to the learner as seeker of knowledge. In addition, it stresses the importance of student acquisition of skills of inquiry and research. And in the study of history this means that students will learn and use historical methodology. To be sure, it is not an attempt to turn students into professional historians. It is intended to aid students to become critical inquirers in keeping with the basic concepts of historical study, and it is premised on the grounds that the study of history must include an understanding of the nature of history and historical research as well as the substantive content of history.

The discovery or inquiry method is also calculated to develop an attitude of openness about historical knowledge. "It is better they [students] should not allow . . . knowledge to freeze in their minds, while the world changes, and historical

[5] Herbert B. Adams, "Special Methods of Historical Study," in *Methods of Teaching*, ed. Hall, p. 120; italics in original.

183

science changes—better that they should not thirty years later be holding too rigidly in their memory the things learned so long before," argues Sir Herbert Butterfield.[6] Perhaps the problem is not even so much that knowledge will become frozen but that it will fade and soon be forgotten. We cannot prevent the attrition of memorized facts, as every history teacher is aware. What have many people gained, then, after two or three years of history in secondary schools and an additional year in college if the history courses have been based upon retention of factual knowledge? It would be far better if students had acquired a positive attitude toward studying the past, and the discovery or inquiry method is intended to promote just such an attitude. As one writer pointed out more than half a century ago: "The study of a subject in accordance with the method of discovery necessarily involves freedom and originality of thinking, fosters the spirit of inquiry, and develops the capacity for self-exertion. Students brought up in this method will give unmistakable indication of free thinking, self-help, originality, and inquisitiveness."[7]

As the word *inquiry* suggests, questioning is an important tool in the learning process. The inquiry approach thus further enhances the historical attitude. As R. G. Collingwood notes, "the questioning activity . . . is the dominant factor in history, as it is in all scientific work."[8] Since the basic work of the historian deals with evidence, Collingwood further explains: "You can't collect your evidence before you begin thinking . . . thinking means asking questions . . . and nothing is evidence except in relation to some definite question."[9] And because of the tentative nature of historical knowledge, it is as important that students learn to ask meaningful questions as it is for them to give answers. Questions also lead into research for answers, and as Carl Becker contends, "no one can profit by historical research, or not much, unless he does some for himself. Historical knowledge, however richly stored in books

[6] Herbert Butterfield, *History and Human Relations* (New York, The Macmillan Company, 1952), pp. 172–73.
[7] Benoy Kumar Sarkar, *Introduction to the Science of Education*, trans. B. D. Basu (London: Longmans, Green, and Co., 1913), p. 80.
[8] R. G. Collingwood, *The Idea of History* (New York, Oxford University Press, 1956), p. 273.
[9] Collingwood, *The Idea of History*, p. 281.

or in the minds of professors of history, is no good to me unless I have some of it." [10]

Although we have discussed historical methodology in detail in Part I, it may be helpful here to touch on the major points again in reference to a model of inquiry which can be used in the history class.

1. Identifying the problem: This may consist of a gap in knowledge, that is, something which has not previously been researched; or it may be a controversial issue on which a new interpretation will shed light; or it may be the availability of new evidence which will warrant a reinterpretation.
2. Formulating the hypothesis: This step will come after some preliminary reading leads to a working guess which will provide a broad guide to the search for evidence.
3. Searching for evidence: This consists of an investigation into appropriate sources, both secondary and primary. It requires an understanding of the nature of historical facts and of external and internal criticism of the sources.
4. Interpreting the evidence: This begins as the researcher isolates what happened and questions why it happened. The problems of frame of reference, objectivity, bias, and judgment must be taken into account.
5. Presenting the account: This consists of an imaginative reconstruction in writing with conclusions clearly expressed.

Naturally, students can apply this model *fully* only to a local problem, since time and access to pertinent sources are crucial considerations. And even then it can be accomplished in a *polished* form best by able students. It is nevertheless useful on larger problems of history, and for average and less capable students, it is important as a general model for the criticism of documents, secondary accounts, and textbooks. Moreover, application of the model is necessary for the development of the intellectual skills identified in the classificatory scheme of objectives given on pages 152–56. The close correlation between the inductive model of historical inquiry and the taxonomy of instructional objectives is obvious when the two are compared. Although the steps in the model

[10] Carl L. Becker, "What Are Historical Facts?" *The Western Political Quarterly,* 8 (September 1955): 337.

of inquiry do not coincide precisely with the levels of skill objectives, the former requires the application of all of the various skills at one point or another. Thus when the model is established as a general mode of operation in historical inquiry, students can develop the ability to identify historical problems, formulate and test hypotheses, search for and analyze evidence, interpret sources, detect bias and frames of reference, devise plans of procedure, evaluate historical accounts, and apply the canons of historical research in general within the spirit of searching for an approximation of the truth about past events.

Basically, the inquiry method is inductive—that is, it requires students to move from the particular to the general, or from evidence to conclusions or generalizations. In a strict sense, of course, students will often start with a given generalization and reverse the process by testing the generalization against conflicting interpretations and against the evidence. The generalization then becomes a hypothesis and is accepted or refuted as students employ the processes of historical inquiry. Nevertheless, the important point is that they are not simply taking all historical generalizations as established truth but instead are making of history a process of investigating the past. The onus is thereby placed upon students to involve themselves in the search for truth.

Critics of the method of inquiry instruction argue that students must have a background of knowledge before they can use the inquiry method. That is true only in part. For what the critics usually mean is that students must have gone through several lecture courses in history before they are prepared to engage in inquiry. While a certain amount of background information is necessary, it is neither feasible nor mandatory that students "store up" all historical knowledge prior to inquiry exercises. If we await that golden day, we shall never even begin to touch upon inquiry—either in secondary schools or in the survey courses in college. The average human mind simply does not store that much knowledge of historical facts. And besides, historians do not work that way. As M. M. Postan indicates: "By refusing to pitch camp until they have reached the ultimate frontier of knowable facts historians merely condemn themselves to an eternity in the wilderness with the promised land of final and definitive history receding ever further away." [11] The historical process is an interplay of facts, hypotheses, and tentative conclusions. The inquiry approach emphasizes the search for facts (evidence) to support or refute a hypothesis, not to deposit them in the mind with the hope that some day they will become useful. Factual knowledge is not thereby downgraded; it simply becomes more purposeful and meaningful, thereby insuring greater retention. Moreover, as we have previously suggested, the necessary background can be built into a lesson through readings, handouts, or audio-visual materials. Some memorization is still necessary; it always will be!

Although, as we noted in a previous chapter, the inquiry method can be used with the textbook, it is enhanced by accessibility to documents, reference sources, and a wide range of reading material. It likewise assumes that students can read such materials. For these two reasons, opponents of the method charge that it has highly limited utility. This is an understandable reaction, but again, it does not represent the whole truth. The paperback book revolution, the availability of press materials, and the imaginative use of accessible resources nullify the argument against the inquiry method on the charge of its demands for reading materials. The matter of reading ability is a more telling limitation of the method. The alternative of reading the textbook in the traditional way, however, does not effectively counter the argument. What does become necessary, of course, is the procurement of a variety of reading materials and the application of more illustrative materials. The task is undeniably difficult, but if history is to be renewed as a subject of study, we cannot simply ignore the challenge and continue down the present path, which is not better only because it is easier to tread.

Alarmists argue that the inquiry method is dangerous because it makes students sceptical and undermines their faith in the *Truth* of history. Uncritical scepticism is, of course, as undesirable as uncritical acceptance of every word of authority. To possess a healthy attitude of reasonable scrutiny and cautious suspension of judgment until the evidence has been carefully weighed, however, is a mark of maturity. The spirit of

[11] M. M. Postan, *Facts and Relevance: Essays on Historical Method* (Cambridge: Cambridge University Press, 1971), p. 51.

historical inquiry does not lead to cynicism but to an open, tolerant point of view which simply says, "Let us find out for ourselves if this is true." The very nature of historical study is antithetical to dogmatism or to the belief that one has captured the absolute truth. Truth spelled with a capital "T" is outside the domain of the study of human activities in the past, but that does not mean that we must forthwith reject all truth. What historical inquiry fosters is an understanding that we can only approximate the truth and that our experience is richer because we realize that we must constantly quest after knowledge of the past.

To the critics who argue that the inquiry approach intellectualizes history to the point of ignoring the affective side of man, we would reply that this need not necessarily be the case. It is in fact the traditional method of instruction in history which so often deprives students of empathy for the people of the past by stressing names, dates, and lists of abstract generalizations. As we have previously noted, the inquiry approach seeks to help us understand man better, and to understand him better we must be exposed to the gamut of man's behavior in the past. It is only when we see that man has stooped to the basest deeds and risen to the noblest actions that we can understand him for what he is. Taken in its proper perspective, the inquiry approach will thrust students into a deeper quest for understanding both the rational and the irrational behavior of man through the ages. Man is as much an emotional creature as he is a rational being—and perhaps often more so. Thus we must re-emphasize that instruction in history is incomplete if it fails to include objectives which deal with attitudes, appreciations, and values.

Finally, the opponents of the discovery or inquiry approach contend that students will grow weary of the method. Given an overdose, they certainly will. But to conclude that the only alternative is narrative instruction in history is simply to offer a different kind of overdose, not to prescribe an antidote. A balanced diet is needed if we are to contribute to the intellectual growth of students. The inquiry-oriented approach still leaves room for some narration, telling, explaining, informing, memorizing, and acquisition of factual knowledge. Wisely employed, it affords an opportunity to involve students more directly, stimulate critical thinking, and revitalize the study of the past.

INTRODUCING THE STUDY OF HISTORY

We have argued that students must possess some understanding of the nature of historical inquiry if they are to appreciate history. For this reason, then, they must be introduced to the study of history in a way which opens their minds to the nature of historical evidence, sources, frame of reference, generalization, causation, and other basic elements of the discipline. And the teacher must begin at the outset of the study of history to develop skills of inquiry in accord with the classification of instructional objectives. Thus in the initial lessons he must include objectives designed to promote interpretation, application, analysis, synthesis, and evaluation, and he must afford opportunities for students to begin development of desirable attitudes toward historical study. Moreover, if history is to be understood as a humanistic study, the teacher must establish a setting in which students understand the value of others' feelings and the importance of seeing the worth of the individual as a human being. The following series of lessons is offered as an example of how the study of history can be introduced in keeping with the foregoing ideas.[12]

LESSON I: READING TRACES FROM THE PAST

OBJECTIVES: Students should be able to

1. Distinguish between trace, fact, inference, and interpretation
2. Identify types of evidence
3. Draw inferences on the nature of society from traces in a fictionalized account of a destroyed nation
4. Demonstrate appreciation of the role of perspective in the scrutiny of evidence

INSTRUCTIONAL MATERIALS: Slides 3–5; one-cent coin; Reading I, "Traces from the Past"

PROCEDURES:

1. Show Slide 3 (Figure 3 below).

[12] For other examples, see Edwin Fenton, *Teaching the New Social Studies* (New York: Holt, Rinehart and Winston, 1966), pp. 150–74; the same lessons appear in a revised form in John M. Good, *The Shaping of Western Society: An Inquiry Approach*, Holt Social Studies Curriculum Series, ed. Edwin Fenton (New York: Holt, Rinehart and Winston, 1968), pp. 17–33.

FigURE 3.   *Tracks in the Desert.*

From E. A. R. Ennion and N. Tinbergen, *Tracks* (Oxford: The Clarendon Press, 1967), p. 16. Reproduced by permission of The Clarendon Press, Oxford.

2. Direct students to study the picture, and then raise such questions as the following:
    a. What do you see in the picture? [*animal tracks*]
    b. Where do you think the picture was made? [*a desert*]
    c. What kinds of creatures made the tracks? [*an adder, a crow, and a Natterjack toad*]
    d. Which creature came across the sand first? second? third? [*crow, adder, toad*]
    e. How can you establish the time sequence in which the creatures moved across the spot?
    f. Are the tracks traces or facts? How do they qualify as evidence? What inferences must you make about the tracks if they are to have any meaning?
    g. In what ways is this evidence similar to that used by historians of the ancient past?
3. Distribute an American one-cent coin (preferably of same year) to each student in the class, and ask him to pretend that he is an archeologist who has discovered the coin in the year 3500 A.D. in a

FIGURE 4.   *A Lonely Politician.*
From *Life*, March 3, 1972, p. 68. Reproduced by permission of the Winter Haven (Fla.) *Daily News-Chief.*

land which was destroyed by a great earthquake around 2000 A.D. Then raise such questions as the following:

a. On the obverse (front) side of the coin, what might you infer from the words "IN GOD WE TRUST" over the head of a man?

b. On the reverse side, what might you infer from the language on the coin? What might you infer from the monument on the coin?

c. What facts can you state about the coin simply from the trace or coin itself?

d. What can you infer about its function or use? Does this suggest anything about the nation from which it came?

4. Distribute Reading I, "Traces from the Past," for the class to read.

5. Now raise the following questions with students:

a. What are the traces of evidence in this account?

b. What are some reasonable inferences which you can make about the following: the uses of the objects? the social status of its owner? the nature of the society in which the owner lived?

c. What other evidence would you need to corroborate your inferences? Does the evidence provide any clues to the religious, intellectual, and political aspects of the society?

[These questions can be discussed in small groups to maximize

191

participation. Then the teacher can ask one person from each group to report the findings of his group.]

6. Show Slide 4 (Figure 4 above), direct students to study the picture, and ask:
    a. What seems to be going on here? [*a politician delivering a speech*]
    b. How many observers can you count?
    c. What can you infer from this picture?
7. Show Slide 5 (Figure 5 below).
8. Direct students to study the picture, and proceed as follows:
    a. What seems to be going on here? [*a politician delivering a speech*]
    b. Explain that it is the same politician in the same location and at the exact same time but that the second photograph was taken from a different spot.
    c. What can you infer from these two pictures?

FIGURE 5. *Seeing It like It Was.*

From *Life*, March 3, 1972, p. 68. Reproduced by permission of the Winter Haven (Fla.) *Daily News-Chief.*

192

d. What difference does perspective make in looking at the evidence? Can this occur when two or more witnesses observe an automobile wreck? In a court of law, then, how difficult is it to determine who is telling the truth when the testimony of eyewitnesses conflicts?

e. What problem does perspective present to the historian as he examines his evidence?

9. Summary: What can you conclude about the nature of historical evidence from the exercises we have done today?

READING I
"TRACES FROM THE PAST"

I. The Setting

It is the year 2350 A.D. You have been invited to travel with an archeological expedition from your home in South Sea Island to a large continent which archeologists call North Frigid Land. Scholars believe that this is the same land referred to in some older documents as the U.S.A. A prosperous nation seems to have flourished there before the coming of the Great Flood about 350 years ago. The flood, caused by the melting of the huge ice caps of the North Polar Lands, raised the level of the oceans so high that most northern lands were wiped out completely.

After arriving in the barren land, you and members of the expedition spend several days exploring and digging on sites which you have identified as likely spots for discovering past evidence of the civilization. You finally uncover some objects, one of the most interesting of which is a bag-shaped item. The bag contains a broken strap which appears to have been used for the purpose of carrying the bag, and it is made of a shiny material which appears to be a kind of leather. The bag appears to have two interlocking snaps to hold it shut, though by now the snaps are badly corroded and rusty.

II. The Evidence

You return the bag to the expedition campsite and begin carefully to remove its contents. The contents are then itemized, and your list contains the following:

1. a small round box, flat on top and bottom, containing a small fluffy piece of cloth and a caked, beige-colored powder
2. a small tube with removable top, containing a firm reddish substance that easily smears onto paper

3. a moderately flexible object containing numerous "teeth" or "spines," about eight inches in length
4. several small, black metallic objects which appear to be a type of clip
5. a metallic object about four inches in length, rough on either side for about three inches to the point; the smooth end is rounded and contains a small notch
6. several small metallic objects on a small metal ring; each object is of the same general shape, but each contains grooves on the flat sides and notches on one edge
7. a folding piece of leather which contains "pockets"; inside this item are several objects, namely:
    a. two paper items: Though they are badly faded, it can be determined that these items were greenish on one side and white and black on the opposite side; the following marks can be determined on the first item: On one side is a picture with a caption underneath containing the letters "Was———on," a "1" in four corners, and some visible lettering at the top, "FEDE—— RES—— NOTE"; on the other side is an eye at the top of a triangular shaped symbol and a birdlike figure holding arrows in one claw (the other side of the bird is illegible); and, finally, on that side are the visible words "IN GOD WE TRUST." The other paper item is similar, but the only discernible marks are a picture on one side and the numerals "5" in each of four corners.
    b. three plastic cards, each with raised letters: One contains the words "GULF TRAVEL CARD, Land and Sea, Mrs. Arthur Jones"; another contains "Mastercharge" and a series of numbers; the third reads "Bank Americard, First National Bank of Miami, Florida," and contains a series of numbers.
    c. four paper cards, only one of which contains any visible lettering, namely: "Georgia Operator's License; Mrs. Arthur R. Jones; Birth Date: 4-12-55; Fee: $2.50; Sex: F; Eyes: Brown; Height: 5′2″; Weight: 125 lbs."
8. a pocket-shaped piece of paper containing on the outside a small reddish picture affixed to the upper right-hand corner and containing the letters "U.S. Postage" and "10 cents." Also on the outside are the letters: Mrs. Arthur Jones, 125 Candler Av—— Atl——, ——a. Inside is a folded piece of paper which contains only the following lettering:

"Dear Betsy,
     Well, Dad retired today after 30 yrs. with Woolworth's; he had served as V-P longer than any man in the history of the

organization, and they gave him a beautiful set of golf clubs as a retirement gift. He can hardly wait to go south to try them out.

Dad traded in the old Chevrolet for a new Chrysler, so our trip to Miami should be a real joy.

We can hardly wait to see you and Bob. We should arrive there next Thursday. Let's plan to dine at the Regency-Hyatt one evening. Will John be home from Stanford for the Easter break when we arrive? And we hope Sue will be back from her vacation in Paris by then. But if we miss them this time, we'll fly up to Atlanta again in June.

No doubt we'll miss our old home and friends, but we will be happy to get away from N.Y. since the welfare crop has just about ruined the city. I don't know what's gotten into people; they just don't want to work anymore. But I won't burden you with that kind of talk. We're worried about the constantly rising tide, but I heard on the radio today that scientists expect the ice to stop melting soon.

Bye for now. See you soon.

Love from Mom"

LESSON II: PLAYING THE ROLE
OF DETECTIVE

OBJECTIVES: Students should be able to

1. Identify internal clues as to the origin of written documents from ancient civilizations
2. Develop a working hypothesis on the origin of the documents
3. Suggest reference sources to be checked in proving the origin of the documents
4. Develop greater appreciation for the role of the historian's discipline in effective citizenship

INSTRUCTIONAL MATERIALS: Reading II, "A Father Talks to His Son," and Reading III, "You Say Our Gods Are Dead"

PROCEDURES:

1. Distribute copies of Reading II (given below), and direct students to read it. [The reference *must* be omitted, of course, on the handout and given only after students have completed the exercise.]

READING II
"A FATHER TALKS TO HIS SON" [13]

"Where did you go?"

"I did not go anywhere."

"If you did not go anywhere, why do you idle about? Go to school, stand before your 'school-father,' recite your assignment, open your schoolbag, write your tablet, let your 'big brother' write your new tablet for you. After you have finished your assignment and reported to your monitor, come to me, and do not wander about in the street. Come now, do you know what I said?"

"I know, I'll tell it to you."

"Come, now, repeat it to me."

"I'll repeat it to you."

"Come on tell it to me."

"You told me to go to school, recite my assignment, open my schoolbag, write my tablet, while my 'big brother' is to write my new tablet. After finishing my assignment, I am to proceed to my work and to come to you after I have reported to my monitor. That's what you told me."

"Come now, be a man. Don't stand about in the public square, or wander about the boulevard. When walking in the street, don't look all around. Be humble and show fear before your monitor. When you show terror, the monitor will like you."

. . . .

"You who wander about in the public square, would you achieve success? Then seek out the first generations. Go to school, it will be of benefit to you. My son, seek out the first generations, inquire of them."

"Perverse one over whom I stand watch—I would not be a man did I not stand watch over my son—I spoke to my kin, compared its men, but found none like you among them."

"What I am about to relate to you turns the fool into a wise man, holds the snake as if by charms, and will not let you accept false phrases. Because my heart has been sated with weariness of you, I kept away from you and heeded not your fears and grumblings—no, I heeded not your fears and grumblings. Because of your clamorings, yes, because of your clamorings—I was angry with you—yes, I was angry with you. Because you do not look to your humanity, my heart

---

[13] Samuel Noah Kramer, *History Begins at Sumer* (Garden City, N.Y.: Doubleday Anchor Books, 1959), pp. 13–15. Reprinted by permission of Samuel Noah Kramer.

was carried off as if by an evil wind. Your grumblings have put an end to me, you have brought me to the point of death."

"I, never in all my life did I make you carry reeds to the canebrake. The reed rushes which the young and the little carry, you, never in your life did you carry them. I never said to you 'Follow my caravans.' I never sent you to work as a laborer. 'Go, work and support me,' I never in my life said to you."

"Others like you support their parents by working. If you spoke to your kin, and appreciated them, you would emulate them. They provide 10 gur (72 bushels) barley each—even the young ones provided their fathers with 10 gur each. They multiplied barley for their father, maintained him in barley, oil, and wool. But you, you're a man when it comes to perverseness, but compared to them you are not a man at all. You certainly don't labor like them—they are the sons of fathers who make their sons labor, but me—I didn't make you work like them."

2. Ask students to name the possible civilizations from which this reading could have originated. Write these on the board. (Usually they will name Rome, Greece, Palestine, Arabia, Persia, Mesopotamia, China, and India.)

3. Ask students to name the internal clues relevant to identifying the civilization from which the material came. (These include the following: "school," "tablet," "monitor," "street," "public square," "boulevard," "first generations," "holds the snake as if by charms," "an evil wind," "reeds," "caravans," "gur," and "barley, oil, and wool." *Note:* It is important that the teacher elicit these from students rather than name them himself. Take plenty of time, and make it an enjoyable exercise.)

4. Ask students if any of the clues fit some civilizations better than others and whether some civilizations can be eliminated at this point.

5. Ask students to identify some possible sources where they can begin to search for the principal features of these civilizations in an attempt to see if the clues fit with the identified characteristics. (*Note:* The teacher will find it profitable to terminate the investigation at this point and assign students the task of doing some research on the subject before the next class meeting. However, he can end this portion of the lesson here by giving students the source.)

6. Hand out Reading III (given below), and direct students to read it carefully with a view to identifying its source. (The reference *must* be omitted, of course, until the end of the exercise.)

197

READING III
"YOU SAY OUR GODS ARE DEAD" [14]

You say
that we know not
the Master of the Everywhere
Creator of the heavens and of the earth.
You say
that ours are not the true gods.
These are strange words
which you speak.
We are perturbed by them,
we are annoyed by them.
Because our forefathers,
those who have been here,
those who have lived upon this earth,
did not speak thus.
They gave us
their precepts of life,
they held as true,
they paid homage to,
they worshiped the gods.
They inculcated us with
all their forms of veneration,
all their ways of worshiping (the gods). . . .
But, if as you tell us,
our gods are now dead,
let us die now
let us now perish,
for now our gods are dead. . . .

7. Ask students to identify clues in this reading which indicate its origin. (*Note:* The clues are considerably different in this reading, and students will have to focus more on its "meaning" than on key words and phrases.)

8. Direct students to formulate a working hypothesis on the origin of the reading and list some sources where they will begin to search for evidence. (*Note:* If the teacher wishes, he can assign half of the class to work on Reading II and the other half to work on Reading

[14] "Mythology of Ancient Mexico" by Miguel Leon-Portilla. Copyright © 1961 by Doubleday & Company, Inc., from *Mythologies of the Ancient World* by Samuel Noah Kramer. Reprinted by permission of Doubleday & Company, Inc.

III. Students will conduct their actual research as an extraclass activity.)

9. Summary: Ask students to reflect on their activities and indicate how the historian may be considered a sort of detective.

LESSON III: VIEWING THE PAST
THROUGH DIFFERENT LENSES
(for two class periods)

OBJECTIVES: Students should be able to

1. Define interpretation, frame of reference, *Zeitgeist* or climate of opinion, bias, objectivity, and judgment as related to historical inquiry
2. Detect the factors listed in 1, above, in selected excerpts from three historians' treatment of Akhenaton
3. Develop an initial appreciation of the utility of differing interpretations
4. Comprehend the need for open-mindedness concerning the finality of conclusions and the need for continuous revision

INSTRUCTIONAL MATERIALS: Transparencies I–IX

PROCEDURES:

1. Show Transparency I (given below).

I

O sole god, like whom there is no other!
Thou didst create the world according to thy desire,
Whilst thou wert alone:
All men, cattle, and wild beasts,
Whatever is on earth, going upon (its) feet,
And what is on high, flying with its wings. . . .

---

2. Ask such questions as the following:
    a. Where do you think this reading came from? (Students will usually say, "the Bible.") Why do you say so?
    b. Were the Hebrews the only monotheists (worshippers of one god) in ancient times?
3. Project Transparency II (given below).
4. Explain that this is a continuation of the same reading (or verse), and then ask such questions as these:

    a. Now, does this appear to be from the Hebrew Scriptures? Why not?

    b. What is the object of worship?

5. Project Transparency III (given below).

II

Thy rays suckle every meadow.
When thou risest, they live, they grow for thee.
Thou makest the seasons in order to rear all that thou hast
    made,
The winter to cool them,
And the heat that they may taste thee.
Thou hast made the distant sky in order to rise therein,
In order to see all that thou dost make.
Whilst thou wert alone,
Rising in thy form as the Living Aton,
Appearing, shining, withdrawing or approaching,
Thou madest millions of forms of thyself alone. . . .

III

All work is laid aside when thou settest in the west.
(But) when (thou) risest (again),
[Everything is] *made to flourish for the king,* . . .
Since thou didst found the earth
And raise them up for thy son,
Who came forth from thy body:
the King of Upper and Lower Egypt, . . . *Ak-hen-Aton,* . . .
    and the Chief Wife of the
King . . . *Nefert-iti, living and youthful forever and ever.*[15]

---

6. Explain that this is the end of the same reading, and ask such questions as these:

    a. According to this "hymn," who is the Creator?

[15] These three selections from "Egyptian Hymns and Prayers," trans. John A. Wilson in James B. Pritchard, ed., *Ancient Near Eastern Texts Relating to the Old Testament*, 3rd. ed. with Supplement (Princeton: Princeton University Press, 1969), pp. 370–371. Copyright © 1969 by Princeton University Press and reprinted by their permission.

b. Who is the *special* creation of Aton on earth? Where does he reign?

7. Explain that Akhenaton is the name taken by the Pharaoh Amenhotep IV and that it means "He-Who-is-Serviceable-to-the-Aton." [16] Then explain that Akhenaton (also spelled "Ikhnaton") has been described by several historians and that now we will see what three historians have said about the man.

8. Show Transparency IV (given below).

IV
A DESCRIPTION BY JAMES H. BREASTED [17]

[Akhenaton was] . . . the most remarkable figure in earlier oriental history. The sumptuous inscriptions on his beautiful coffin . . . call him "the living Aton's beautiful child who lives forever and is true (or just, or righteous) in sky and earth." To his own nation he was afterwards known as "the criminal of Akhenaton"; but however much we may censure him for the loss of the empire, which he allowed to slip from his fingers, however much we may condemn the fanaticism with which he pursued his aim, even to the violation of his own father's name and monuments, there died with him such a spirit as the world had never seen before—a brave soul, undauntedly facing the momentum of immemorial tradition, and thereby stepping out from the long line of conventional and colorless Pharaohs, that he might disseminate ideas far beyond and above the capacity of his age to understand. Among the Hebrews, seven or eight hundred years later, we look for such men; but the modern world has yet adequately to value or even acquaint itself with this man, who, in an age so remote and under conditions so adverse, became not only the world's first idealist and the world's first individual, but also the earliest monotheist, and the first prophet of internationalism—the most remarkable figure of the Ancient World before the Hebrews.

---

9. Ask such questions as the following:
   a. What are some key words which Breasted used to describe

---

[16] John A. Wilson, *The Culture of Ancient Egypt* (Chicago: The University of Chicago Press, 1956), p. 215.
[17] James H. Breasted, "Ikhnaton, the Religious Revolutionary," *The Cambridge Ancient History* (Cambridge: The University Press, 1926), 2: 127–128.

Akhenaton? [*Note:* List these on the board. Encourage students to use a dictionary for unfamiliar words.]

   b. Can you find any indications of favorable bias in Breasted's description?

10. Show Transparency V (given below).

V
A DESCRIPTION BY HARRY R. HALL[18]

The son of Amenhotep III and Tii was no Egyptian warrior like his ancestors. Of mixed race, with, probably, the alien blood of Aryan Mitanni inherited from his father and of the wild desert tribes . . . derived from his mother running in his veins as well as the ichor of the descendants of Ra, the son of a luxurious and art-loving father and of a clever and energetic mother, he was brought up under strong feminine influence. All the requisites for the creation of a striking and abnormal character were present. Amenhotep IV was a man of entirely original brain, untrammelled on account of his position by those salutary checks which the necessity of mixing with and agreeing with other men of lesser mental calibre imposes on those not born in the purple. His genius had full play. And the result was disaster. So insensate, so disastrous, was his obliviousness to everything else but his own "fads" in religion and art that we can well wonder if Amenhotep IV was not really half insane. Dithyrambs have been penned, especially in late years, in praise of this philosophic and artistic reformer, "the first individual in ancient history." We might point out that others have an equal right to this characterization, for instance [Hammurabi], Hatshepsut, or [Thutmose III]. . . . Certainly Akhenaten was the first doctrinaire in history, and, what is much the same thing, the first prig.

---

11. Raise such questions as these:

   a. What are some words used by Hall to describe Akhenaton? [*Note:* List these on the board. Encourage students to use a dictionary for unfamiliar words.]

   b. What evidence of racism can you find in Hall's description?

   c. How does Hall's description differ from Breasted's?

12. Project Transparency VI (given below).

[18] Harry R. Hall, *The Ancient History of the Near East*, 11th ed. (London: Methuen & Company, 1950), p. 298.

VI
A DESCRIPTION BY JOHN A. WILSON [19]

The self-centered nature of Akh-en-Aton's faith, the fact that only the royal family had a trained and reasoned loyalty to the Aton, and the fact that all of pharaoh's adherents were forced to give their entire devotion to him as a god-king explain why the new religion collapsed after Akh-en-Aton's death. Political and economic factors were also important, but . . . we cannot believe that [the courtiers] cherished within their bosoms the teaching about a benevolent and sustaining sole god, the Aton, when all of their religious exercise was exhausted in worship of Akh-en-Aton. . . .

Two important questions face us. Was this monotheism? If so, was it the world's first ancestral monotheism, and did it come down to us through the Hebrews? Our own answer to each question is in the negative, even though such an answer may rest upon definitions of the terms, and such definitions must necessarily be those of modern distinctions. . . .

The Amarna texts call the Aton the "sole god, like whom there is no other." This, however, was nothing new in Egyptian religious address. The form of expression was a fervid exaggeration or concentration, which went back to the earliest religious literature more than a thousand years before Akh-en-Aton's time. . . .

13. Ask the following questions:
     a. Why does Wilson's account seem more "detached" or "objective" than those of Hall and Breasted? Does Wilson focus more on Akhenaton or upon the religion of Aton?
     b. Explain that students have now seen three different and sometimes conflicting interpretations of Akhenaton and his religion. Ask them to assume that all three historians had access to the same sources and facts. Now, ask them *why* the historian's differ in their interpretations. (*Note:* List students' comments on the board. These will probably include such factors as these: educational training, background of experience, personal interests, religious and philosophical beliefs, views on man, the time in which the authors lived and wrote,

[19] Wilson, *The Culture of Ancient Egypt*, pp. 224–225. Copyright © 1951 by the University of Chicago. Reprinted by permission of The University of Chicago Press.

nationality, and cultural experiences.) Now, explain that we can call these factors a *frame of reference* and that every historian possesses a frame of reference or a way of viewing matters as determined by his own individual and group experiences.

14. To validate your statement, inform students that you will now show them biographical data on each of the three historians.

   a. Project Transparencies VII–IX one at a time, and direct students to compare the biographical information in each case with the historian's description of Akhenaton (as listed on the board).

   b. As students examine the information, ask them to indicate instances of *Zeitgeist,* bias, objectivity, and judgment as found in their comparison of the data on each author with his interpretation.

VII
INFORMATION ON JAMES H. BREASTED [20]

Born at Rockford, Illinois, 1865; received A.B. degree, North Central College (Illinois), in 1888; pursued graduate studies in Hebrew and Oriental languages at Chicago Theological Seminary—later awarded honorary bachelor of divinity degree (1899); received A.M. degree, Yale University, in 1892; received Ph.D. degree, University of Berlin, in 1894; wrote dissertation on Akhenaton; made hand copies of all Egyptian inscriptions in European museums (1900); led expedition to Egypt (1905–07) to copy and photograph inscriptions from ancient Nubia; author of more than one dozen books on ancient Egypt; he believed "that social and moral development was first seen in Egypt and that the key to the origins of modern ethics and philosophy might well be found in the sands along the Nile"; died in 1935.

---

15. Summary: Ask students to define frame of reference and to relate how it affects the historian's writing. Ask them to define *Zeitgeist,* bias, objectivity, and judgment as those terms apply to the study of history. Stress the importance of understanding that history is an *interpretation* of the past and not merely an account of facts.

[20] Based on *The National Cyclopaedia of American Biography* (New York: James T. White and Company, 1941), 29: 257–258.

VIII
INFORMATION ON HARRY R. HALL[21]

Born at Fulham, England, 1873; as a young boy he indicated interest in ancient history; graduated with honors from St. John's College, Oxford, 1891—concentrated his studies in the language and history of ancient Egypt; appointed assistant at British Museum (1896) in the department of ancient Egyptian and Assyrian materials; became an outstanding authority on objects from the ancient Near East; participated in expeditions in Egypt (1903–06, 1910, 1925) and in Iraq (1918–19); became director of department of ancient Egyptian and Assyrian materials in the British Museum (1924); author of numerous articles and books on Egypt, Babylonia, and the Aegean—wrote *The Ancient History of the Near East*; died in 1930.

IX
INFORMATION ON JOHN A. WILSON [22]

Born at Pawling, New York, 1899; received A.B. degree, Princeton University, 1920; A.M., American University, Beirut, Syria, 1923; Ph.D., University of Chicago, 1926 (studied under James H. Breasted); epigrapher, Epigraphic Expedition, Oriental Institute, under auspices of University of Chicago, 1926–31; professor of Egyptology, University of Chicago, 1931–present; author of *The Burden of Egypt* (1951)—later republished as *The Culture of Ancient Egypt*—and *Signs and Wonders upon Pharaoh* (1964).

LESSON IV: STARTING WITH HUNCHES

OBJECTIVES: Students should be able to

1. Recognize that historical sources may include nonwritten materials as well as written documents

---

[21] From J. R. H. Weaver, ed., *Dictionary of National Biography, 1922–1930* (Oxford: The Clarendon Press, 1937), pp. 387–388. By permission of the Clarendon Press, Oxford.
[22] From *Who's Who in America*, 37th ed. (Chicago: A. N. Marquis Company, 1970–1971), 36: 2473. Copyright © 1972 Marquis Who's Who, Inc.

2. Develop further their understanding of the concepts of *Zeitgeist*, bias, objectivity, and judgment in historical study
3. Develop skill in stating hypotheses from nonwritten historical sources
4. Develop some appreciation for the excitement and challenge inherent in coping with historical sources that touch directly on human needs

INSTRUCTIONAL MATERIALS: Slides 6–19

PROCEDURES:

1. Show Slide 6 (Figure 6 below).

FIGURE 6.   *Orpheus the Savior (Domitilla Catacomb, 3rd century A.D.).*

From Ludwig von Sybel, *Christliche Antike* (Marburg: N. G. Elwert, 1906–1909), vol. I, p. 155. Reproduced from Joseph Campbell, *The Masks of God: Creative Mythology,* (New York: The Viking Press, 1968). Courtesy of Joseph Campbell and The Viking Press, Inc.

2. Stress the fact that this drawing was taken from a catacomb in Rome and that it dates from the third century A.D. Then explain that catacombs were used by early Christians as burial sites and sometimes as places of refuge from persecution by Roman authorities. Then ask students to identify as many scenes in the panel as they can.

   a. Explain the scenes which they cannot identify. [The scenes are as follows: *center panel*—Orpheus the Savior, pagan poet and purported founder of the Greek mystery religion called Orphism, here subduing animals with the magical power of his lyre and song; *surrounding panels*—four scenes from Old and New Testaments (David holding sling, Moses striking rock, Daniel in Lion's den, and Jesus at tomb of Lazarus); these alternate with four scenes depicting animals, two of which are the sacrificial bull of pagan rites and two of which are rams which are frequently cited in the Old Testament; *panels outside the circle*—eight heads of sacrificed rams with vegetal spray; *four corners*—dove from Noah's ark, bearing olive branch.] [23]

   b. Ask students to develop a working hypothesis about this figure in light of where it was found and on the basis of the mixture of scenes. (*Note:* Raise questions wherever appropriate to stimulate thought. These may include such questions as these: If this is a Christian painting, why does Orpheus rather than Jesus appear as the central figure, perhaps the "savior"? Why are elements of the Hebrew religion and pagan religion blended in with Christian beliefs?) The goal is to get students to state a hypothesis that this bit of evidence indicates that Christianity borrowed some of its ideas from other religions (in other words, that Christianity is a syncretic or eclectic religion).

   c. Raise the following questions: Does a *new* religion always borrow from older religions? Since this is very limited evidence, what other sources must we consult in order to establish the validity of our hypothesis? Suppose that we search for other evidence, what role will frame of reference, bias, objectivity, and judgment play in our interpretation?

3. Show Slides 7–18 (Figures 7–18 below).

4. Explain that these are all pictures of posters made during World War I. Direct students to observe the posters with a view to

[23] The interpretations are based upon Joseph Campbell's *The Masks of God: Creative Mythology* (New York: The Viking Press, 1968), p. 8.

FIGURE 7. *Haven (Poster of the British Women's Hospital Fund), by Bernard Partridge.*

From *War Posters*, ed. Martin Hardie and Arthur K. Sabin (London: A. & C. Black, Ltd., 1920). Reproduced by permission of the publisher.

FIGURE 8. *Let Us Save Them* (Sauvons-les! *Poster of the National Day for the Benefit of ex-Soldiers Suffering from Tuberculosis), by Jules Abel Faivre.*

From *War Posters*, ed. Martin Hardie and Arthur K. Sabin (London: A. & C. Black, Ltd., 1920). Reproduced by permission of the publisher.

FIGURE 9. *French Women during the War* (La Femme Française pendant la Guerre. *Poster of the Kinematograph Section of the French Army), by G. Capon.*

From *War Posters*, ed. Martin Hardie and Arthur K. Sabin (London: A. & C. Black, Ltd., 1920). Reproduced by permission of the publisher.

FIGURE 10. *For Every Fighter a Woman Worker (Poster of the United War Work Campaign, American Y.W.C.A.), by Adolph Freidler.*

From *War Posters*, ed. Martin Hardie and Arthur K. Sabin (London: A. & C. Black, Ltd., 1920). Reproduced by permission of the publisher.

FIGURE 11. *Remember Belgium (American Bonds Poster, 1918), by Ellsworth Young.*

From *War Posters*, ed. Martin Hardie and Arthur K. Sabin (London: A. & C. Black, Ltd., 1920). Reproduced by permission of the publisher.

FIGURE 12. *Cardinal Merciér Protects Belgium (Le Cardinal Merciér protége la Belgique. Poster published in Paris, 1916), by D. Charles Fouqueray.*

From *War Posters*, ed. Martin Hardie and Arthur K. Sabin (London: A. & C. Black, Ltd., 1920). Reproduced by permission of the publisher.

FIGURE 13. *Music in War-Time (Poster of the Professional Classes War Relief Council), by John Hassall.*

From *War Posters*, ed. Martin Hardie and Arthur K. Sabin (London: A. & C. Black, Ltd., 1920). Reproduced by permission of the publisher.

FIGURE 14. *By Ourselves at Last!* (Enfin seuls . . . ! *Poster of the French "Flag Days," 25th and 26th December, 1915. Organized by Parliament), by Adolphe Willette.*

From *War Posters*, ed. Martin Hardie and Arthur K. Sabin (London: A. & C. Black, Ltd., 1920). Reproduced by permission of the publisher.

FIGURE 15. *At Neuve Chapelle (British Recruiting Poster), by Frank Brangwyn.*

From *War Posters*, ed. Martin Hardie and Arthur K. Sabin (London: A. & C. Black, Ltd., 1920). Reproduced by permission of the publisher.

FIGURE 16. *The Ninth Arrow. Subscribe to the War Loan* (Der 9te Pfeil. Zeichnet Kriegsanleihe. *German War Loan Poster*), *by Erler.*

From *War Posters*, ed. Martin Hardie and Arthur K. Sabin (London: A. & C. Black, Ltd., 1920). Reproduced by permission of the publisher.

FIGURE 17. *No! Never!* (Nein! Niemals! *German Poster*), *by F. K. Engelhard.*

From *War Posters*, ed. Martin Hardie and Arthur K. Sabin (London: A. & C. Black, Ltd., 1920). Reproduced by permission of the publisher.

FIGURE 18. *It takes the last blow to make victory complete! Subscribe to the War Loan!* (Es gilt die letzen Schläge, den Sieg zu vollenden! Zeichnet Kriegsanleihe! *German Poster*), *by Gerd Paul.*

From *War Posters*, ed. Martin Hardie and Arthur K. Sabin (London: A. & C. Black, Ltd., 1920). Reproduced by permission of the publisher.

developing some tentative guesses about what life was like during that time (1914–18).

5. Ask such questions as the following: How did the Allies depict the Germans and vice versa? What was the nature of recruitment appeals? What appeals were made to people on the home front? What role does nationalism play in the posters? What kind of problems were encountered by disabled soldiers? What dress customs are discernible in the posters? (*Note:* Students can do this work in groups, if desired. Each group can take one of the questions.)

6. After students have formulated their hypotheses, raise the following questions: What kind of sources will be needed to test the hypotheses? What problems will be encountered in capturing the mood of the times in which the posters were published?

7. Show Slide 19 (Figure 19 below).

FIGURE 19.   *A U.S. Marine in Vietnam.*

From *Life*, July 9, 1971. Photo by James Pickerell. Reproduced by permission of Black Star, New York, New York.

8. Ask students to give an opinion of what is happening in the picture. Afterwards inform them that the American marine is demanding that this Vietnamese family show him their ID cards. Then direct students to formulate a working hypothesis on the South Vietnamese villagers' reaction to American involvement in their country.

9. After students have stated their hypotheses, ask such questions as these: What special problems does the historian face in writing about a contemporary event, especially one such as this which is laden with emotional conflict? What kind of evidence do we need to test our hypothesis? Is that evidence now available? What does the historian mean when he argues that he needs perspective on an event? How is the historian affected by the time in which he lives and writes?

10. Summary: Ask students to comment upon the potential use of nonwritten historical sources. Reiterate the importance of the hunch or working hypothesis as a starting point of historical inquiry. Stress the need for careful and comprehensive scrutiny of the evidence to support the hypothesis, and emphasize the importance of striving to accept the evidence in the spirit of "what actually happened," and of understanding it within its own time period. Evaluate the problem of dealing with material or evidence which is closely related to human needs, motivation, and feelings.

11. Assign students responsibility for soliciting from three adults their definition of history and their opinions on the value and uses of history. Ask students to write these down and think about them for discussion in the next class period.

LESSON V: REFLECTING ON THE NATURE OF HISTORY

OBJECTIVES: Students should be able to

1. Work out a defensible definition of history which incorporates the fundamentals of historical inquiry as discussed during the previous five lessons

2. Develop further appreciation of the need for a critical, open-minded approach to a study of the past

3. Write an essay on the value and uses of history

INSTRUCTIONAL MATERIALS: Written comments of interviews with three adults

PROCEDURES:

1. Divide students into small groups of four or five each, and instruct them to discuss the definitions and comments upon the value and

uses of history as given by the people they interviewed. Direct students to prepare one list of the definitions and another of the value and uses of history as seen through the eyes of the people they interviewed.

2. Ask students to reassemble as a class, and call upon one person from each group to read the definitions and then to read the comments upon the value and uses of history. (As the reports are presented, write each new definition and comment on the board. Ask each student to add to his own personal list any definition and comment he has not already recorded.)

3. Hold a general critical discussion of the definitions and comments. Then assign students to write a brief essay on their own definition of history and on their personal point of view about the value and uses of history. (Allow remaining class time for students to draw up an outline for their essay. Move about the room to see that students are getting under way, and provide assistance as may be needed. Direct students to complete their essays as an assignment for the following day.)

CHAPTER 11

Selected Illustrative Lessons

Once the teacher has introduced his students to the nature of historical study, he cannot rest content that they will henceforth apply their knowledge to all further historical study. And to revert solely to the traditional method of dispensing historical information after the initial introductory lessons is to assure students that the teacher was not serious about the inquiry orientation. Development of the historian's skills of critical inquiry (translation, interpretation, application, analysis, synthesis, and evaluation) and enhancement of the historical attitude require consistency: Throughout the course history must be treated as a thought process as well as product. As we have previously noted, all lessons do not have to be inquiry oriented, and conventional procedures are still useful on occasion. But an exclusive reliance on expository techniques will not attain the wide range of goals essential to instruction in history.

In this chapter, then, we shall examine selected inquiry lessons in order to provide additional illustrations. These lessons are taken from both United States and world history, and they range over a wide area of content. Intended only to supply further examples and, hopefully, to provide a glimpse through the peephole of unending possibilities, these lessons are not intended to suggest that inquiry is a now-and-then technique. We cannot emphasize too strongly that inquiry is

216

an approach which, to be effective, must undergird instruction in history. Space does not permit us to outline lengthy units of instruction,[1] but that must not be taken as support of infrequent use of the inquiry approach. Each lesson should therefore be viewed as only part of a series of lessons to be developed on a given topic. Two of the examples deal with the concepts of historical causation and prediction; two, with value-laden issues; and a third, with historical interpretation.

ON THE CONCEPTS OF CAUSATION AND PREDICTION

The first lesson deals with the causes for the decline of Rome, and it can be profitably placed at the end of an inquiry unit on the history of the Roman Republic and Empire. It may be spread over a period of three days in order to allow time for the reading and research necessary to cope with some of the accompanying questions.

LESSON I: CAUSES FOR THE DECLINE OF ROME

OBJECTIVES: Students should be able to

1. Analyze major interpretations of the causes for the decline of the Roman Empire in the West
2. Apply the principle of multiple causation to the study of the decline of Rome in the West
3. Identify the assumptions of the authors of a selected extract on the decline of Rome
4. Identify the bias of the authors of the same extract
5. Detect the logical fallacies of argument in the same extract
6. Establish a basis for comparison and contrast of Rome and the United States

INSTRUCTIONAL MATERIALS: Reading IV, "Causes for the Decline of Rome"

PROCEDURES (First Day):

1. Hand out Reading IV (given below), and direct students to read it carefully, making note of the causes for the decline of Rome as cited by the authors of the extract.

[1] For a list of secondary school history textbooks with an inquiry orientation, see Appendix A.

READING IV
CAUSES FOR THE DECLINE OF ROME [2]

It is commonly said that Rome "fell" in A.D. 476. There was no great event or catastrophe at that time such as the invasion of the barbarians. It was not a "fall" but a steady decline which began long before the barbarians were a threat to the Empire.

Many historians place depopulation at the head of the list of causes for the fall of Rome. This had been going on steadily many hundreds of years. First the Punic Wars and then the civil wars of the Republic were responsible for killing off large numbers of young men. Gladiatorial combats and plagues further reduced the population. Large numbers were killed by the barbarians, and often whole provinces were carried into captivity. Race suicide was another cause of depopulation. The result was an ever increasing shortage of man power to cultivate the fields and to fill the ranks in the army.

Slavery had other ill effects on the Empire. When the supply of slave labor fell off, the system of *coloni* began. These were chiefly barbarians who had been conquered in war and reduced to the status of serfs. They were bound to the soil. When the land was for sale they went with it.

Taxation had an evil effect on the material prosperity of the Empire. As wealth became more and more concentrated, fewer people were able to pay taxes and so the burden fell increasingly upon the curials, the old senatorial class. Furthermore, the emperors began the practice of making them responsible for collecting the taxes, and if they were unable to collect the required amount, they were forced to make it up out of their own fortunes. In order to increase this class of people the middle class, when they had acquired a certain amount of wealth, were forced to become curials. There was no incentive to become wealthy. Many went bankrupt and others migrated to barbarian countries.

There was an increasing scarcity of money because it was sent to foreign countries to pay for luxuries and other products which the Romans wanted. They had no products to offer in exchange for these. As metals were scarce, emperors began mixing cheaper metals with gold and silver. This reduced the purchasing power of coins, which in turn demoralized business.

Though some of the emperors were good, none of them were democratic. Immorality was common and human rights were unknown. The old religion had been declining since the later days of the Republic, and Christianity could not be practiced openly before the

[2] William Lee Neff and Mabel Gertrude Planner, *World History for a Better World*, rev. ed. (Milwaukee: The Bruce Publishing Company, 1958), pp. 153–154.

time of Constantine. Rulers were concerned with their own selfish interest, and the populace with material prosperity. Had there been more people who measure up to Plato's ideal of a good ruler, or be faithful to Cicero's statement of the natural law, or know and practice the precepts of Christ's teaching, Rome might not have fallen. As it was, the decay, begun in the days of the Republic, gained momentum with the years, and when the barbarians began knocking at the gates of Rome there was no one strong enough to keep them out.

2. Ask students to name the causes given by the authors in the reading, and list these on the board.

3. Structure an inquiry into the reading by raising such questions as the following:

   a. What do you think the authors mean by the phrase "race suicide"? Does racial intermarriage result in the decline of a nation? What evidence can you present to support your argument?

   b. Was the Roman system of taxation a *cause* for decline, or was it the *effect* of other factors? Did debasement of the coinage system lead to decline? Has the United States debased its coinage system in recent years? Does this necessarily lead to decline?

   c. What bias do the authors hold toward a democratic form of government? Toward Christianity? Does it necessarily follow that nondemocratic and non-Christian nations must decline? What evidence can you offer to support your argument?

   d. Do the authors apply a fair standard in their consideration of the decline of Rome when they base their judgment on the grounds that it was not democratic, that Christianity got off to a slow start, and that human rights were not observed? What is a reasonable standard by which the Romans might be judged at the time of their existence?

   e. Is immorality a cause of decline, or is it the effect of something else? What do the authors mean by immorality? Should we apply our standards of morality to the Romans?

4. Assign students to read selected histories on the causes for the decline of Rome in the West. (This must be done carefully, and the works must be chosen and assigned according to the abilities of students.[3] Direct each student to list in writing the causes cited by the author of the passage he is assigned to read.

[3] An excellent choice of selections can be found in Bernard Feder, *Viewpoints in World History* (New York: American Book Company, 1968), pp. 25–48.

PROCEDURES (Second Day):

1. Divide students into small groups of four or five each, and direct them to synthesize their findings in a written list. Also request that they compare their list with Reading IV, focusing on these questions:
   a. Are the authors of Reading IV correct in their statement that "Many historians place depopulation at the head of the list of causes for the fall of Rome"?
   b. To what extent did gladiatorial combats reduce the population?
   c. Did you find any evidence to support their argument for "race suicide"?
   d. Do other authors agree with Reading IV regarding the effect of the system of taxation?
   e. Do other authors agree with Reading IV regarding the effects of immorality and the gradual acceptance of Christianity?
   f. What role did slavery play in the decline of Rome according to Reading IV, and does that square with the other readings?
2. After students have completed their group work, direct a spokesman for each group to report on their conclusions.
3. Ask students to summarize their findings under the following headings: economic, political, social, religious, and other causes for decline. List these on the board, and direct students to take notes.
4. Assign students to write a short essay on the comparisons and contrasts between the societies of ancient Rome and present-day United States.

PROCEDURES (Third Day):

1. Call upon students to report the conclusions of their essays, listing the generalizations under the two rubrics of "Similarities" and "Differences."
2. Ask students if historical comparisons or analogies are valid. This should lead to the identification of a number of fallacies of historical comparison (e.g., differences in forms of government and society, the uncertainty of the future of a current society, the problem of *interpretation* of causes, and the difficulty of judging a past civilization by the standards of a present society).
3. Return to the two lists on the board, requesting students to eliminate, modify, or allow to stand the generalizations which have been drawn.

The second lesson deals with the topic of historical prediction. It will fit well into a discussion of the recent history of the Soviet Union or of the Cold War. In either case it can be used as a culminating lesson which occupies two class periods.

LESSON II: TYRANNIES AND THE LESSONS OF HISTORY

OBJECTIVES: Students should be able to

1. State the limitations of historical prediction
2. Analyze deductively evidence offered in support of a historical prediction
3. Identify the spirit of the time (*Zeitgeist*) in which a selected magazine article was written
4. Appreciate the peculiar historical evolution of a selected form of society and government for a given nation

INSTRUCTIONAL MATERIALS: Reading V, "Tyrannies Must Fall"

PROCEDURES (First Day):

1. After students have spent several days of inquiry into the history of the U.S.S.R. or of the Cold War, assign Reading V (given below) as homework on the day before this lesson.

READING V
TYRANNIES MUST FALL[4]

. . . It would be an error to say that the two systems, Soviet Dictatorship and Western Freedom, cannot coexist, for they have in fact coexisted for 33 years. But they cannot coexist indefinitely without radical change in one. . . .

Either Freedom will win, or Dictatorship will win.

The Soviet Union is confident of the breakdown of the non-Communist world. It is certain that our economy will collapse, our bourgeois capitalism will follow feudalism into ruin, and our government will surrender to "world revolution." We of the free nations are equally confident that the tyrannical Communist dictatorship must yield to a better order. Already Russian Communism has exhibited two distinct phases. It began with the early semi-idealistic stage under Lenin and Trotsky; it moved on to the harsh aggressive imperialism of Stalin. We are certain that the Russian people must and will win their way to a new system of government.

[4] Allan Nevins, "Tyrannies Must Fall," *Colliers*, October 20, 1951, pp. 16–19.

221

Between the two rival expectations, however, lies a vital difference. The Kremlin bases its belief in our early downfall upon the theories of Marx and Lenin as footnoted by Stalin. We base our confidence in a coming Russian revolution on plain historical facts and established historical principles.

History does not assert that, in such a tense cold-war situation as now exists, a hot war is inevitable. On the contrary, an armed truce, a balance of forces, has sometimes kept the peace until the aggressive power has given up its hope of military conquest. Nor does history insist that in a land like Soviet Russia the iron grip of dictatorship can be relaxed only by a sudden violent overturn. A process of bloodless evolution, perhaps with revolutionary incidents, may do the work.

But every lesson of history does go to show that—not for one reason, but several—such a system as is enthroned in Moscow, with its concentration of military, political and economic power in a despotic oligarchy, with its police terror, with its suppression of free discussion, and with its fettering of seven or eight satellite states, must in no long time undergo a sharp transformation. It is as unstable as an inverted pyramid. . . . The South African leader [Jan Smuts] stated his own conviction: "Dictatorship can only be tolerated as a temporary expedient, and can never be a permanent substitute for free self-government. Freedom is the most ineradicable craving of human nature."

Let us look at the various reasons why, unless the Soviet dictatorship permits a steady, bloodless evolution, Russia will suffer what Smuts predicted—"a cataclysm." It may be that this aggressive despotism, bent on domination, is the strongest and most efficiently led in human annals; nevertheless, its ultimate fate is predictable.

To begin with, we have a long and melancholy history to prove that no government and no system can subjugate all Europe, much less the whole globe. Every power that has tried it has not only failed, but has half or totally ruined itself in trying. Charles V, whose motto was "Still further," attempted to establish an Austro-Spanish supremacy over half of mankind. It was a preposterous effort. In 1544, he seemed to have Europe and Spanish America at his feet; in 1556, worn out by failures, he abdicated. His "ramshackle empire" of Germans, Italians, Spaniards, Flemings and Dutch simply could not be held together.

Nor was Louis XIV a whit more fortunate. He, too, wished to dominate Europe. He enlarged the French domains along the Rhine, seizing Strasbourg. He took a slice of Flanders. He brought a great part of Italy under his influence. Placing his grandson on the throne of Spain, he boasted that he had erased the Pyrenees. Yet the tough little Dutch nation under William III held him at bay; and when Marlborough took the field, Louis XIV met a series of defeats—Blenheim, Ramillies, Audenaarde, Malplaquet—which left France exhausted, and which, as he accepted a dictated peace, closed his reign in humiliation and gloom.

As these two ambitious despots failed, so did Napoleon and Hitler. They brought to their undertakings a measure of genius, however misshapen and wicked, that their predecessors had lacked. They worked in a revolutionary period, and for years each made rich profits out of the blunders of his antagonists. When Napoleon saw his star in the zenith at Austerlitz, and when Hitler strode under the Arc de Triomphe, each believed he had European dominion within his grasp. Yet all history goes to show that such an attempt to handcuff long separate nations, no matter how seemingly helpless, must eventually break down.

. . . the Soviet dictatorship is caught in a nasty dilemma. If it maintains its aggressive policies, it runs the risk of war—and disaster. If it comes to terms with the West, it will lose all excuse for the vast armies, the million or more secret police, the concentration camps, and the rest of the apparatus of crisis and terror by which its power is supported.

The second reason for our confidence in a coming Russian revolution—or a rapid evolution with revolutionary incidents—is this: that no power has ever succeeded in holding in permanent subjection a chain of satellite countries as Russia is holding her neighbors. The situation in the East European chain of Soviet satrapies, however disguised, is essentially a revolutionary forcing-bed, which will someday blossom into widespread plots, demonstrations and uprisings.

The Soviet dictatorship is trying to erase an established sense of nationality in all surrounding countries. İt wants "friendly" neighbors, and by "friendly" it means enslaved. It holds not only Poland, Bulgaria, Slovakia and the Baltic States, which are mainly Slavic, as vassals, but also Hungary, which is Magyar; the ancient Bohemia of the Czechs, who are of mixed stocks and Western outlook; Romania, whose people likewise have mixed origins and boast their Latinized tongue; and the East Germans. They are pinned down by a combination of terror and propaganda. They are not only chained to the war chariot of the Soviet Union, but are doing a great deal to pull it.

Poland, Czechoslovakia and Hungary in particular are, by a series of Five-Year Plans, being compelled to sacrifice culture, decent living standards and social freedom to the forced development of heavy industry, so that the Politburo can make them bear a great part of the burden of Communist armaments.

The movement for liberation may come gradually, or suddenly and violently, but it will come. Then, too, the day will dawn when the misled people of Russia will realize that it does not pay to hold a ring of subjugated, sullen, unhappy people in bondage. History shows that it never has paid. . . .

The third reason for our confidence in a coming Russian revolution, violent or peaceable, is that no power has ever yet been able to prevent the entry of ideas from other lands. The Soviet dictatorship could not exist without its Iron Curtain. General knowledge of the superior living conditions of the West, and of the blessings of freedom of movement, freedom of mind and freedom to choose work, would crumble its foundations. Hence the furious zeal of the Politburo to make the Iron Curtain impenetrable. "The Terror joins hands with the Inquisition," writes an Englishman. But history proves that an iron curtain always has chinks and rustholes; that a fabric which looks airtight always yields to the invisible osmosis of information.

Dictatorships for centuries have used exile, death, prison, censorship, book burnings, control of schools and universities, and the systematic falsehoods of a propaganda machine—and always, in the long run, in vain. No doubt the Politburo has brought indoctrination to a new pitch of perfection. No doubt it has molded the minds of millions from infancy. But then modern science has also brought the power of ideas to ride the radio waves to a new pitch of perfection.

Philip II and the Spanish Inquisition tried to crush freedom of thought; but they failed. The French Bourbons were implacably hostile to ideas; but the Enlightenment came in nonetheless—with revolution in its train. Napoleon III exiled Victor Hugo, chained the French press, and steam-rollered the universities; but he finally had to give up his repression as creating five new Hydra heads for every one it cut off. Hitler burned a mountain of books, exiled thousands of intellectuals from Thomas Mann down, muzzled all editors, and filled the concentration camps with men who dared to think; but he could not stop the movement of ideas in Germany.

The fact is that intellectual repression defeats itself by creating suspicion and skepticism, the parents of revolt. . . .

We have still another reason for believing that a drastic transformation is sooner or later inevitable in Russia. If history demonstrates anything, it is that any country which cannot adjust itself constantly and even radically to internal change—that is, any dictatorship which tries to keep a frozen political and social system—is certain to be overtaken by revolution. *No regime has ever lasted unless it had the power of self-criticism and self-reform.* That is precisely the power which Stalinism lacks.

A dictatorship always looks highly efficient—for a time. It has rapidity, directness, discipline and energy; it enlists a compact body of enthusiastic supporters. But as a matter of fact it always proves inefficient.

Why is it, for example, that a dictatorship always resorts to an arbitrary system of justice—or rather injustice? Because it is too inefficient and too cowardly to make a decent system of justice work. Louis XIV's regime in France used *lettres de cachet,* secret arrest, imprisonment without trial or hope of release, and inhuman punishments. That system was not so bad as Russia's today. . . .

We thus see that totalitarian Russia suffers from at least four great weaknesses. It is ambitious to dominate Europe and the world, and no power has ever yet pursued that goal without meeting disaster. It is trying to enthrall and exploit a chain of vassal nations, and Yugoslavia's defiance shows that this leads to armed revolt. It is attempting to cut Russia off from the flow of world ideas, which must finally prove irresistible. And it has established the worst repressions in history to punish internal criticism and block peaceable change. The pressures in the boiler will mount dangerously. Unless the policies are altered, what Jan Smuts called a "cataclysm" is certain. . . .

2. Ask students to identify the four reasons why the author of the reading argued that the Soviet Union must change from a totalitarian to a democratic form of government. List these across the board. Then direct them to cite the evidence which the author gives for each of his four arguments, and write these under each of the items on the board.
3. Ask students to identify the logic of the author's argument, using the syllogism. (If students have not already been introduced to the deductive logic of the syllogism, give one or two simple examples, for instance: "All men are mortal. /Socrates is a man./ Socrates is mortal." If they are unable to get started, give them the initial premise: "Tyrannies must fall." The second premise is, "The Soviet Union is a tyranny." The conclusion is, "The Soviet Union must fall." [5]
4. Follow through with a discussion of syllogisms, and then ask the following:
    a. Is it correct to label the Soviet Union as a tyranny in the 1950's? What are the characteristics of a tyranny?
    b. Can you name any other present-day states which are tyrannies? Must they fall? Is it inevitable that the Soviet Union fall or that it modify itself into a democratic society?
5. Ask: What was the spirit of the time in which the author wrote his article? What was the mood of the United States at that time?
6. Assign students to read selected passages on the Soviet Union from 1953 to the present. Direct them to write a two-page essay on the predictions of Reading V which have been borne out and those which have not as yet. Ask them to include a final speculative paragraph on what they feel will occur in the Soviet Union within the next two decades, basing their views on historical evidence.

[5] See W. Oliver Martin, "The Structure of Knowledge in the Social Sciences," in Stanley Elam, ed., *Education and the Structure of Knowledge* (Chicago: Rand McNally and Company, 1964), pp. 188–220.

PROCEDURES (Second Day):

1. Ask students to indicate whether they are in basic agreement with Reading V. Divide class into two groups: those in basic agreement and those opposed to the arguments of Reading V. Allow each group to discuss its arguments for a few minutes and select two students from each side to debate the issue.
2. Allow each debate team a maximum of ten minutes to argue its position.
3. Summarize the arguments for the class, emphasizing the particular historical evolution of the society and government of Russia and the U.S.S.R. Reemphasize the limitations of historical prediction.

ON ISSUES INVOLVING VALUE POSITIONS

The proper study of history inevitably touches upon issues which evoke controversy over values. To attempt to avoid such issues because of public opinion or for fear of controversy is to ignore one of the most important reasons for studying history. Since historical inquiry is designed to probe situations as they really were, teachers and students must face up to them. The challenge, of course, is to approach them within the spirit of the historical attitude. Such issues are controversial mainly because they tend to remain current and because they elicit emotional responses. It is the job of the history teacher to face the issue squarely and to seek to develop an attitude of rational historical inquiry. This is not to suggest that the issues should be stripped of their emotional content but only to remind the history teacher that one of his major functions is to promote an attitude of free and open inquiry.

The following lessons are designed to deal with value-laden issues in a United States history course. The first series of lessons deals with the American Indian, and it is intended to be spread over five days.

LESSON III: SPEAKING THE FEELINGS
OF THE AMERICAN INDIAN

OBJECTIVES: Students should be able to

1. Analyze a primary source in order to understand the frame of reference of its author

226

2. Recognize and appraise the values of the American Indian in Washington Territory as reflected in an address by Chief Seattle in the nineteenth century
3. Evaluate the treatment of the American Indian in Washington Territory in the nineteenth century
4. Form a value judgment about the treatment of the American Indian in Washington Territory
5. Develop a working hypothesis on the general treatment of American Indians by white Americans
6. Muster evidence to support the working hypothesis

INSTRUCTIONAL MATERIALS: Reading VI, "Chief Seattle's Speech"

PROCEDURES (First Day):

1. Distribute copies of Reading VI (given below), and direct students to read it.

READING VI
"CHIEF SEATTLE'S SPEECH" [6]

Brothers: That sky above us has pitied our fathers for many hundreds of years. To us it looks unchanging, but it may change. Today it is fair. Tomorrow it may be covered with cloud.

My words are like the stars. They do not set. What Seattle says, the great chief in Washington can count on as surely as our white brothers can count on the return of the seasons.

The White Chief's son says his father sends words of friendship and good will. This is kind of him, since we know he has little need of our friendship in return. His people are many, like the grass that covers the plains. My people are few, like the trees scattered by the storms on the grasslands.

The great—and good, I believe—White Chief sends us word that he wants to buy our land. But he will reserve us enough so that we can live comfortably. This seems generous, since the red man no longer needs a large country. Once my people covered this land like a flood tide moving with the wind across the shell-littered flats. But that time is gone, and with it the greatness of tribes now almost forgotten.

But I will not mourn the passing of my people. Nor do I blame our white brothers for causing it. We too were perhaps partly to blame. When our young men grow angry at some wrong, real or imagined,

[6] Reprinted from William Arrowsmith, "Teaching and the Liberal Arts: Notes Toward an Old Frontier," in Donald N. Bigelow, ed., *The Liberal Arts and Teacher Education* (Lincoln, Neb.: University of Nebraska Press, 1971). Copyright © 1971 University of Nebraska Press and reprinted by their permission.

they make their faces ugly with black paint. Their hearts too are ugly and black. They are hard and their cruelty knows no limits. And our old men cannot restrain them.

Let us hope that the wars between the red man and his white brothers will never come again. We would have everything to lose and nothing to gain. Young men view revenge as gain, even when they lose their own lives. But the old men who stay behind in time of war, mothers with sons to lose—they know better.

Our great father in Washington—for he must be our father now as well as yours, since George has moved his boundary northward—our great and good father sends us word by his son, who is surely a great chief among his people, that he will protect us if we do what he wants. His brave soldiers will be a strong wall for my people, and his great warships will fill our harbors. Then our ancient enemies to the north—the Haidas and Tsimshians—will no longer frighten our women and old men. Then he will be our father and we will be his children.

But can that ever be? Your God loves your people and hates mine. He puts his strong arm around the white man and leads him by the hand, as a father leads his little boy. He has abandoned his red children. He makes your people stronger every day. Soon they will flood all the land. But my people are an ebb tide, we will never return. No, the white man's God cannot love his red children or he would protect them. Now we are orphans. There is no one to help us.

So how can we be brothers? How can your father be our father, and make us prosper and send us dreams of future greatness? Your God is prejudiced. He came to the white man. We never saw him, never even heard his voice. He gave the white man laws, but he had no word for his red children whose numbers once filled this land as the stars filled the sky.

No, we are two separate races, and we must stay separate. There is little in common between us.

To us the ashes of our fathers are sacred. Their graves are holy ground. But you are wanderers, you leave your fathers' graves behind you, and you do not care.

Your religion was written on tables of stone by the iron finger of an angry God, so you would not forget it. The red man could never understand it or remember it. Our religion is the ways of our forefathers, the dreams of our old men, sent them by the Great Spirit, and the visions of our sachems. And it is written in the hearts of our people.

Your dead forget you and the country of their birth as soon as they go beyond the grave and walk among the stars. They are quickly forgotten and they never return. Our dead never forget this beautiful earth. It is their mother. They always love and remember her rivers, her great mountains, her valleys. They long for the living, who are lonely too and who long for the dead. And their spirits often return to visit and console us.

No, day and night cannot live together.

The red man has always retreated before the advancing white man, as the mist on the mountain slopes runs before the morning sun.

So your offer seems fair, and I think my people will accept it and go to the reservation you offer them. We will live apart, and in peace. For the words of the Great White Chief are like the words of nature speaking to my people out of great darkness—a darkness that gathers around us like the night fog moving inland from the sea.

It matters little where we pass the rest of our days. They are not many. The Indians' night will be dark. No bright star shines on his horizons. The wind is sad. Fate hunts the red man down. Wherever he goes, he will hear the approaching steps of his destroyer, and prepare to die, like the wounded doe who hears the steps of the hunter.

A few more moons, a few more winters, and none of the children of the great tribes that once lived in this wide earth that roam now in small bands in the woods will be left to mourn the graves of a people once as powerful and as hopeful as yours.

But why should I mourn the passing of my people? Tribes are made of men, nothing more. Men come and go, like the waves of the sea. A tear, a prayer to the Great Spirit, a dirge, and they are gone from our longing eyes forever. Even the white man, whose God walked and talked with him as friend to friend, cannot be exempt from the common destiny.

We may be brothers after all. We shall see.

We will consider your offer. When we have decided, we will let you know. Should we accept, I here and now make this condition: we will never be denied the right to visit, at any time, the graves of our fathers and our friends.

Every part of this earth is sacred to my people. Every hillside, every valley, every clearing and wood, is holy in the memory and experience of my people. Even those unspeaking stones along the shore are loud with events and memories in the life of my people. The ground beneath your feet responds more lovingly to our steps than yours, because it is the ashes of our grandfathers. Our bare feet know the kindred touch. The earth is rich with the lives of our kin.

The young men, the mothers, and girls, the little children who once lived and were happy here, still love these lonely places. And at evening the forests are dark with the presence of the dead. When the last red man has vanished from this earth, and his memory is only a story among the whites, these shores will still swarm with the invisible dead of my people. And when your children's children think they are alone in the fields, the forests, the shops, the highways, or the quiet of the woods, they will not be alone. There is no place in this country where a man can be alone. At night when the streets of your towns and cities are quiet, and you think they are empty, they will throng with the returning spirits that once thronged them, and that still love these places. The white man will never be alone.

So let him be just and deal kindly with my people. The dead have power too.

(Seattle's speech was delivered, in 1856, in his native Duwamish before an audience which included Isaac Stevens, governor of Washington Territory. It was translated on the spot by a Dr. Henry Smith of Seattle, who later published a highly "improved" version of Seattle's speech in the *Seattle Star* (October 29, 1877). Nonetheless, the speech in Smith's version evidently followed the original closely. The version printed here is my "translation" of Henry Smith's Victorian English. What I have done is simply to remove verbal flourishes and obvious Victorian poeticisms; the various embellishments which successive editors gradually intruded into Seattle's speech as reported by Smith have also been removed.)[7]

2. Raise such questions as the following:
    a. Do you believe Seattle is sincere in his expressions of gratitude to the federal government, or do you think his expression is tongue-in-cheek? What evidence can you give to support your position?
    b. What did Seattle mean by such expressions as: "The White Chief's son . . . ," "since George has moved his boundary northward . . . ," "our great and good father sends us word by his son . . ."?
    c. Is there any trace of bitterness in Seattle's speech? What is his image of white people and their religion? What is his belief about race?
    d. How would you characterize the religion of Seattle and his people? What role does nature play in it? Based on this view, how must the natural environment be treated? Can we take a lesson from this today?
    e. What indication of a "generation gap" can you find in Seattle's speech? Is this inevitable in all societies?
    f. What did Seattle mean by the statement, "Your dead forget you. . . . Our dead never forget. . . ."?
    g. What elements of despair can you find in Seattle's speech?
    h. Why is Seattle's speech so eloquent?
    i. Who made decisions in Seattle's tribe?
    j. Seattle said, "There is no place in this country where a man can be alone. . . . The white man will never be alone. . . . The dead have power too." What do you think he meant by this?

[7] Note by William Arrowsmith, "Teaching and the Liberal Arts," p. 26.

3. Assignment for next day: Assume that Chief Seattle's address reflects the feeling of most members of his tribe. On this assumption write an essay (of from one to two pages) in which you identify the values of the American Indian in Washington Territory, and tell how these seem to differ from the values of most white Americans at that time. Also include a paragraph in which you give your opinion of the values of the Indians in Washington Territory.

PROCEDURES (Second Day):

1. Place three columns on the board under the following headings:

I. VALUES OF	II. VALUES OF	III. OPINIONS OF
SEATTLE'S	WHITE	INDIAN
PEOPLE	AMERICANS	VALUES

Then call upon individual students to state items which go under each heading. After this has been completed, seek to reconcile any differences, and where differences remain, call upon dissenting students to justify their arguments.
2. Ask students to reflect upon the problems of moral judgments in history. (See Part I, pp. 54–56 for comments upon these problems.)
3. Assignment for next day: Write a brief essay in which you evaluate the treatment of the American Indian in Washington Territory as implied in Chief Seattle's speech. Then develop a working hypothesis on the general treatment of American Indians by white Americans. (Note: Explain that the term "white Americans" is used purely for the purpose of distinguishing between the aboriginal Americans and those who came later.)

PROCEDURES (Third Day):

1. Divide the class into groups of five, and direct students to discuss their evaluations and working hypotheses.
2. Request that a spokesman for each group report upon the consensus for his group. Then work for refinement of the hypotheses until satisfied that students are ready to submit them to a test.
3. Supply students with a list of sources to be consulted for evidence pertinent to their hypotheses.
   These may include excerpts from the following books which have been published or reprinted in recent years:
   Ralph K. Andrist, *The Long Death: The Last Days of the Plains Indians* (New York: Collier Books, 1968).
   Robert F. Berkhofer, Jr., *Salvation and the Savage* (Lexington: University of Kentucky Press, 1965).
   William Brandon, *The American Heritage Book of Indians* (New York: American Heritage Publishing Company, 1961).

Vine Deloria, *Custer Died for Your Sins* (New York: The Macmillan Company, 1969).

Louis Filler and Allen Guttman, eds., *The Removal of the Cherokee Nation* (Lexington, Mass.: D. C. Heath and Company, 1962).

Jack D. Forbes, ed., *The Indian in America's Past* (Englewood Cliffs, N.J.: Prentice-Hall, 1964).

Henry B. Fritz, *The Movement for Indian Assimilation, 1860–1890* (Philadelphia: University of Pennsylvania Press, 1963).

William T. Hagan, *American Indians* (Chicago: University of Chicago Press, 1961).

Reginald Horsman, *Expansion and American Indian Policy, 1783–1812* (East Lansing: Michigan State University, 1967).

Helen Hunt Jackson, *A Century of Dishonor* (New York: Harper & Row, 1965).

Alvin M. Josephy, Jr., *The Patriot Chiefs: A Chronicle of American Indian Resistance* (New York: The Viking Press, 1969).

Roy H. Pearce, *The Savages of America* (Baltimore: The Johns Hopkins University Press, 1953).

Francis P. Prucha, *American Indian Policy in the Formative Years* (Cambridge: Harvard University Press, 1962).

Lewis O. Saum, *The Fur Trader and the Indian* (Seattle: University of Washington Press, 1966).

Edward H. Spicer, *Cycles of Conquest* (Tucson: University of Arizona Press, 1962).

Edward H. Spicer, *A Short History of the Indians of the United States* (New York: Van Nostrand, 1969).

Ruth Underhill, *Red Man's America* (Chicago: University of Chicago Press, 1953).

Wilcomb Washburn, ed., *The Indian and the White Man* (Garden City, N.Y.: Doubleday & Company, 1964).

PROCEDURES (Fourth Day):

Check students' work and assist those who need guidance. Allow them to use entire period for research.

PROCEDURES (Fifth Day):

1. Select six students to report the findings of their research. Involve other students by encouraging them to comment upon the reports, giving opposing evidence or corroborating conclusions as appropriate.
2. Spend latter half of period in discussion of the following questions:
   a. Do we have any moral obligation to the American Indian today?
   b. What would you propose that we do?

The next lesson likewise deals with "feelings" and values. Centered upon the plight of the migrants to California in the 1930's, the poignant pictures of Dorothea Lange express better than words can describe the hardships of those who made the long trek westward. The lesson can be used to study the domestic problems of the United States in the 1930's, and it can be tied to current problems of the nation.

LESSON IV: LIFE OF THE MIGRANT IN THE 1930'S

OBJECTIVES: Students should be able to

1. Use pictures as a primary source of evidence in reconstructing the era of migration to California
2. Demonstrate empathy for the hardships suffered by migrants
3. Develop a working hypothesis on the plight of migrants to be tested by examining additional evidence

INSTRUCTIONAL MATERIALS: Slides 20–23

PROCEDURES:

1. Begin by projecting a transparency which provides data on migrations to California in the 1930's. Then ask students to conjecture why such large-scale migration occurred at that time. (They should record these in their notes in order to check them against evidence at a later point.)
2. Project Slides 20–23 (given below), allowing sufficient time for students to study each one carefully. Ask them to observe the elements of human suffering and misery in the pictures.

FIGURE 20. *"There's lots of ways to break a man down."*

From Dorothea Lange and Paul Schuster Taylor, *An American Exodus* (New York: Reynal & Hitchcock, 1939), p. 50; rev. ed. (New Haven: Yale University Press, 1969), p. 46. Reproduced by permission of Paul Schuster Taylor.

FIGURE 21. *"Section after section dried up and blowed away."*

From Dorothea Lange and Paul Schuster Taylor, *An American Exodus* (New York: Reynal & Hitchcock, 1939), p. 95; rev. ed. (New Haven: Yale University Press, 1969), p. 77. Reproduced by permission of Paul Schuster Taylor.

FIGURE 22. *Entering California through the Desert.*

From Dorothea Lange and Paul Schuster Taylor, *An American Exodus* (New York: Reynal & Hitchcock, 1939), p. 108; rev. ed. (New Haven: Yale University Press, 1969), p. 88. Reproduced by permission of Paul Schuster Taylor.

FIGURE 23. *Squatter Camp on Outskirts of Holtville, California.*

From Dorothea Lange and Paul Schuster Taylor, *An American Exodus* (New York: Reynal & Hitchcock, 1939), p. 117; rev. ed. (New Haven: Yale University Press, 1969), p. 92. Reproduced by permission of Paul Schuster Taylor.

3. Ask students to indicate their feelings about the conditions evident in the slides. Then raise such questions as these:
    a. Do you think this could have been prevented? Why do you say so?
    b. Is this simply one of the unavoidable outcomes of a capitalist society? What evidence can you give to support your contention?
    c. Do you believe these people could have found work if they had tried hard enough? Is the same true for the thousands upon thousands of unemployed and poverty-stricken people today? How can you justify your answer?
4. Direct each student to formulate a working hypothesis regarding the migrant workers of the 1930's. Then assign them the task of

examining other evidence (over the next two or three days) to support or refute their hypotheses. One factor they must check out is how representative the pictures are. It will also be very helpful to direct their attention to related statistical data on median national income, agricultural production, unemployment, etc.

5. Assign selected students to read John Steinbeck's *Grapes of Wrath*, or if the movie of the same title can be obtained, have all students see it. A report on the book or a follow-up session on the movie can be used to culminate the lessons.

ON INTERPRETING THE AMERICAN REVOLUTION

Certainly few topics are dearer to Americans than the Revolution for Independence, but likewise no topic in American history is fraught with more mythic notions. That in part is unavoidable because the Revolution deals with our origins as a nation. As we have elsewhere noted, however, the popular (and sometimes the scholarly) interpretation of the American Revolution has been narrow and highly parochial. Thus a series of inquiry lessons on the topic can go a long way toward broadening students' conception of the American struggle for independence.

The following approach affords an opportunity for students to probe into some of the primary sources and the interpretations for themselves. Each of the lessons is designed to cover one regular class period. Aimed primarily for above-average students, these particular lessons are intended to follow a study of the background of the American Revolution and the Revolutionary War, and they occupy a total of five class periods. Although a similar approach can be used with other students, the readings in these lessons assume a fairly sophisticated level of reading skills.[8]

[8] For a more extensive historiographical treatment of the causes of the American Revolution, see Bernard Feder, *Viewpoints: USA* (New York: American Book Company, 1967), pp. 18–32. An excellent book, *Viewpoints* can be used with students of average ability. Also, see Allan O. Kownslar and Donald B. Frizzle, *Discovering American History* (New York: Holt, Rinehart and Winston, 1967), pp. 98–192, for a valuable "discovery" approach to the Revolution. And, for less capable students, see Edwin Fenton, Allan O. Kownslar et al., *The Americans* (New York: American Heritage Publishing Company, 1970), pp. 56–81.

LESSON V: CAUSES OF THE AMERICAN REVOLUTION: INTERPRETATIONS IN CONFLICT

OBJECTIVES: Students should be able to

1. Determine the thesis of each of three interpretations of the American Revolution
2. Identify the frame of reference of the authors of the three interpretations
3. Understand the complexity of causes for the American Revolution
4. Analyze selected documents related to the era of the American Revolution
5. Weigh these documents as evidence in support of or against three selected interpretations of the American Revolution provided in the previous lesson
6. Appreciate the utility of primary sources in historical inquiry
7. Prepare a written comparison of the three selected interpretations of the American Revolution with the account given in the class textbook

INSTRUCTIONAL MATERIALS: Reading VII, "The Traditional View of the American Revolution," Reading VIII, "The Role of Social and Economic Factors in the American Revolution," and Reading IX, "The Problems of Colonial Empire"; books of documents; history textbook.

PROCEDURES (First Day):

1. Hand out Readings VII, VIII, and IX (given below), and direct students to read each carefully. Ask them to determine the thesis of each historian.

READING VII
"THE TRADITIONAL VIEW OF THE AMERICAN REVOLUTION" [9]

The hour of the American Revolution was come. The people of the continent with irresistible energy obeyed one general impulse, as the earth in spring listens to the command of nature, and without the appearance of effort bursts forth to life in perfect harmony. The change which Divine wisdom ordained, and which no human policy or force could hold back, proceeded as uniformly and as majestically as the laws of being, and was as certain as the decrees of eternity. The movement was quickened, even when it was most resisted; and its fiercest adversaries worked together effectually for its fulfilment. The

[9] From George Bancroft, *History of the United States,* 10 vols. (Boston: Little, Brown and Company, 1834–1874), 7: 21–24; footnotes omitted.

indestructible elements of freedom in the colonies asked room for expansion and growth. Standing in manifold relations with the governments, the culture, and the experience of the past, the Americans seized as their peculiar inheritance the traditions of liberty. Beyond any other nation they had made trial of the possible forms of popular representation; and respected the activity of individual conscience and thought. The resources of the vast country in agriculture and commerce, forests and fisheries, mines and materials for manufactures, were so diversified and complete, that their development could neither be guided nor circumscribed by a government beyond the ocean; the numbers, purity, culture, industry, and daring of its inhabitants proclaimed the existence of a people, rich in creative energy, and ripe for institutions of their own. . . . When all Europe slumbered over questions of liberty, a band of exiles, keeping watch by night, heard the glad tidings which promised the political regeneration of the world. A revolution, unexpected in the moment of its coming, but prepared by glorious forerunners, grew naturally and necessarily out of the series of past events by the formative principle of a living belief. And why should men organize resistance to the grand design of Providence? Why should not the consent of the ancestral land and the gratulations of every other call the young nation to its place among the powers of the earth? Britain was the mighty mother who bred and formed men capable of laying the foundation of so noble an empire; and she alone could have formed them. She had excelled all nations of the world as the planter of colonies. The condition which entitled her colonies to independence was now more than fulfilled. Their vigorous vitality refused conformity to foreign laws and external rule. They could take no other way to perfection than by the unconstrained development of that which was within them. They were not only able to govern themselves, they alone were able to do so; subordination visibly repressed their energies. It was only by self-direction that they could at all times and in entireness freely employ in action their collective and individual powers to the fullest extent of their ever increasing intelligence. Could not the illustrious nation which had gained no distinction in war, in literature, or in science, comparable to that of having wisely founded distant settlements on a system of liberty, willingly perfect its beneficent work, now when no more was required than the acknowledgment that its offspring was come of age, and its own duty accomplished? Why must the ripening of lineal virtue be struck at, as rebellion in the lawful sons? Why is their unwavering attachment to the essential principle of their existence to be persecuted as treason, rather than viewed with delight as the crowning glory of the country from which they sprung? If the institutions of Britain were so deeply fixed in the usages and opinions of its people, that their deviations from justice could not as yet be rectified; if the old continent was pining under systems of authority which were not fit to be borne, and which as yet no way opened to amend, why should not a people be heartened to build a commonwealth in the wilderness, which alone offered it a home? . . .

READING VIII
"THE ROLE OF SOCIAL AND ECONOMIC FACTORS IN THE AMERICAN REVOLUTION" [10]

The blows aimed at colonial merchant capitalism through the strengthening of the Acts of Trade and Navigation, the promulgation of the Proclamation Line of 1763 and the passage of the Currency Act of 1764 precipitated the crisis in the imperial-colonial relations: and merchant capitalists (whether land speculators or traders) were soon converted from contented and loyal subjects into rebellious enemies of the crown. But, to be successful, the revolutionary host had to be swelled from the ranks of the lower middle-class small farmers and traders and the working-class artisans, mechanics, seamen, fishermen and lumbermen. This was not difficult: for the material well-being of the lower classes was tied to the successful enterprising of the upper, and contraction of economic opportunity in the higher sphere was bound to bring want and suffering in the lower.

The colonies had enjoyed a period of unprecedented prosperity during the Seven Years' War: the expanding market in the West Indies, the great expenditures of the British quartermasters, the illegal and contraband trade with the enemy forces, all had furnished steady employment for workers and lucrative outlets for the produce of small farmers. But with the end of the war and the passage of the restrictive legislation of 1763 and after, depression had set in. With stringency and bankruptcy everywhere confronting merchant capitalists, it was inevitable that mechanics, artisans, seamen and lumbermen should be thrown out of employment, small tradesmen should be compelled to close the doors of their shops, and that small farmers should be confronted with an expanded acreage, a diminished market and heavy fixed charges made even more onerous as a result of currency contraction. Into the bargain, escape into the frontier zones—always the last refuge of the dispossessed—was shut off. Openly abetted by merchants and land speculators, the lower classes moved into the revolutionary host.

It would be a mistake to assume, however, that the working class and lower middle-class groups surrendered up their identities completely and operated only at the behest and with the encouragement

[10] From Louis M. Hacker, "The First American Revolution," *Columbia University Quarterly*, 27 (September 1935): 293–295.

of the merchant capitalists. Under the direction of their own leaders in the Sons of Liberty and the Committees of Correspondence, they were able to articulate their own class demands: the result was, the period of revolutionary crisis saw the development of a radical program which merchants and planters regarded with misgivings and dread but with which they dared not interfere lest, in alienating the underprivileged farmers, tradesmen and workers, they lose that mass support upon which their own destiny so completely was dependent. The lower classes began to look upon the revolution as the instrument for attaining their freedom: from the civil disability of almost universal disfranchisement, from the inequalities of entail and primogeniture, from oppression at the hands of engrossing landlords and from the threatened dominance and exactions of an oversea ecclesiastical authority.

For these and similar class reasons, the lower middle classes and the workers of colonial America joined with the merchants and planters in demonstrations against the imperial program: and when peaceful agitation and pressure proved unavailing, they were ready to take up arms when England resorted to coercion and violence. In 1774 and 1775, through the agencies of the Coercive Acts and the Restraining Acts, England, by striking at the economic life of the colonies directly, virtually opened hostilities. The colonists replied with two declarations of freedom. The first, naturally representing the dominant interest of merchant capitalism, was embodied in a series of resolutions passed by the Second Continental Congress, 6 April, 1776; these nullified the Acts of Trade and Navigation and put an end to the colonial slave trade: and with this single blow colonial merchant capitalism smashed the hampering fetters of the imperial-colonial relations. The second, adopted by the Congress, 4 July, 1776, was the Declaration of Independence: written by the radicals, this was a political manifesto which called upon the masses to defend the revolution. The first American Revolution then moved fully into the stage of armed resistance.

READING IX
"THE PROBLEMS OF COLONIAL EMPIRE" [11]

[C]onfronted with the problem of guaranteeing the necessary security for the extended empire in North America, which it was estimated would involve an annual expenditure of from three to four hundred thousand pounds for the maintenance of ten thousand troops—ac-

[11] From Lawrence Henry Gipson, "The American Revolution As An Aftermath of the Great War for the Empire, 1754–1763." Reprinted with permission from the *Political Science Quarterly*, 65 (March 1950): 96–97, 104.

cording to various estimates made by General Amherst and others in 1764 (to be found among the Shelburne Papers)—the British ministry was impelled to raise the question: Should not the colonials be expected to assume some definite part of the cost? Since the government felt that the colonies were in a position to do so and that the stability of these outlying possessions was a matter of greater concern and importance generally to them, by reason of their proximity, than to the people of the mother country three thousand miles away, the answer was in the affirmative. The reason for this is not hard to fathom. The nine years of war [1754–1763] had involved Britons in tremendous expenditures. In spite of very heavy taxation during these years, the people were left saddled at the termination of hostilities with a national debt of unprecedented proportions for that day and age of over one hundred and forty million pounds. It was necessary not only to service and to retire this debt, in so far as was possible, but also to meet the ordinary demands of the civil government and to maintain the navy at a point of strength that would offer some assurance that France and Spain would have no desire in the future to plan a war to recover their territorial losses. In addition to all this, there was now the problem of meeting the charges necessary for keeping the new possessions in North America under firm military control for their internal good order and for protection from outside interference. . . .

In conclusion, it may be said that it would be idle to deny that most colonials in the eighteenth century at one time or another felt strongly the desire for freedom of action in a wider variety of ways than was legally permitted before 1754. Indeed, one can readily uncover these strong impulses even in the early part of the seventeenth century. Yet Americans were, by and large, realists, as were the British, and under the functioning of the imperial system from, let us say, 1650 to 1750 great mutual advantages were enjoyed, with a fair division, taking everything into consideration, of the financial burdens necessary to support the system. However, the mounting Anglo-French rivalry in North America from 1750 onward, the outbreak of hostilities in 1754, and the subsequent nine years of fighting destroyed the old equilibrium, leaving the colonials after 1760 in a highly favored position in comparison with the taxpayer of Great Britain. Attempts on the part of the Crown and Parliament to restore by statute the old balance led directly to the constitutional crisis, out of which came the War for American Independence. Such, ironically, was the aftermath of the Great War for the Empire, a war that Britons believed, as the Earl of Shelburne affirmed in 1762 in Parliament, was begun for the "security of the British colonies in N. America. . . ."

2. Ask students to identify the thesis or major argument of each of these three historians. [They should arrive at something similar to

the following: *Reading VII* (Bancroft): The proud, self-sufficient colonists had developed ideal institutions of freedom, and they could no longer tolerate suppression by the mother country. Moreover, their fight for independence was inevitable because it had been foreordained by Providence. *Reading VIII* (Hacker): Colonial merchant capitalists became discontented with the increasing restrictions being placed upon their economic advantage by England. They were joined by the lower middle class and the lower class who were also affected by the restrictive measures. But these classes were not mere pawns of the merchant capitalists, for they felt they could gain more civil liberties through independence from the authority of the mother country. *Reading IX* (Gipson): The origins of the conflict are embedded in the great war for British imperial supremacy in North America. The brunt of the cost for security had been borne by British taxpayers, and when the government demanded equalization of the financial burden, the colonists stoutly resisted.]

3. After students have identified the three interpretations, direct them to answer such questions as follow:

   a. Why do these three historians disagree? What seems to be the frame of reference of each one? Do they manifest any bias? [Biographical sketches of each of the authors will be useful here.]

   b. What are the appealing qualities of Bancroft's interpretation? Bancroft subscribes to the "Whig interpretation" of history, i.e., the idea that the country moved in steady progression to the ultimate triumph of democracy. Do you believe such historical progression is inevitable? Why?

   c. How do Hacker and Gipson differ from the popular interpretation that the American Revolution was plainly and simply the struggle of a people to win their rights against an oppressive king and his country?

   d. Can the three interpretations be synthesized? Why or why not? It is possible that a better interpretation may yet appear? Why do you say so?

PROCEDURES (Second and Third Days):

1. Assign students to read selected documents pertinent to the Revolution. [It will be necessary for students to use two class periods and extraclass time to complete the selected readings.] They should focus on the following questions as they read the documents:

   a. What evidence did you find to support the Bancroft thesis? the Hacker thesis? the Gipson thesis?

   b. What are the major arguments of the colonists? the British? What is the position of the Loyalists? What are the arguments of

243

such Englishmen as William Pitt the elder and Edmund Burke in opposition to their own country's colonial policies?

c. What evidence do you find that the colonists are developing their own sense of identity as a people separate from the English?

2. Request that students make notes on their findings. Remind them of the incompleteness of their readings and the tentative nature of any conclusions. Stress the complexity of the issue and the difficulty of determining the actual causes of the Revolution.

Make such works as the following accessible to students:

The Annals of America, Vol. 2, "1775–1783, Resistance and Revolution" (Chicago: Encyclopedia Britannica, 1968), pp. 51–481. [The entire set of the *Annals* is a superb collection of documents, and *every* school should have at least one complete set.]

Henry Steele Commager, ed., *Documents of American History*, 8th ed. (New York: Appleton-Century-Crofts, 1968), pp. 43–105. [An excellent one-volume collection of documents, every school library and preferably every American history teacher should own several copies of this compilation.]

Samuel Eliot Morison, ed., *Sources and Documents Illustrating the American Revolution, 1764–1788*, 2nd ed. (New York: Oxford University Press, 1965), 380 pp. [Also an excellent collection of documents on the topic.]

Other helpful collections include:

Thomas A. Bailey, ed., *The American Spirit: United States History as Seen by Contemporaries* (Boston: D. C. Heath and Company, 1963), pp. 83–120.

Henry Steele Commager and Richard B. Morris, eds., *The Spirit of 'Seventy-Six* (Indianapolis: The Bobbs-Merrill Company, 1958), pp. 1–58.

Louis M. Hacker, *The Shaping of the American Tradition* (New York: Columbia University Press, 1947), pp. 123–210.

J. Rogers Hollingsworth and Bell I. Wiley, eds., *American Democracy: A Documentary Record*, Vol. I, 1620–1865 (New York: Thomas Y. Crowell Company, 1961), pp. 56–107.

Merrill Jensen, ed., *Tracts of the American Revolution, 1763–1776* (Indianapolis: The Bobbs-Merrill Company, 1967), 498 pp.

Richard B. Morris, ed., *The American Revolution, 1763–1783* (Columbia: University of South Carolina Press, 1970), pp. 1–218.

J. R. Pole, ed., *The Revolution in America, 1754–1788: Documents and Commentaries* (London: Macmillan and Co., 1970), pp. 5–40.

PROCEDURES (Fourth and Fifth Days):

Assign students to write a three-page critical essay in which they examine the treatment of the American Revolution in their textbook as compared with the three interpretations previously discussed and documentary evidence which they have examined. [Note: This can serve well in lieu of an examination on the unit of study dealing with the Revolution.]

The thrust of this chapter has been in the direction of developing inquiry-oriented history lessons. The examples have been chosen to illustrate a fairly wide range of objectives which go beyond, but include, the level of memory or recall of knowledge. The lessons are meant to be illustrative only, and the teacher may wish to modify the procedures and locate other instructional materials. The main point, however, is that these types of lessons are essential to the development of intellectual skills and the historical attitude. We cannot deny that imagination and hard work are necessary to develop such lessons, but the teacher will find that his efforts are well rewarded.

CHAPTER 12

Evaluating Achievement in History

The author of the Book of Ecclesiastes has reminded us that there is a time for planting and a time for plucking up. And so it is with the teaching of history. When the fertile seeds of historical inquiry have been sown, an abundant harvest can be expected. But the method of reaping is as crucial as the method of sowing. Thus techniques of evaluating student achievement in historical study must be as carefully chosen and executed as those for planting and nurturing the seeds of the historical attitude. To select outdated and inappropriate machinery of evaluation is to guarantee a sizable loss of the harvest of effective methodology.

The types of tests and other modes of evaluation employed by the teacher quickly reveal to students what approach to history the teacher really believes important and thus what they should concentrate upon in future lessons. If we are to succeed in aiding students to see the value of history, then evaluation must be viewed as a vital component of the teaching and learning process. And as an integral part of the process, it must function harmoniously with all other elements, or like a defective gear, it causes all other parts to malfunction. Since our goal in the teaching of history is to develop skills of critical thinking and foster appropriate attitudes and appreciations as well as to communicate significant historical knowledge, our modes of evaluation must synchronize with all of these processes. If the wheels of evaluation are imbalanced in favor of factual content, the process of developing the historical attitude will quickly break down, and we shall return to the dreary activity of pushing students along in the dilapidated cart of traditional instruction.

Among the most important forms of evaluation is, of course, the classroom test, and the construction of effective tests is a difficult task. The job can be made easier, however, if the teacher observes the basic principles of test construction and if he is willing to apply his imagination and energy to the endeavor. We will find it useful to examine the fundamentals of test construction and to consider a few examples of questions which are designed to measure achievement in history.

OBSERVING BASIC PRINCIPLES

A history test is intended to measure student achievement in the subject, and the history teacher can succeed in measuring such achievement only in relation to the objectives which he has clearly set forth. That is one of the major reasons why in a previous chapter we stressed the importance of formulating well-defined instructional objectives. It is also another reason why we have noted the value of written objectives. If the teacher has explicitly established his aims, then he has a definite base for evaluating the attainment of those aims. Without this base, the teacher is left to choose and construct examination questions in a random and haphazard fashion. Moreover, the absence of clear objectives often results in the selection of an inordinately large number of questions which call only for facts. And nothing is better calculated to suppress students' interest in history than an excess of factual questions. History is, as we have attempted to show, more than a collection of facts, and unless we design tests which transcend the level of memorization of factual content, we succeed only in reinforcing the view that history is "dates and all that stuff."

247

History as a humane subject of study is too valuable to be spoiled by a supersaturation of "stuff."

Once the teacher has established the objectives he will follow in designing his test, he should observe other general principles of test construction. Foremost among these is a consideration of the time element. Given the typical time limit of fifty minutes for a class, one must choose his questions carefully to insure that every student has a chance to respond to all questions on a test. Even experienced teachers sometimes misjudge the amount of time necessary to complete an examination. But two simple rules may be helpful in this regard: (1) A test can usually be only a sampling of what students have learned. (2) It is better to examine thoroughly with a few questions than to test superficially with a larger number of test items. To this we can add that it is a helpful practice for the teacher to write out his own responses to an examination because it will give him some indication of how long it may take his students to do the same. This practice also provides him with a key to scoring and evaluating student answers.

If we bear in mind that a classroom test is designed to determine whether students have learned significant historical knowledge and whether they can employ their intellectual skills rather than how quickly they can complete a test, we shall not fall victim to measuring for speed instead of for achievement. In this same regard we must remember that a history test which requires a high level of reading ability, either by using a difficult vocabulary or by employing sophisticated syntax, does not provide an accurate measure of achievement in history. It may indeed measure vocabulary and reading skill, but in the interest of determining what students have gained from our own course, let us leave that for standardized achievement tests.

Like other teachers, the history instructor is usually burdened with a load of five classes of at least 25 to 30 students in each. Therefore, the testing of 125 to 150 (sometimes as many as 200) students is undeniably a difficult job. For this reason teachers have to make the process of evaluation as easy on themselves as possible. One way to do this is to use good objective questions on history tests. In light of the aims of instruction in history, then, it will be useful to consider the principles of constructing objective test items which measure for the attainment of those aims.

CONSTRUCTING OBJECTIVE TESTS

As critics of objective tests have noted, such tests are not always objective because, except in cases of purely factual questions, the test maker has made a value judgment in selection of the option which is considered to be correct. And of course no test can be completely objective, for in fact the teacher's frame of reference always determines the selection not only of the options included but also of the questions or the items themselves. At the same time, this is also true for subjective or essay tests because the teacher's frame of reference intrudes equally into the choice of questions and even more so into the evaluation of students' responses to an essay question. Perhaps we would be better off simply to consider that evaluation is a tricky and difficult business any way we go about it. Moreover, because it is difficult, we may be wise to consider the different ways to evaluate. And considering the average heavy load carried by teachers, the choices are fairly clear. Even if teachers are persuaded that "essay" tests are better than "objective" tests, few of them can find time to evaluate 150 essays several times during a semester. College professors, many of whom constitute the largest group of critics, should have the "opportunity" to exchange places with school teachers; their views on the use of objective tests could be remarkably modified.

We should not build our case for the use of some objective test items merely upon their expediency, however, for good objective test items also offer other advantages. One of these is that objective items permit the teacher to cover or sample a broad range of learning because more items can be included than on an essay test. Thus the teacher can evaluate achievement more completely. In addition, the well-constructed objective test item can be used very effectively to measure certain types of achievement, measurement which, because of limitations of class time, cannot be accomplished through essay items only. The key to the whole business lies, of course, with

249

the word *good*. Poorly constructed objective items are a bane to effective evaluation. If we can think only of our instructional aims and forget the somewhat spurious appellation of "objective," we can proceed to do the best job possible with one of the most difficult aspects of teaching, that is, evaluation of learning.

More than any other objective item, the true-false or alternative-response question has saddled objective testing with a bad name. No other type of test item deserves criticism as much as the true-false question. In fact, we can go so far as to say that it has no legitimate use in testing for achievement in history. It is first of all antithetical to the spirit of historical inquiry because it assumes a simple "either-or" dichotomy. And to rub salt into the wound, it stresses factual learning, exacerbating the injury even further by equating the trivial and insignificant with the important in historical learning. For these reasons alone, the true-false test should be discarded as a measure of learning in history.

But these are not the only deficiencies of the true-false test. One of its major shortcomings is its inability to induce thought. This has been epitomized in the comic strip "Peanuts." Upon learning that his teacher will give a true-false test, Linus exclaims that "Taking a 'true or false' test is like having the wind at your back!" And so it is: The probability of *guessing* is quite high. This can be illustrated further by playing the little game of flipping a coin to see how many times it will turn up heads, and how many times, tails. In ten tosses of a coin, for example, it is not unusual for one or the other side of the coin to turn up in a ratio of, say, seven to three. On the same principle it is possible for a student to *guess* correctly on seven out of ten true-false items. As the number of tosses is increased, of course, the probability of heads and tails begins to equalize. Thus in one hundred tosses of the coin, the ratio of heads to tails will approach 50–50. In other words, to reduce guessing, the teacher would have to include a large number of true-false items—at least a minimum of fifty to seventy-five items. The advantage does not always favor the student, of course, since on a ten-item true-false test the odds may go against him. Or in other words, he gets only three "heads" and seven "tails." It was that situation which beset poor Linus, and he was forced to declare dejectedly on the next day, "I Falsed when I should have Trued!"

As if these deficiencies were not sufficient to cause any thoughtful history teacher to reject true-false tests, we shall add two more. Any true-false item which is other than factual in nature depends upon a source of authority for its validity. The following item will serve as an example:

T   F   The Industrial Revolution was the single most dynamic force of the nineteenth century.[1]

Obviously, not all historians agree with this statement, which supposedly is to be marked "True." It becomes a matter, then, of responding on the basis of the interpretation of the authors of the textbook from which it was taken. The student is given no opportunity to present an opposing argument. Thus if he desires to get the answer correct, he is compelled to acquiesce to the authority of a statement which, while not necessarily wrong, is at least open to debate. The final shortcoming of the true-false test lies in the difficulty of phrasing items. As an example, let us examine the following items:

T   F   The North wanted to capture Vicksburg, and the South wanted to capture Richmond.
T   F   With more emphasis on individual rights all restrictions on voting were dropped.

In the first instance the question is two pronged: Supposedly the student must respond with "False," since part of the question is untrue. If nothing else, the item could be divided into two questions; but in any case, the triviality of the question is obvious. In the second instance a student would be well advised to respond "False," since the qualifier *all* rarely typifies any historical situation. Additionally, the question is vague because it fails to denote the specific time in history when the situation was supposed to have occurred. Several other examples of poorly worded items could be given, but we need not flog the horse any more, since he is incapable of pulling his load anyway.

The completion test is only slightly better than the true-

[1] This and all other illustrative test items in this chapter are taken directly from actual classroom tests. In a few instances they have been altered slightly for illustrative purposes.

false examination. It can pull its share of the load, but taken alone, it is not up to the task. When recall of factual information is required, the completion test has some value. Because guessing is reduced to a minimum, chance plays a small role in the completion test: If a student does not know the correct answer or if he cannot make an "educated guess," he has no coin to flip. On the other hand, we must recognize that the ability to recall specific facts is not synonymous with understanding.

Probably the single greatest mistake made in the construction of a completion test item is ambiguity. The following item is an example:

The leader of the Aztec nation was _____ .

Presumably, the test maker wants the answer "Montezuma," but it would be also correct to respond "killed by the Spaniards," or even "an elected monarch." The item can be made incontestable by phrasing it in question form thus: "Who was the leader of the Aztec nation at the time of the Spanish conquest?"

Other common errors in construction of completion items include the following: (1) blanks which conform closely to the length of the word(s) required as an answer, thereby providing a clue that the answer is a short or a long word or phrase; (2) omission of too many words in a sentence or paragraph, thus mutilating a statement to the point that it loses its meaning; (3) the appearance of a clue preceding a blank (such as a or an), hence restricting the response to a word which must be compatible with it; (4) exclusion of trivial rather than significant words; and (5) dispersion of blanks throughout the statement rather than in a column, thereby increasing the difficulty of scoring. Even when these errors are avoided, however, it must be remembered that the completion item measures only the ability to recall information; it does not even provide the student with an opportunity to recognize the correct answer from among several choices. That is to say, given a choice of five answers, the student may be able to recognize the proper response, even though he could not recall it when needed. For this reason both matching and multiple-choice questions tend to be better than completion items.

Matching tests allow teachers to cover a fairly wide range

of material, and they are easy to score. The major problems with such tests are threefold: (1) Clues are often included (unwittingly). (2) Students tend to perform either very well or very poorly on matching tests. (3) Matching tests tend to be time-consuming. By examining the following matching test, we can observe instances of these problems.

____ 1.	Founder of the American Red Cross.	A. Susan B. Anthony
____ 2.	Wrote songs about blacks and the deep South.	B. Grover Cleveland
____ 3.	Leader in the fight for women's suffrage.	C. Jane Addams
____ 4.	Wrote many famous marches.	D. Samuel Gompers
____ 5.	Established Hull House in Chicago.	E. Populist Party
____ 6.	Famous orator who ran unsuccessfully for President three times.	F. Sherman Antitrust Act
____ 7.	Wrote entertaining stories and books on American life.	G. Suffrage
____ 8.	Elected President two times by the Democratic Party.	H. William McKinley
____ 9.	A minor political party supported by the farmers.	I. Wm. J. Bryan
____ 10.	A law passed in 1890 designed to break up combinations of companies.	J. Interstate Commerce Act
____ 11.	A law passed in 1887 which made certain harmful practices of interstate railroads illegal.	K. John P. Sousa
____ 12.	The right to vote.	L. Mark Twain
		M. Stephen Foster
		N. Clara Barton

Upon close examination it will become apparent that a student can score high on this test without having prepared for it. Item 9, for example, calls for the name of a political party, and option E is clearly the only party mentioned. Items 10 and 11 both call for names of laws, and options F and J are obviously laws; it remains only a 50–50 choice of one or the other. Moreover, since railroads are a form of "Commerce," the choice is even more certain. Item 12 calls for a term, and the only one appearing among the list of options is G (suffrage). Thus through such a process of elimination, the student can *guess* at many items without any prior study.

We can point out another problem by using the same example. Suppose a student responds to item 6 by matching it with option B. He has thereby used the option which is correctly matched with item 8. The result is that he will miss two items unless he uses option B twice—and that is usually not the case. If he should do the same on another item, he will miss four answers rather than only two. This is the reason why students tend to do either very well or very poorly on matching items.

Another disadvantage of the matching test is that it requires an inordinate amount of time to complete, especially when the test includes more than seven or eight items. The time factor can be reduced, however, by giving two or three groups with no more than, say, five to seven items. In addition, items can be grouped more homogeneously. One group, for example, could contain important names; another, only laws and amendments; another, only terms; and so on. Not only does this practice reduce the time required to answer, it also cuts down on the number of clues and hence decreases the possibility of guessing.

Actually, a better form of matching is the key-list item, which is a blend of matching and multiple choice. The following item provides an example:

I. DIRECTIONS: For each quotation listed below (Nos. 1–7) identify the civilization which is correctly associated with it. Record the letter of the civilization by the appropriate number on your answer sheet. Any one of the civilizations may be used more than once or not at all.

    A. Egyptian
    B. Hebrew
    C. Mesopotamian
    D. Minoan
    E. Persian

(C)1.   "From above in heaven/ One could no more make out man and man./ The gods were afraid before the stormflood,/ Fled, and mounted up to the heaven of Anu."

(A)2.   "Hail to thee mighty god, lord of Righteousness! I am come to thee, oh my Lord: I have brought myself that I may look upon thy glory. I know thee, and I know the name of the forty-two gods who make their appearance with thee in the Hall of Righteousness. . . ."

(C)3.   "Who is there who can grasp the will of the gods of heaven?/ The plan of a god is full of mystery— who can understand it?/ How can mortals learn the ways of a god? He who is still alive at evening is dead the next morning. . . ."

(E)4. "Now the two primal Spirits, who revealed themselves in vision as Twins, are the Better and the Bad in thought and word and action. And between these two the wise one chose aright, the foolish not so."

(B)5. "Assemble yourselves and come; draw near together, you that are escaped of the nations: they have no knowledge that set up the wood of their graven image, and pray unto a god that cannot save."

(A)6. "During the flood, the people shows its joy; every heart is happy . . . , the divine cycle speaks through you. . . ."

(C)7. "If a man has stolen ox or sheep or ass or pig or ship, whether from the temple or from the palace, he shall pay thirtyfold; if he stole from a commoner, he shall render tenfold. If the thief cannot pay, he shall be put to death."

Such an item reduces guessing because any option may be used more than once, or it may not be used at all. But the key list affords another advantage, namely, testing for the skill of application. In this particular instance students had not seen the quotations before the examination. Instead they had studied the characteristics of each civilization, and now on this test they were required to apply their understanding of the ancient civilizations. In item 6, for example, students would be expected to know that the ancient Egyptian looked favorably upon the annual inundation of the Nile and conceived of life as recurring over and over again in cycles. That contrasts, for example, with ancient Mesopotamia where catastrophic floods occurred irregularly and fostered a pessimistic attitude about life. And it contrasts with the ancient Hebrews too because life was viewed as purposeful, moving in linear (as opposed to cyclical) fashion toward a divinely ordained goal. The items in this key list thus go beyond the knowledge level to one of intellectual skills, but, of course, the skill is premised upon the use of knowledge. Other tests of this kind can be developed at a less sophisticated level, but without eliminating the necessity for using the skill of application.

Let us now consider the multiple-choice test as the last of the so-called objective measures of achievement. On a comparative basis it is clearly the best among the objective tests—though it is not free from fault, as we shall see. The greatest strength of the multiple-choice item is its relative flexibility, allowing for evaluation of achievement both in learning knowledge and in developing intellectual skills. It is the latter of these two advantages which makes it superior to the other forms of objective testing. On the other hand, it contains the problems related to all types of objective tests. Good multiple-choice items are difficult to construct, especially those intended to test for criticial thinking ability. As the test maker moves into the areas of interpretation, application, analysis, synthesis, and evaluation, he will encounter the problem of selecting responses which do not reflect his own subjective views. Nevertheless, the well-designed multiple-choice test can be very useful. For purposes of illustration, we can examine a variety of multiple-choice items.

The following item is an example of a knowledge-level question:

> (a) Who were the coauthors of the *Communist Manifesto?*
>   a. Marx and Engels
>   b. Marx and Lenin
>   c. Trotsky and Lenin
>   d. Lenin and Stalin
>   e. Stalin and Khrushchev

The question is relatively easy and simply calls for recognition of the names properly associated with drafting the *Communist Manifesto.* Such items are not difficult to construct. But the crucial point is that they test only for factual information, and if history is to be taught in keeping with the ideas we have previously outlined, the teacher must establish a judicious balance of such questions with others which test for development of intellectual skills.

Since historical understanding includes a sense of time or the order in which events occurred, the teacher should include questions which test for that understanding. Too often teachers have taken a cumbersome approach to time-order questions. The following is typical:

> Place these events in the order of their occurrence by marking 1 by the first, 2 by the second, and so on through 5 for the final event:

256

(3) Stock market crash of 1929
(5) Japanese attack on Pearl Harbor
(4) Election of Roosevelt as President
(1) Formation of the League of Nations
(2) Election of Hoover as President

If a student should mark the first answer incorrectly, however, the others will automatically be out of place. Thus this item is extremely difficult to grade. This can be avoided by arranging the question as follows:

(c) Which one of the following occurred *fourth* in order of time?
   a. Stock market crash of 1929
   b. Japanese attack on Pearl Harbor
   c. Election of Roosevelt as President
   d. Formation of the League of Nations
   e. Election of Hoover as President

Such an arrangement, however, does not assure that the student knows the complete sequence. The following multiple-choice item is better yet:

(b) Which is the correct sequence in which the following events occurred?
   A. Stock market crash of 1929
   B. Japanese attack on Pearl Harbor
   C. Election of Roosevelt as President
   D. Formation of the League of Nations
   E. Election of Hoover as President

a. E, A, D, C, B
b. D, E, A, C, B
c. A, E, D, B, C
d. D, A, E, B, C
e. E, D, C, B, A

The question calls for one response and can be easily scored by the teacher. More time is required to respond to the time-order question than to answer most multiple-choice questions, however, and the teacher should bear that in mind when considering the length of the examination.

The ability to translate symbolic data into verbal form is a useful instructional objective in history. This can be evaluated by using a cartoon, as in the following example:

Study the cartoon below, and then respond to the following question.

(d) The mood portrayed in this cartoon by Herblock is representative of a period in United States history which is often called:

a. Anti-Nazism
b. Anti-Semitism
c. Patriotism
d. McCarthyism
e. Trumanism

The question requires a knowledge of events circa 1946 to 1956 and the ability to transfer that knowledge from a political cartoon into verbal form.

Closely related to this type of question is one which requires the interpretation of data, as, for example, in the next question.

The following table indicates the ability of five countries in the mid-1930's to produce the amount of foodstuffs which were consumed at home, or in other words, the self-sufficiency of each country.

Country	Percent of Foodstuffs* Produced at Home
I	25
II	67
III	83
IV	95
V	100

* Adapted from *The Economic Development of Western Civilization* by Shepard B. Clough, p. 430. Copyright © 1959 by the McGraw-Hill Book Company. Used with permission of McGraw-Hill Book Company.

(a) Which country would represent Great Britain?
a. I
b. II
c. III
d. IV
e. V

Based on knowledge of the economic self-sufficiency of major countries before the outbreak of World War II, this question

"FIRE!"

FIGURE 24.   *"Fire!"*

By Herblock, from *The Washington Post*, June 1949. Reprinted in *The Herblock Book* (Beacon Press, 1952). Reproduced by permission of Herbert Block.

requires an interpretation of data. While the precise percentages are insignificant, it is important to realize that Great Britain depended heavily upon foreign trade for foodstuffs which she did not produce in sufficient quantities at home. The error commonly made by teachers, however, is to require students to memorize data. That not only runs counter to the historical attitude, it is also meaningless—and as every teacher knows when he is honest with himself, the information will soon be forgotten. What is more important, of course, is that students comprehend the economic situation of the major nations at that time, since it had far-reaching effects. Similar questions can be constructed around such data as the rise of political parties (e.g., the British Labor Party or the National Socialist German Workers' Party), or an extrapolation question can be centered on data related to growth and fluctuations in national income.[2] Map questions are also appropriate for this kind of item.

Another useful multiple-choice question is one which tests for understanding of concepts. Too frequently, teachers simply ask for recall in a completion question, as for example:

(anthropomorphism): The name for the belief that gods have human qualities.

The question can be phrased differently to test for both knowledge and application, as in the following item:

(e) The people "imagine their gods to be born, and to have raiment [clothing], voice, and body, like themselves. . . ." This description by an ancient writer suggests that the people he mentioned conceived of their gods as
a. mythological
b. supernatural
c. humble
d. democratic
e. anthropomorphic

The purpose of such a question is to determine if students can go beyond definitions to transfer of knowledge.

Comparisons often provide a useful key to understanding of historical knowledge by requiring the student to relate ideas. The following item illustrates how comparative questions can be constructed:

[2] See Norris M. Sanders, *Classroom Questions: What Kinds?* (New York: Harper & Row, 1966) and Benjamin S. Bloom *et al., Taxonomy: Handbook I, Cognitive Domain* (New York: David McKay Company, 1956), for other examples.

(d) What did the Egyptian belief about the god P'tah have in common with the Hebrew belief about the god Yahweh?
  a. Each god made a covenant with his people.
  b. Each god was a personification of nature.
  c. Each god was transcendent.
  d. Each god spoke the world into being.
  e. Each god was impersonal.

This question assumes that the teacher has not pointedly made these comparisons; otherwise, it simply becomes a matter of recall. If a student is forced both to recall the information for each belief and to draw the comparisons for himself, he is required to utilize an intellectual skill.

Another type of question requires the application of the principles of historical inquiry. The following question assumes that students have been introduced to the nature of historical study but that neither of the two specific quotations has been used in class:

Read the following statements, and then answer the question given below them.
". . . there developed a regime that was a popular government in name but one ruled by the first citizen in fact, a monarchical leadership on a democratic base. . . ."
—G. Busolt (1893)

"Athens was not . . . at any time a perfect democracy. But that it was far more democratic and far less aristocratic in the time of Pericles than is generally assumed and asserted is certain."
—L. R. Van Hook (1918)

(d) These two statements, though based on the same facts, are clearly contradictory. Assuming that each historian employed the scientific method in his research, what probably accounts for the different interpretations?
  a. One author is trying to predict; the other is trying to interpret.
  b. Their hypotheses are different.
  c. One author is using primary sources; the other, secondary sources.
  d. Their frames of reference are different.
  e. They disagree on the meaning of "democracy."

261

Such a question helps the teacher to evaluate understanding of the process of historical inquiry. It can likewise be tested through an analogy item:

(c) Regarding historical sources on the reign of Louis XIV, primary source is to secondary source as
  a. Bossuet is to Saint-Simon
  b. Voltaire is to Bossuet
  c. Saint-Simon is to Voltaire
  d. Madame Roland is to Arthur Young
  e. Louis XIV is to Colbert

The purpose of this question is to get students to recognize the difference between primary and secondary sources and to associate these correctly with the given individuals who have written about Louis XIV. Naturally, these individuals should have been encountered in an inquiry lesson, using sources from each of them.

In keeping with the historical attitude, it is important that students recognize the distinction between facts and generalizations. This can be evaluated in a question such as the following:

(e) Which one of the following is a historical fact about the reign of Louis XIV?
  a. Louis XIV was God's lieutenant on earth, a king by Divine Right.
  b. Louis XIV made a mistake by revoking the Edict of Nantes.
  c. The most fundamental step taken by Louis XIV was to assure himself of control of the army.
  d. Louis XIV's vanity and great love of admiration were his ruin.
  e. *Lettres de cachet*, issued by Louis XIV, allowed for arbitrary arrest and imprisonment.

Only by testing for the intellectual ability to apply the historical attitude can the teacher be assured of having attained that objective.

To test for the ability to analyze historical material, the following type of multiple-choice question can be used:

(a) Which of the following lines best typifies Romanticism?

a. "Never saw I, never felt, a calm so deep!
   The river glideth at his own sweet will."
b. "Say first, of God above, or Man below,
   What can we reason, but from what we know?"
c. "Ask of thy mother earth, why oaks are made
   Taller or stronger than the weeds they shade?"
d. "Vast chain of Being! which from God began,
   Natures ethereal, human, angel, man. . . ."
e. "It is only by the exercise of reason, that man
   can discover God. Take away that reason, and he
   would be incapable of understanding anything."

The initial option ("a") expresses man's desire to be attuned with nature and thus illustrates the Romantic attitude. The third option ("c") also refers to nature, but it illustrates the mechanical spirit of Realism. Options "b" and "e" likewise illustrate Realism by their emphasis upon "reasoning," and option "d" expresses the Realist conception of Deism or God as First Principle. Again, it is important that students be afforded the opportunity to deal with the substantive matter of Realism and Romanticism in an inquiry context so that they grasp these concepts for themselves rather than having them "handed" to them by the teacher.

Another useful kind of analytical exercise can be built around a passage which requires the student to identify the assumption(s) of the writer. This can be illustrated in the following multiple-choice question:

Read the following excerpt from a book written in 1885 by the American clergyman Josiah Strong:

It seems to me that God, with infinite wisdom and skill, is training the Anglo-Saxon race for an hour sure to come in the world's future. Heretofore there has always been in the history of the world a comparatively unoccupied land westward, into which the crowded countries of the East have poured their surplus populations. But the widening waves of migration, which millenniums ago rolled east and west from the valley of the Euphrates, meet to-day on our Pacific coast. There are no more new worlds. The unoccupied arable lands of the earth are limited, and will soon be taken. The time is coming when the pressure of population on the means of subsistence will be felt here as it is now felt in Europe and Asia. Then will the world enter upon a new stage of its history—*the final competition of races, for which the Anglo-Saxon is being schooled.* Long before the thousand millions are here, the mighty *centrifugal* tendency, inherent in this stock and strengthened in the United States, will assert itself. Then this race of unequaled energy, with all the majesty of numbers and the might of wealth behind it—the representative, let us hope, of the largest liberty, the purest Christianity, the highest civilization—having developed peculiarly aggressive traits calculated to impress its institutions upon mankind, will spread itself over the earth. [*Italics in original.*]

(b) Which one of the following assumptions is NOT made by the author of the foregoing passage?
   a. The United States has been peculiarly blessed by God.
   b. Civilization is strengthened by increases in population.
   c. The Darwinian concept of "survival of the fittest" applies to nations.
   d. Race may be defined by cultural and language characteristics.
   e. History is an account of the progress of Christianity.

As with many of the questions designed to test for development of skills, this item requires more time for a response than the typical factual question. Students will have to read the excerpt carefully, weigh each of the assumptions stated in the options, and finally eliminate the one which does not apply.

At this point we must note a limitation of the multiple-choice question in testing for attainment of high-level cognitive objectives. Suppose, for example, that a student wishes to include an assumption not among the alternatives in the foregoing multiple-choice item. The structure of the question simply does not permit him that freedom. Thus as we move into questions related to skills of synthesis and evaluation, the multiple-choice question becomes less useful, and the written or essay test becomes increasingly more appropriate.

Before we proceed to discuss the so-called subjective test, however, we should consider a few important principles in the construction of the multiple-choice test. First, the "stem" of a multiple-choice item should be complete enough to make sense independently of the options, as has been done in each of the previous examples. In other words, avoid the following type of item:

_____ The economic depression of the 1930's was
a.   Slowed by loans from foreign countries
b.   World-wide
c.   Caused by Herbert Hoover
d.   The result of the "Five-Year Plan"
e.   None of the above

Because the stem does not stand on its own, the student must read through all options as though he were working on a completion item. But that is not the only fault of the item. Notice the difference in length of options: Since "b" is much shorter than the others, students will be attracted to it, and thus guessing will tend to override knowledge. Alternatives or options should be approximately equal in length to reduce guessing in favor of excessively short or overly long responses.

At the same time the sample question is faulty on another count. Option "d" is not a plausible answer, at least not if students have any knowledge of the Five-Year Plans of the Soviet Union. To include entirely implausible options is to increase the possibility of guessing. Thus if the teacher includes a ridiculous response, he may manifest his wit, but he also increases the possibility of chance selection of the correct answer. Option "e" likewise plays into the hands of the student who has not prepared well for the examination. This is so for the following reason: If a student recognizes that any option is correct, then he can automatically eliminate option "e." The same principle is applicable to the use of the option "All of the above": If a student recognizes that two options are correct but is unsure of the other two, then he can automatically choose "All of the above." In other words, these options tend to help the "guesser." If the teacher wishes to include more than one correct response, the following options could be used in lieu of the last two in our example:

d.   a and b only
e.   b and c only

This arrangement is also superior to the multiple-response item because it still calls for a single response. The multiple-response item would allow a student to select any one *or* more of the options given. Thus in a hypothetical question if responses "c" and "d" are correct, the student is required to place both letters in the appropriate blank. A problem arises, however, when the student chooses "a" and "c" or when he chooses "a," "c," and "d." Obviously, he has gotten part of the answer correct; but how does the teacher score the question? It is better to stick to the one-response item and avoid any further headaches of evaluation.

Throughout our examples of multiple-choice items we have used five options or alternatives. This is not merely a matter of preference. Since our goal in construction of tests is to measure student achievement, we must reduce the guessing factor as much as possible. Thus a three-option multiple-choice question is better than a two-option true-false item; and a four-choice item decreases guessing even further, while the five-option item makes guessing an even more hazardous business. As a practical matter, however, a multiple-choice item with four *good* alternatives is better than one with four good ones and a bad one. So the teacher hard-pressed for time may find it more feasible to use four-choice items. We will say more about multiple-choice options in a subsequent section on scoring and grading tests.

CONSTRUCTING SUBJECTIVE TESTS

As we have previously suggested, "objective" and "subjective" are not really appropriate terms of distinction among types of tests. Nevertheless, the terms remain in vogue, and we shall use them for convenience. By "subjective," we mean those tests which require a written response and allow for more freedom to organize and structure the "answer" in keeping with high-level cognitive skills. In other words, the subjective test ideally permits the student to express himself creatively on a given topic. Moreover, it presents the student with an opportunity to probe an idea or topic in some degree of depth.

If the history teacher employs the lessons we have outlined in chapters 10 and 11 or if he employs similar lessons, he will have the opportunity of "testing" for some of the higher level cognitive skills through the written exercises required of students in those lessons. When the inquiry approach is used, evaluation can be viewed as more encompassing than standard testing. And in another sense, the teacher will often find it helpful to evaluate student progress toward development of the historical attitude by observing the oral remarks of students and by noting their willingness to proceed according to the spirit of historical inquiry. Nevertheless, the written test remains an integral part of instruction in history.

History teachers, from the junior high school to the college level, often complain that students are unprepared to write acceptable essay tests. Weeping and gnashing of teeth will not improve the situation, however, and neither will playing the game of "they should have learned how before they got here." Students need opportunities to write, and only practice in writing essays properly will improve their abilities. It is not always the case that students have taken too many objective tests and not enough written tests. The problem is as much the kind as it is the frequency of written tests. Contributing to the low status of the written test is the question which calls for discussion but amounts to no more than an excessively lengthy fill-in-the-blank answer. In other words, when students are expected to repeat the teacher's lecture on a given topic, no mental skill is exercised. And too often the reward of a good grade has gone to the student who memorizes *more* than the next fellow. Questions which do not require students to engage in interpretation, application, analysis, synthesis, and evaluation do not contribute to the development of inquiry skills.

The variety of written tests which open the door to evaluation of intellectual abilities and attitudes is manifold. We shall attempt to illustrate only the most important of them here. Let us begin with a question which requires the use of analytical skills. On pages 263–64 we gave a statement by Josiah Strong on the role of Anglo-Saxon nations, especially the United States, in colonization of the "uncivilized" countries of the world. Instead of structuring the question into a multiple-choice item, the teacher could give the same excerpt and request that students identify the assumptions of the writer. Students would thus be required to ferret out the assumptions for themselves rather than simply to respond to those identified by the teacher. The same kind of skill can be tested in the following item:

The following excerpt is taken from Sir Ernest Barker, *Oliver Cromwell and the English People* (Cambridge: Cambridge University Press, 1937). Read it over carefully and then respond as directed below.

"There is a sense in which the English Puritan Revolution of the seventeenth century and the German National Socialist Revolution of recent years have their analogies. Cromwell came upon an England which was bitterly divided in regard to the ultimate foundations of national life. Monarchism quarrelled with parliamentarianism; both of them quarrelled with incipient democratic doctrines of the sovereignty of the people, and even with incipient communistic doctrines of the ownership of the people's land: Anglicanism, Presbyterianism and Independency jostled together. For a time, if only for a time, Cromwell gave unity: he drew his country together, in a common "assimilation" to a dominant trend: he insisted on a common foundation of common "fundamentals." In the same way, it may be said, the leader of National Socialism came upon a Germany which was equally divided: in the same way he drew his country together: in the same way he insisted on a unity of fundamentals."

What is the "spirit of the times" in which Barker is writing? What assumption(s) does he make regarding the uses of history? Do you agree with Barker's interpretation? Why?

Other questions of this nature can be centered around hypotheses and generalizations which require the student to draw upon evidence to support or refute them. The next item is an example of this:

The following hypothesis is posed: "Christianity and the Church from the time of Paul the Apostle to that of the thirteenth century suppressed freedom of thought."

Take a stand for or against this hypothesis and illustrate how it is true or false by using evidence and examples to support your position.

Or a broader kind of item can be used as part of a final examination over the first half of a course in world history:

"Men have always had some kind of religion. Whatever the form of religious expression, men have needed to feel 'at home' in the universe." Defend or reject this generalization by giving examples which support your argument.

In each instance the student must *select* evidence and examples carefully. While answers to the questions are more difficult for the teacher to evaluate, since they may vary considerably, the questions allow the student to demonstrate his ability to muster evidence, present a logical argument, and express himself effectively. In addition, the questions discourage the rote repetition of "notes."

From this kind of skill we can move to the related ability to synthesize information. A fairly basic question of this nature follows:

> What do all of the early civilizations have in common regarding the type of questions they asked about life and the world? Support your points with evidence or examples. Why were the questions answered differently in each civilization? Does this have any significance for us today? Why?

This question requires the student to pull together information and ideas about the ancient civilizations he has studied. Again, however, if this has already been done by the teacher, then the question falls to the lower level of recall, and no mental skills are necessary to respond to it.

A more personalized approach to testing ability to synthesize can be accomplished through the next question:

> You have just heard a radio commentator argue that the Cold War was precipitated or begun by the Soviet Union and that the United States shares no responsibility at all for bringing on the Cold War. Write a letter of response to him indicating what arguments he has failed to include in his comments. Even if you are in basic agreement with the commentator, demonstrate to him what counter arguments he has omitted.

The object of this test item is to force students to consider the interpretations of some historians who argue that the United States cannot be exculpated on the question of responsibility for the Cold War. It is worded so as to permit the student to stand on his own position if he chooses; but it also obliges him to clarify his view, present a cogent argument, and face the reality of conflicting opinions. Premised upon the idea that lessons have been devoted to probing into the issue of the Cold War, the test item also requires that he synthesize the pro and con arguments of historians and pertinent data from primary sources which he has studied in class.

Another approach to testing for the skill of synthesis, combined with the skill of evaluation, is the "if . . . then" question. This can be accomplished through the following type of question:

> Study the following generalization: If the United States had joined the League of Nations, then the League would have succeeded in controlling events which led to the outbreak of World War II. Write an essay in which you illustrate how this generalization is acceptable.

Requiring knowledge of the major events between 1919 and 1939, the question calls for a careful synthesis. But it goes further by asking students to construct a logical hypothetical argument on the basis of possibilities which were real or viable alternatives at the time of the events. As with other "open" questions of this nature, answers are more difficult to evaluate than they are for standard questions which call only for a list of causes, for example, or only for a "discussion" that necessitates no originality of thought. Evaluation of such essays will be subjective, of course, but that is not to be taken as being synonymous with "undesirable"; history is not a "positive" science. As we move toward the upper end of the hierarchy of cognitive skills, the process of evaluation becomes increasingly more difficult.

This brings us now to testing for attainment of the highest category of cognitive skills, the ability to evaluate. To illustrate how this can be done, let us examine two test items.

1. By what standards should we determine whether the Industrial Revolution was a "blessing or a curse to the working man"? Utilizing these standards, develop and defend your personal position on the issue.
2. Respond to the following as indicated. Make your answer concise, but do not omit major points. (Your answer should take no more than perhaps three pages.)
   1. In what two major ways were the peace settle-

ments after World War I and World War II
similar?
2. In what two major ways were the peace settlements after World War I and World War II
different?
3. *Evaluate* the effect or significance of the similarities and differences which you list.

(*Suggestion:* set up two categories with two parts to
each—one for *similarities* and your *evaluation* and another for *differences* and your *evaluation*. Write in general
terms, not in specifics; that is, when you list "territorial
losses," do not attempt to give all of the specific territorial
losses—just enough to establish your point. An example
is given below. The example given should also be used;
the similarity and the evaluation have not been completed
in this example.)

Similarities	*Evaluation*
1. Germany lost territory each time; in W.W.I she lost all of her colonial possessions and a considerable amount of her contiguous territory (such as Alsace-Lorraine); while in W.W.II she lost . . .	1. The most significant effect of these losses of W. W. I was . . . In a way this action seems to be justified (or unjustified) because . . . The losses of W.W.II . . .

The first of these items requires the student to establish
standards or criteria of evaluation before he proceeds to
evaluate the issue. Thus while the item permits the student to
state a value position, it taxes his ability to devise a basis for
his belief. The second item makes it necessary for the student
to draw comparisons and recognize contrasts between significant historical events and, finally, to make a reasoned
judgment on the historical effects of those events.

As is obvious, the latter examples which we have cited
also involve the affective side of instruction in history. We
have previously noted the difficulty of dealing with this area of
instruction, but we have also stressed its importance. One final
example will perhaps suffice to show how the instructional
objective of attitudes and appreciations can be evaluated.

What was Martin Luther's concept of liberty? Do you
believe this is good or bad? Why?

This question attempts to combine the cognitive and affective areas of learning. It gives the student a chance to deal with a moral question within the context of a historical occurrence. What is important, of course, is not the position he takes but how well he thinks through and presents his judgment. Also it would elicit one more bit of evidence that the student is acquiring a historical attitude.

Essay tests, subjective tests, or whatever we choose to call them, are necessary components of instruction in history. They are most useful when they provide evidence of the student's ability to apply intellectual skills and to clarify his attitudes and appreciations. Moreover, they afford the student an opportunity to develop his writing ability and thereby prepare him to perform more effectively on tasks expected of him in future years. Carefully constructed subjective tests thus open an important dimension of evaluation of achievement in history.

SCORING AND GRADING

The primary purpose of testing is to determine how well students are acquiring knowledge, developing mental abilities, and enlarging their attitudes and appreciations. We must be concerned, then, with the effectiveness of tests. A beginning point is a check on the validity of test items. This is no easy task, and it is especially difficult for subjective items. Nevertheless, we must do the best we can, and a few simple procedures may help us to accomplish the task.

A valid test item is one which measures what it is supposed to measure. To a certain extent, the validity of an item can be determined by its correspondence with instructional objectives. Thus if we are testing for the ability to use the skill of application, our test item must in fact be designed to do just that. Another measure of its validity, however, can be ascertained by its degree of difficulty and by the extent to which it discriminates among the levels of ability to respond correctly to it. These two factors can be determined for objective tests by relatively easy procedures. Let us take the following item for illustrative purposes:

10. (c) The fact that sixteenth and seventeenth century leaders sometimes sacrificed religious loyalties to political expediency is shown most strikingly by

    a. the war of Charles V against the Schmalkaldic League
    b. the Dutch revolt against Spain
    c. France's participation in the Thirty Years' War
    d. Danish intervention in the Thirty Years' War
    e. Elizabeth's aid to Dutch Protestants

On an actual test in a class of twenty-five students, this item proved to be difficult, but the more able students tended to do very well on it. Let us examine how this information was derived.

First, the objective items on *all* papers were scored. Then 30 percent of the highest scores and 30 percent of the lowest scores were recorded (or seven in each group). These were designated as the high group and the low group, respectively. After this, the next step was to tally the number of incorrect responses made by members of the sample groups to each option for *every* item. When this was completed, the following information was obtained for Item 10:

Item	Option	No. Missed High Group	No. Missed Low Group
10.	a.	2	2
	b.	0	0
	c. [Correct Answer]		
	d.	1	1
	e.	0	4
Total		3	7

A total of ten students (from the sample of fourteen) missed the item—three in the high group and seven in the low group. Its degree of difficulty can thus be determined by using the following formula:

$$\text{DIFF.} = \frac{\text{NO. MISSED (LOW GROUP)} + \text{NO. MISSED (HIGH GROUP)}}{\text{TOTAL NO. IN SAMPLE}}$$

$$\text{DIFF.} = \frac{7 + 3}{14} = \frac{10}{14} = .71 \text{ or } 71 \text{ percent}$$

The degree of difficulty of the item is therefore 71 percent. Its discrimination index can be derived through the following formula:

$$\text{DISC.} = \frac{\text{NO. MISSED (LOW GROUP)} - \text{NO. MISSED (HIGH GROUP)}}{\text{TOTAL NO. IN SAMPLE}}$$

$$\text{DISC.} = \frac{7 - 3}{14} = \frac{4}{14} = .286 \text{ or } .29$$

The discrimination index for the item therefore is .29. (For clarity the latter has been stated as a decimal figure rather than as a percentage as for the difficulty factor.)

Obviously, the item is fairly difficult, but it discriminates in favor of the more able students. If the item had exceeded 85 percent in its degree of difficulty, we should raise two questions: (1) Was instruction related to this item effective? (2) Is the item faulty, thereby causing students to choose the "wrong" option? If, on the other hand, the degree of difficulty of the item were very low, say, only 5 percent, we should probably raise a question regarding its value, that is, its ability to function effectively in measuring knowledge about the content covered by the question. These figures are arbitrary, of course, and the teacher can establish other limits if he wishes. Let us also suppose that the discrimination index had been reversed and that more students in the high than in the low group had missed the item. In that case we would find it necessary to raise a question regarding the choices. When an item discriminates negatively—in other words, students in the high group have found some (probably justifiable) reason to select the "wrong" answer—upon further scrutiny the teacher will probably find a faulty option. If an item proves to be too difficult or if it discriminates negatively, the best course of action is to omit it and rescore the papers.

As we examine item 10 further, we will note that option "b" was not chosen by any student, which means that the option is nonfunctional or not a plausible choice. Since our item contains five options, the loss of one does no great harm.

Suppose, however, that no student selected option "d" as well. In that case the probability of a correct guess would be increased. By making a tally of responses for each item, we will know when an option should be modified before it is included on another test. And that brings us to observe that the effort put into construction of good multiple-choice items should not be wasted. The items can be used again and again. By keeping each item on an index card and by recording the difficulty and discrimination indices, the teacher can build a file of questions which will be useful in future semesters. This means, of course, that students should not be allowed to retain tests so that the items remain secure. Such a procedure is a wise investment of energy and time. It should not, however, prevent the teacher from "going over" the test with students after he has graded it because it is useful to have students correct their mistakes. It is also a double-check against errors in grading by the teacher. When students record their responses on an answer sheet, the teacher can retain the test booklets. Naturally, students and their parents are entitled to see the test if they wish, but test booklets need not be taken from the classroom.

Subjective tests present special problems of grading. Research studies have indicated, for example, that teachers are inconsistent in assigning marks to papers. In addition, teachers are influenced by such extraneous factors as poor handwriting, incorrect grammar, and misspelled words, tending to score papers lower when these factors are present in written tests. It has also been demonstrated that teachers are subject to a sort of halo effect: If a student does well on the first question or if he does poorly, then there is a tendency to assume he will do well or poorly on all other questions. Such problems can never be eliminated completely, but the teacher should be aware of them if he is to attempt to grade as fairly as possible.

To minimize the halo effect, the teacher can grade one essay through all papers, then return to a second question and do the same, and so forth. Each item is thus considered on its own merits. Not only is this procedure useful for reducing the halo effect, but it also helps the teacher concentrate on one question for a sustained period of time and thereby permits him to compare student performance on the question at hand. Furthermore, the teacher can take a break after scoring one question throughout the papers and lessen worry about unduly penalizing any single student.

It should be remembered that the standard grading practice was not divinely revealed to teachers; it is an arbitrary system which has become accepted as custom. If the history teacher constructs tests of the nature we have suggested, then he should be prepared to adopt a different scale of marking. Thus a grade of 60 percent on a fairly rigorous test may indeed represent average performance. Since the test will not be padded with items which every student will successfully complete, the teacher must consider the difficulty of each test and assign grades accordingly. Any score above 85 percent, for example, may become an "A," and a failing grade may be any score below 50 percent. In short, the teacher should use his imagination to determine what is a reasonable expectation of performance on any given test.

In the final analysis of evaluation, the effectiveness of a test is to be determined by how well it measures achievement in relation to instructional objectives. A test is only a means, not an end, of instruction in history. Tests and grades should never be used as devices to coerce students into an appreciation of history. In fact, when employed as the ends of instruction, they are more likely to create distaste for the subject. History is a humanizing study; let us not destroy it by confusing means with ends. Let us make it a pleasurable study, something which is edifying and enlightening.

APPENDIX A

Selective List of Textbooks Designed for Inquiry in History

Bartlett, Irving, et al. A New History of the United States: An Inquiry Approach. Holt Social Studies Curriculum Series, ed. Edwin Fenton. New York: Holt, Rinehart and Winston, Inc., 1969.

Branson, Margaret Stimmann. Inquiry Experiences in American History. Boston: Ginn and Company, 1970.

Brown, Richard H., and Halsey, Van R., eds. "The Amherst Project Units in American History." Menlo Park, Calif.: Addison-Wesley Publishing Company, 1970.

Burns, Robert E., et al. Episodes in American History: An Inquiry Approach. Lexington, Mass.: Ginn and Company, 1973.

Eibling, Harold H., Jackson, Carlton, and Perrone, Vito. Foundations of Freedom: United States History to 1877. River Forest, Ill.: Laidlaw Brothers, 1973.

——. Challenge and Change: United States History: The Second Century. River Forest, Ill.: Laidlaw Brothers, 1973.

Feder, Bernard. Viewpoints: USA. New York: American Book Company, 1967.

——. Viewpoints in World History. New York: American Book Company, 1968.

Fenton, Edwin. 32 Problems in World History. Chicago: Scott, Foresman and Company, 1964.

——, and Kownslar, Allan O., eds. The Americans: A History of the United States. New York: American Heritage Publishing Co., Inc., 1970.

Ford, Richard B. *Tradition and Change in Four Societies: An Inquiry Approach.* Holt Social Studies Curriculum Series, ed. Edwin Fenton. New York: Holt, Rinehart and Winston, Inc., 1968.

Freidel, Frank, and Drewry, Henry N. *America: A Modern History of the United States.* Lexington, Mass.: D. C. Heath, 1970.

Good, John M. *The Shaping of Western Society: An Inquiry Approach.* Holt Social Studies Curriculum Series, ed. Edwin Fenton. New York: Holt, Rinehart and Winston, Inc., 1968.

Gordon, Alice K. *The Promise of America.* Chicago: Science Research Associates, Inc., 1970.

Kane, Ralph J., and Glover, Jeffrey A. *Inquiry: USA.* New York: Globe Book Company, Inc., 1971.

Kownslar, Allan O., and Frizzle, Donald B. *Discovering American History.* New York: Holt, Rinehart and Winston, Inc., 1967.

Massialas, Byron G., and Zevin, Jack. *Looking Into History.* World History Through Inquiry Series. Chicago: Rand McNally & Company, 1969.

Oliver, Donald O., and Newman, Fred M. The Public Issues Series, Harvard Social Studies Project. (Selected Units in United States and World History.) Columbus, Ohio: American Education Publications, 1967–.

Sandler, Martin W., Rozwenc, Edwin C., and Martin, Edward C. *The People Make a Nation.* Boston: Allyn and Bacon, Inc., 1971.

Weisberger, Bernard A. *The Impact of Our Past: A History of the United States.* New York: American Heritage Publishing Co., Inc., 1972.

Bibliography

A. HISTORIOGRAPHY

Acton, John E. E. D. *Essays on Freedom and Power*. Selected by Gertrude Himmelfarb. Boston: Beacon Press, 1948, 1949.

Adams, Herbert Baxter. *Methods of Historical Study*. Studies in Historical and Political Science, Second Series, No. 11. Baltimore: Johns Hopkins University, 1884.

Angus-Butterworth, Lionel Milner. *Ten Master Historians*. Reprinted. Freeport, New York: Books for Libraries Press, 1969.

Aron, Raymond. "Evidence and Inference in History." In *Evidence and Inference*, ed. Daniel Lerner. Glencoe, Ill.: Free Press, 1959.

————. *Introduction to the Philosophy of History*. Boston: Beacon Press, 1962.

Auerbach, Jerold S. "New Deal, Old Deal, or Raw Deal?: Some Thoughts on the New Left Historiography." *Journal of Southern History*, 35 (February 1969): 18–30.

Austin, Norman, ed. *The Greek Historians*. New York: Van Nostrand-Reinhold Company, 1969.

Ausubel, Herman. *Historians and Their Craft*. New York: Columbia University Press, 1950.

Aydelotte, William O. *Quantification in History*. Reading, Mass.: Addison-Wesley Publishing Company, Inc., 1971.

Bagby, Philip. *Culture and History*. Berkeley: University of California Press, 1959.

Barnes, Harry E. *A History of Historical Writing.* Rev. ed. New York: Dover Publications, 1961.

Barzun, Jacques, and Graff, Henry F. *The Modern Researcher.* Rev. ed. Harcourt, Brace and World, 1970.

Bass, Herbert J., ed. *The State of American History.* Chicago: Quadrangle Books, Inc., 1970.

Beard, Charles A. *The Discussion of Human Affairs.* New York: The Macmillan Company, 1936.

————. *The Nature of the Social Sciences.* New York: Charles Scribner's Sons, 1934.

————. "Written History as an Act of Faith." *American Historical Review,* 39 (January 1934): 219–31.

Becker, Carl. "Everyman His Own Historian." *American Historical Review,* 37 (January 1932): 221–36.

Bellot, H. Hale. *American History and American Historians: A Review of Recent Contributions to the Interpretation of the History of the United States.* Norman: University of Oklahoma Press, 1952.

Benson, Lee. *Toward the Scientific Study of History.* Philadelphia: J. B. Lippincott Company, 1972.

————. *Turner and Beard: American Historical Writing Reconsidered.* Glencoe, Ill.: Free Press, 1960.

Berkhofer, Robert F., Jr. *A Behavioral Approach to Historical Analysis.* New York: The Free Press, 1969.

Berlin, Isaiah. *Historical Inevitability.* New York: Oxford University Press, 1945.

————. "History and Theory: The Concept of Scientific History." *History and Theory,* 1 (1960): 1–31.

Black, J. B. *The Art of History: A Study of Four Great Historians of the Eighteenth Century.* New York: Russell & Russell, Inc., 1965.

Blake, Christopher. "Can History be Objective?" *Mind,* 64 (1955): 61–78.

Bloch, Marc L. *The Historian's Craft.* New York: Alfred A. Knopf, 1953.

Bock, Kenneth E. *The Acceptance of Histories.* Berkeley: University of California Press, 1956.

Bolingbroke, Henry Saint-John, Lord Viscount. *Letters on the Study and Use of History.* Paris: Theophilus Barrois, Jr., 1808.

Bowles, Edmund, ed. *Computers in Humanistic Research.* Englewood Cliffs, N.J.: Prentice-Hall, Inc., 1967.

Bremner, Robert H., ed. *Essays on History and Literature.* Columbus, O.: Ohio State University Press, 1966.

Brinton, Crane. *The Anatomy of Revolution.* Rev. ed. New York: Random House, 1965.

Brooks, Philip C. *Research in Archives: The Use of Unpublished Primary Sources.* Chicago: University of Chicago Press, 1969.

Burke, Peter. *The Renaissance Sense of the Past.* New York: St. Martin's Press, 1969.

Bury, J. B. *The Ancient Greek Historians.* New York: Dover Publications, 1958.

———. "Cleopatra's Nose." In *Selected Essays of J. B. Bury,* ed. H. Temperley. Amsterdam: A. M. Hakkert, 1964; Chicago: Argonaut, 1967.

Butterfield, Herbert. *The Historical Novel.* Cambridge: The University Press, 1924.

———. *History and Human Relations.* New York: The Macmillan Company, 1952.

———. "History as the Organization of Man's Memory." In *Knowledge Among Men,* ed. Paul H. Oehser. New York: Simon and Schuster, Inc., 1966.

———. *Man on His Past: The Study of the History of Historical Scholarship.* Cambridge: Cambridge University Press, 1955.

———. *The Whig Interpretation of History.* New York: Charles Scribner's Sons, 1951.

Cahnman, Werner J., and Boskoff, Alvin, eds. *Sociology and History.* New York: Free Press of Glencoe, 1964.

Cairns, Grace. *Philosophies of History.* Foreword by Pitirim A. Sorokin. New York: Philosophical Library, 1962. Reprint. London: Peter Owen Limited, 1963.

Callcott, George H. *History in the United States, 1800–1860: Its Practice and Purpose.* Baltimore: The Johns Hopkins Press, 1970.

Carr, Edward H. *What Is History?* New York: Alfred A. Knopf, 1962.

Cheyney, Edward P. *Law in History and Other Essays.* New York: Alfred A. Knopf, 1927.

Child, Arthur. "Moral Judgment in History." *Ethics,* 61 (July 1951): 297–308.

Cochran, Thomas C. *The Inner Revolution: Essays on the Social Sciences in History.* New York: Harper & Row, Torchbooks, 1964.

Cohen, Morris R. *The Meaning of Human History.* 2nd ed. La Salle, Ill.: The Open Court, 1961.

Collingwood, R. G. *Essays in the Philosophy of History.* Ed. William Debbins. Austin: University of Texas Press, n.d.

————. *The Idea of History.* New York: Oxford University Press, 1949.

Commager, Henry S. *The Nature and the Study of History.* Columbus, O.: Charles E. Merrill Books, Inc., 1965.

Conkin, Paul K., and Stromberg, Roland N. *The Heritage and Challenge of History.* New York: Dodd, Mead & Company, 1971. ˙

Cunliffe, Marcus, and Winks, Robin W., eds. *Pastmasters: Some Essays on American Historians.* New York: Harper and Row, 1969.

Curtis, L. P., Jr., ed. *The Historian's Workshop.* New York: Alfred A. Knopf, 1970.

Danto, Arthur C. "On Historical Questioning." *Journal of Philosophy,* 51 (February 1954): 89–99.

Dardel, Eric. "History and Our Times." *Diogenes,* 21 (March 1958): 11–25.

Dentan, Robert C., ed. *The Idea of History in the Ancient Near East.* New Haven: Yale University Press, 1955.

Dollar, Charles M., and Jensen, Richard J. *Historian's Guide to Statistics.* New York: Holt, Rinehart and Winston, Inc., 1971.

Donagan, Alan. "Explanation in History." *Mind,* 64 (1957): 146–64.

Dorson, Richard M. *American Folklore and the Historian.* Chicago: University of Chicago Press, 1971.

Dovring, Folke. *History as a Social Science: An Essay on the Nature and Purpose of Historical Studies.* The Hague: Martinus Nijhoff, 1960.

Dray, William. *Laws and Explanation in History.* New York: Oxford University Press, 1957.

————, ed. *Philosophical Analysis and History.* New York: Harper and Row, 1966.

Droysen, Johann Gustav. *Outline of the Principles of History.* Trans. E. Benjamin Andrews. Boston: Ginn & Company, 1893.

Duberman, Martin. *The Uncompleted Past.* New York: Random House, 1969.

Durant, Will and Ariel. *The Lessons of History.* New York: Simon and Schuster, 1968.

Eisenstadt, A. S., ed. *The Craft of American History: Selected Essays.* 2 vols. New York: Harper and Row, 1966.

Eliade, Mircea. *Cosmos and History.* New York: Harper and Row, 1959. (Originally published as *The Myth of the Eternal Return,* 1954.)

Elton, G. R. *Political History: Principles and Practice.* New York: Basic Books, Inc., 1970.

Erikson, Erik H., "On the Nature of Psycho-Historical Evidence: In Search of Gandhi." *Daedalus,* 97 (Summer 1968): 695–730.

————. *Young Man Luther: A Study in Psychoanalysis and History.* New York: W. W. Norton & Company, 1958.

Fell, Albert Prior, ed. *Histories and Historians.* Edinburgh: Oliver & Boyd, 1968.

Finberg, H. P. R., ed. *Approaches to History.* London: Routledge and Kegan Paul, 1962.

Fischer, David Hackett. *Historians' Fallacies.* New York: Harper & Row, 1970.

Fitzsimmons, Matthew A., Pundt, Alfred G., and Nowell, Charles E., eds. *The Development of Historiography.* Harrisburg, Pa.; The Stackpole Company, 1954. Reprint. Port Washington, N.Y.: Kennikat Press, 1967.

Fling, Fred Morrow. *Outline of Historical Method.* Lincoln, Neb.: J. H. Miller, 1899.

————. *The Writing of History.* New Haven: Yale University Press, 1920.

Fogel, R. W. "The New Economic History: Its Findings and Its Method." *Economic History Review,* 19, No. 3 (1966): 642–56.

Frankel, Charles. *The Case for Modern Man.* Boston: Beacon Press, 1959.

Freeman, Edward Augustus. *The Methods of Historical Study.* London: Macmillan and Co., 1886.

Galbraith, V. H. *An Introduction to the Study of History.* London: C. A. Watts & Co., Ltd., 1964.

Gallie, W. B. *Philosophy and the Historical Understanding.* New York: Schocken Books, 1964.

Gardiner, Patrick. *The Nature of Historical Explanation.* New York: Oxford University Press, 1952.

————, ed. *Theories of History.* New York: Free Press of Glencoe, 1959.

Gargan, Edward T., ed. *The Intent of Toynbee's History.* Chicago: Loyola University Press, 1961.

Garraty, John A. *The Nature of Biography*. New York: Alfred A. Knopf, 1957.

Gay, Peter. *A Loss of Mastery: Puritan Historians in Colonial America*. Berkeley: University of California Press, 1966.

————, and Cavanaugh, Gerald J., eds. *Historians at Work*. Vol. I, *Herodotus to Froissart*. New York: Harper & Row, 1972.

————, and Wexler, Victor G., eds. *Historians at Work*. Vol. II, *Valla to Gibbon*. New York: Harper & Row, 1972.

George, Hereford B. *Historical Evidence*. Oxford: Clarendon Press, 1909.

Geyl, Pieter. *Debates With Historians*. Cleveland: World Publishing Company, 1958.

————. *Use and Abuse of History*. New Haven: Yale University Press, 1955.

————, Toynbee, Arnold J., and Sorokin, Pitirim A. *The Pattern of the Past: Can We Determine It?* New York: Greenwood Press, 1968.

Gilbert, Felix, and Graubard, Stephen R., eds. *Historical Studies Today*. New York: W. W. Norton & Company, 1972.

Gooch, G. P. *History and Historians in the Nineteenth Century*. Boston: Beacon Press, 1959.

Gordon, David C. *Self-Determination and History in the Third World*. Princeton: Princeton University Press, 1971.

Gottschalk, Louis, ed. *Generalization in the Writing of History*. Chicago: University of Chicago Press, 1963.

————. *Understanding History*. Rev. ed. New York: Alfred A. Knopf, 1969.

————, Kluckhohn, Clyde, and Angell, Robert. *The Use of Personal Documents in History, Anthropology, and Sociology*. Bulletin No. 53. New York: Social Science Research Council, [1945].

Gould, Clarence P. "History—A Science?" *The Mississippi Valley Historical Review*, 32 (1946): 375–88.

Gould, J. B. "Hypothetical History." *Economic History Review*, XXII, No. 2 (1969): 195–207.

Gray, Wood, *et al. Historian's Handbook: A Key to the Study and Writing of History*. 2nd ed. Boston: Houghton Mifflin Company, 1964.

Gustavson, Carl G. *A Preface to History*. New York: McGraw-Hill, 1955.

Halperin, S. William, ed. *Some 20th Century Historians: Essays* on *Eminent Europeans*. Chicago: University of Chicago Press, 1961.

Handlin, Oscar, *et al. Harvard Guide to American History*. Cambridge: Harvard University Press, Belknap Press, 1954.

Harrison, Frederic. *The Meaning of History and Other Historical Pieces*. New York: The Macmillan Company, 1902.

Hempel, Carl G. "The Function of General Laws in History." *Journal of Philosophy*, 39 (1942): 35–48.

Hexter, J. H. *Doing History*. Bloomington: Indiana University Press, 1971.

———. *The History Primer*. New York: Basic Books, Inc., 1971.

———. *Reappraisals In History*. Evanston: Northwestern University Press, 1961.

Higham, John. *Writing American History: Essays on Modern Scholarship*. Bloomington: Indiana University Press, 1970.

Higham, John, *et al. History*. Englewood Cliffs, N.J.: Prentice-Hall, Inc., 1965.

Hockett, Homer C. *The Critical Method in Historical Research and Writing*. New York: The Macmillan Co., 1955.

Hofstadter, Richard. *The Progressive Historians: Turner, Beard, Parrington*. New York: Alfred A. Knopf, 1968.

Hook, Sidney. *The Hero in History*. New York: John Day Company, 1943.

———, ed. *Philosophy and History: A Symposium*. New York: New York University Press, 1963.

Hoover, Dwight W., ed. *Understanding Negro History*. Chicago: Quadrangle Books, 1968.

Hughes, H. Stuart. *History As Art and As Science*. New York: Harper & Row, 1964.

Hulme, Edward Maslin. *History and Its Neighbors*. New York: Oxford University Press, 1942.

Ibn Khaldun. *The Muqaddimah: An Introduction to History*. Trans. Franz Rosenthal. Princeton: Princeton University Press, 1967.

Jackson, Gabriel. *Historian's Quest*. New York: Alfred A. Knopf, 1969.

Jameson, J. Franklin. *The History of Historical Writing in America*. New York: Antiquarian Press, 1961.

Jaspers, Karl. "The Axial Age of Human History." *Commentary*, 6 (1948): 430–35.

———. *The Origin and Goal of History*. New Haven: Yale University Press, 1953.

Jerome, Thomas Spencer. *Aspects of the Study of Roman History.* New York: G. P. Putnam's Sons, 1962.

Johnson, Allen. *The Historian and Historical Evidence.* New York: Charles Scribner's Sons, 1926.

Journal of Contemporary History, 3 (April 1968). (Entire issue on historical and social science methodology.)

Jouvenel, Bertrand de. *The Art of Conjecture.* Trans. Nikita Lary. London: Weidenfeld and Nicolson, 1967.

Joynt, C. B., and Rescher, N. "The Problem of Uniqueness in History." *History and Theory,* 1 (1961): 150–63.

Kennan, George F. "The Experience of Writing History." *Virginia Quarterly Review,* 36 (Spring 1960): 205–14.

Kent, George O. "Clio the Tyrant: Historical Analogies and the Meaning of History." *Historian,* 32 (November 1969): 99–106.

Kent, Sherman. *Writing History.* 2nd ed. New York: Appleton-Century-Crofts, 1967.

Kitson Clark, George. *The Critical Historian.* New York: Basic Books, Inc., 1967.

Kohn, Hans. *Reflections on Modern History: The Historian and Human Responsibility.* Princeton: D. Van Nostrand, 1963.

Komarovsky, Mirra, ed. *Common Frontiers of the Social Sciences.* Glencoe, Ill.: The Free Press, 1957.

Kracauer, Siegfried. *History: The Last Things Before the Last.* New York: Oxford University Press, 1969.

Kraus, Michael. *The Writing of American History.* Norman: University of Oklahoma Press, 1953.

Kroeber, A. L. *An Anthropologist Looks at History.* Berkeley: University of California Press, 1963.

Lambert, Henry C. M. *The Nature of History.* London: Oxford University Press, 1933.

Lamprecht, Karl. *What is History?* Trans. E. A. Andrews. London: The Macmillan Company, 1905.

Lamprecht, Sterling P. *Nature and History.* New York: Columbia University Press, 1950.

Landes, David S., and Tilly, Charles. *History as Social Science.* Englewood Cliffs, N.J.: Prentice-Hall, Inc., 1971.

Langer, William L. "The Next Assignment." *American Historical Review,* 64 (January 1958): 283–304.

Langlois, Charles V., and Seignobos, Charles. *Introduction to the Study of History.* Trans. G. G. Berry. New York: Henry Holt and Company, 1898. Reprint. New York: Barnes & Noble, Inc., 1966.

Lee, Dwight E., and Beck, Robert N. "The Meaning of 'Historicism'." *American Historical Review,* 59 (April 1954): 568–77.

Leff, Gordon. *History and Social Theory.* University, Ala.; University of Alabama Press, 1969.

Levin, David. *History As Romantic Art.* Stanford: Stanford University Press, 1959.

Liddell Hart, B. H. *Why Don't We Learn from History?* New York: Hawthorn Books, 1971.

Lipset, Seymour M., and Hofstadter, Richard, eds. *Sociology and History: Methods.* New York: Basic Books, Inc., 1968.

Loewenberg, B. J. "Some Problems Raised by Historical Relativism." *Journal of Modern History,* 21 (1949): 17–23.

Lucey, William L. *History: Methods and Interpretation.* Chicago: Loyola University Press, 1958.

Lukacs, John. *Historical Consciousness.* New York: Harper & Row, 1968.

Lynd, Helen M. "The Nature of Historical Objectivity." *Journal of Philosophy,* 47 (1950): 29–43.

Mandelbaum, Maurice. *The Problem of Historical Knowledge.* New York: Harper & Row, 1967.

Manuel, Frank E. *Freedom from History.* New York: New York University Press, 1971.

Marcus, John T. *Heaven, Hell, and History.* New York: The Macmillan Company, 1967.

Marczewski, Jean. "Quantitative History." *Journal of Contemporary History,* 3 (April 1968): 179–91.

Marrou, Henri. *The Meaning of History.* Trans. Robert J. Olsen. Dublin: Helicon Press, 1966.

Marwick, Arthur. *The Nature of History.* London: Macmillan and Company, 1970.

Mazlish, Bruce, ed. *Psychoanalysis and History.* Englewood Cliffs, N.J.: Prentice-Hall, 1963.

―――. *The Riddle of History.* New York: Harper & Row, 1966.

―――. "What Is Psycho-History?" In *Transactions of the Royal Historical Society.* Fifth Series, vol. 21. London: Royal Historical Society, 1971.

Mehta, Ved. *Fly and the Fly-Bottle.* Boston: Atlantic–Little, Brown & Company, 1963.

Meiland, Jack W. *Scepticism and Historical Knowledge.* New York: Random House, 1965.

Meyerhoff, Hans. "On Psychoanalysis and History." *Psychoanalytic Review,* 49 (Summer 1962): 3–20.

————, ed. *The Philosophy of History in Our Time*. Garden City, New York: Doubleday, Anchor Books, 1959.

Mises, Ludwig von. *Theory and History*. New Haven: Yale University Press, 1957.

Montagu, M. F. Ashley, ed. *Toynbee and History: Critical Essays and Reviews*. Boston: Porter Sargent, 1956.

Montell, W. Lynwood. *The Saga of Coe Ridge: A Study in Oral History*. Knoxville: The University of Tennessee Press, 1970.

Morison, Samuel Eliot. "Faith of a Historian." *American Historical Review*, 56 (January 1951): 261–75.

————. "History as a Living Art." In his *By Land and By Sea*. New York: Alfred A. Knopf, 1953.

————. *Vistas of History*. New York: Alfred A. Knopf, 1964.

Muller, Herbert J. *The Uses of the Past*. New York: Oxford University Press, 1957.

Nagel, Ernest, "Some Issues in the Logic of Historical Analysis." *Scientific Monthly*, 74 (March 1952): 162–70.

Namier, Lewis Bernstein. *Avenues of History*. London: H. Hamilton, 1952.

Nash, Ronald H., ed. *Ideas of History*. New York: E. P. Dutton, 1969.

Neff, Emery. *The Poetry of History*. New York: Columbia University Press, 1947.

Nevins, Allan. *The Gateway to History*. Garden City, N.Y.: Doubleday, Anchor Books, 1962.

Nordau, M. *The Interpretation of History*. New York: Moffat, Yard and Company, 1911.

Norling, Bernard. *Towards a Better Understanding of History*. Notre Dame, Ind.: University of Notre Dame Press, 1960.

Oakeshott, Michael. "The Activity of Being an Historian." In his *Rationalism in Politics*. New York: Basic Books, Inc., 1962.

Oman, Charles W. C. *On the Writing of History*. New York: Barnes and Noble, 1969.

Ortega y Gasset, José. *History as a System*. New York: W. W. Norton & Company, Inc., 1961.

————. *The Modern Theme*. New York: Harper & Row, 1961.

Pares, Richard. *The Historian's Business and Other Essays*. Ed. R. A. and Elizabeth Humphreys. New York: Oxford University Press, 1961.

Passmore, J. Z. "The Objectivity of History." *Philosophy*, 33 (1958): 97–110.

Plekhanov, George V. *The Role of the Individual in History*. New York: International Publishers, 1940.

Plumb, J. H. *The Death of the Past.* Boston: Houghton Mifflin Company, 1970.

Popper, Karl R. *The Open Society and Its Enemies.* 2 vols. 4th rev. ed. Princeton: Princeton University Press, 1963.

————. *The Poverty of Historicism.* Boston: Beacon Press, 1957.

Postan, M. M. *Fact and Relevance: Essays on Historical Method.* Cambridge: Cambridge University Press, 1971.

Renier, Gustaf J. *History: Its Purpose and Method.* Boston: Beacon Press, 1950.

Riasanovsky, Alexander V., and Riznik, Barnes, eds. *Generalizations in Historical Writing.* Philadelphia: University of Pennsylvania Press, 1963.

Robinson, James Harvey. *The New History.* New York: The Macmillan Company, 1912.

Rowney, Don Karl, and Graham, James Q., Jr., eds. *Quantitative History.* Homewood, Ill.: The Dorsey Press, 1969.

Rowse, A. L. *The Use of History.* Rev. ed. New York: The Macmillan Co., 1963.

Salmon, Lucy M. *Historical Material.* New York: Oxford University Press, 1933.

————. *Why Is History Rewritten?* New York: Oxford University Press, 1929.

Salvemini, Gaetano. *Historian and Scientist.* Cambridge: Harvard University Press, 1939.

Sanders, Jennings B. *Historical Interpretations and American History.* Yellow Springs, Ohio: Antioch Press, 1966.

Santayana, George. *Reason in Science.* Vol. 5, *Life of Reason.* New York: Charles Scribner's Sons, 1942.

Saveth, E. N., ed. *American History and the Social Sciences.* Riverside, N.J.: The Free Press, 1964.

Schaff, Adam. "Historical Facts and Their Selection." *Diogenes,* 69 (March 1970): 99–125.

————. "Why History Is Constantly Rewritten." *Diogenes,* 30 (June 1960): 62–74.

Schevill, Ferdinand. *Six Historians.* Chicago: University of Chicago Press, 1956.

Schlesinger, Arthur, Jr. "The Historian and History." *Foreign Affairs,* 41 (April 1963): 491–97.

————. "The Historian as a Participant." *Daedalus,* 100 (Spring 1971): 339–58.

————. "The Humanist Looks at Empirical Social Research." *American Sociological Review,* 27 (December 1962): 768–71.

Schmitt, Bernadotte. *The Fashion and Future of History.* Cleveland: Western Reserve University Press, 1960.

Scott, Ernest. *History and Historical Problems.* London: Oxford University Press, 1925.

Seligman, Edwin R. A. *The Economic Interpretation of History.* 2nd ed. New York: Columbia University Press, 1924.

Shafer, Boyd C., *et al. Historical Study in the West.* New York: Appleton-Century-Crofts, 1968.

Shafer, Robert J., ed. *A Guide to Historical Method.* Homewood, Ill.: The Dorsey Press, 1969.

Shorter, Edward. *The Historian and the Computer: A Practical Guide.* Englewood Cliffs, N.J.: Prentice-Hall, 1971.

Shotwell, James T. *The History of History.* Rev. ed. New York: Columbia University Press, 1939.

Simpson, Leslie Byrd. *The Writing of History, A Dialogue.* Berkeley: University of California Press, 1947.

Singleton, Charles S., ed. *Interpretation: Theory and Practice.* The Johns Hopkins Humanities Seminars. Baltimore: Johns Hopkins Press, 1969.

Skotheim, Robert Allen. *American Intellectual Histories and Historians.* Princeton: Princeton University Press, 1966.

————, ed. *The Historian and the Climate of Opinion.* Reading, Mass.: Addison-Wesley Publishing Company, 1969.

Small, Melvin. *Public Opinion and Historians.* Detroit: Wayne State University Press, 1970.

Smith, Page. *The Historian and History.* New York: Alfred A. Knopf, 1964.

Snyder, Phil L., ed. *Detachment and the Writing of History: Essays and Letters of Carl L. Becker.* Ithaca: Cornell University Press, 1958.

Squire, John Collings, ed. *If: Or History Rewritten.* New York: Kennikat Press, 1964.

Stern, Fritz, ed. *Varieties of History.* Cleveland: Meridian Books, 1965.

Stover, Robert. *The Nature of Historical Thinking.* Chapel Hill: The University of North Carolina Press, 1967.

Strayer, Joseph, ed. *The Interpretation of History.* New York: Peter Smith, 1950.

Stubbs, William. *Seventeen Lectures on the Study of Medieval and Modern History.* Oxford: The Clarendon Press, 1886.

Swierenga, Robert P. "Clio and Computers: A Survey of Computerized Research in History." *Computers and the Humanities,* 4 (September 1970): 1–21.

————, ed. *Quantification in American History: Theory and Research*. New York: Atheneum Publishers, 1970.

Taft, William H. *Newspapers as Tools for Historians*. Columbus, Mo.: Lucas Brothers Publishers, 1970.

Teggart, Frederick J. *Theory and Processes of History*. Berkeley: University of California Press, 1962.

Tholfsen, Trygve R. *Historical Thinking*. New York: Harper & Row, 1967.

Thompson, James W., and Holm, Bernhard J. *A History of Historical Writing*. 2 vols. New York: The Macmillan Company, 1942.

Thomson, David. *The Aims of History*. London: Thames & Hudson, 1969.

Toulmin, Stephen, and Goodfriend, June. *The Discovery of Time*. New York: Harper & Row, 1965.

Toynbee, Arnold J. *A Study of History*. Abridgments of vols. I–VI, VII–X, by D. C. Somervell. New York: Oxford University Press, 1947–1957.

Trevelyan, George Macaulay. *An Autobiography & Other Essays*. London: Longmans, Green and Company, 1949.

————. *Clio, A Muse and Other Essays*. Freeport, N.Y.: Books for Libraries Press, 1968.

Unger, Irwin, "The 'New Left' and American History." *American Historical Review*, 72 (July 1967): 1237–63.

Vansina, Jan. *Oral Tradition: A Study in Historical Methodology*. Trans. H. M. Wright. Chicago: Aldine Publishing Company, 1965.

Vico, Giambattista. *The New Science*. Rev. ed. Trans. Thomas Goddard Bergin and Max Harold Fisch. Ithaca: Cornell University Press, 1968.

Vincent, John Martin. *Aids to Historical Research*. New York: D. Appleton-Century Company, 1934.

————. *Historical Research*. New York: Holt, 1911.

Walsh, Warren B. *Perspectives and Patterns: Discourses on History*. Syracuse: Syracuse University Press, 1962.

Walsh, W. H. *Philosophy of History: An Introduction*. New York: Harper & Row, 1960.

Webb, Walter Prescott. "History as High Adventure." *American Historical Review*, 64 (January 1959): 265–81.

Wedgwood, C. V. *The Sense of the Past*. New York: The Macmillan Company, 1967. (Originally published as *Truth and Opinion*, 1960.)

Weiss, Paul. *History: Written and Lived.* Carbondale: Southern Illinois University Press, 1962.

White, Morton. *Foundations of Historical Knowledge.* New York: Harper & Row, 1965.

Widgery, Alban G. *Interpretations of History: Confucius to Toynbee.* London: Allen and Unwin, 1961.

Williams, William A. *The Contours of American History.* Cleveland: World Publishing Company, 1961.

Wilson, Edmund. *To the Finland Station: A Study in the Writing and Acting of History.* London: M. Secker & Warburg, 1940.

Winks, Robin W., ed. *The Historian as Detective.* New York: Harper & Row, 1968.

Wolman, Benjamin B. *The Psychoanalytic Interpretation of History.* New York: Basic Books, Inc., 1971.

Woodward, C. Vann. "The Age of Reinterpretation." *American Historical Review,* 66 (October 1960): 1–19.

————. *American Attitudes Toward History.* Oxford: Clarendon Press, 1955.

————, ed. *The Comparative Approach to American History.* New York: Basic Books, 1968.

Zinn, Howard. *The Politics of History.* Boston: Beacon Press, 1970.

B. PEDAGOGY

Allen, Rodney F., Fleckenstein, John V., and Lyon, Peter M., eds. *Inquiry in the Social Studies.* Social Studies Readings, no. 2. Washington, D.C.: National Council for the Social Studies [1968].

American Council of Learned Societies and National Council for the Social Studies. *The Social Studies and the Social Sciences.* New York: Harcourt, Brace and World, Inc., 1962.

American Historical Association, Service Center for Teachers. The entire *Pamphlet Series.* New York: The Macmillan Company, various dates. (Now succeeded by pamphlet series *Discussions on Teaching.*)

Anderson, H. R., Linquist, E. F., and Heenan, David K. *Selected Test Items in World History.* Rev. ed. Bulletin no. 9. Washington, D.C.: National Council for the Social Studies, 1960.

Anderson, H. R., Linquist, E. F., and Stull, Harriet. *Selected Test*

Items in American History. Rev. ed. Bulletin no. 6. Washington, D.C.: National Council for the Social Studies, 1964.

Anthony, Albert S. "Pedagogical Limitations of the Source Materials Approach to the Teaching of History." *The Social Studies,* 60 (February 1969): 51–56.

Association of Social Studies Teachers of New York City. *A Handbook for Social Studies.* 3rd ed. New York: Holt, Rinehart and Winston, 1967.

Ballard, Martin, ed. *New Movements in the Study and Teaching of History.* Bloomington: Indiana University Press, 1970.

Barnes, Mary Sheldon. *Studies in Historical Method.* Boston: D. C. Heath & Company, 1899.

Bauer, Nancy W., ed. *Revolution and Reaction: The Impact of the New Social Studies.* Bloomfield Hills, Mich.: The Cranbrook Press, 1966.

Baxter, Maurice Glen, *et al. Teaching of American History in High School.* Bloomington: Indiana University Press, 1965.

Beck, Earl R. *On Teaching History in Colleges and Universities.* Tallahassee: Florida State University Press, 1966.

Berg, Harry D., ed. *Evaluation in Social Studies.* Thirty-fifth Yearbook. Washington, D.C.: National Council for the Social Studies, 1965.

Beyer, Barry K. *Inquiry in the Social Studies Classroom: A Strategy for Teaching.* Columbus: Charles E. Merrill, 1971.

Billington, Ray Allen, *et al. The Historian's Contribution to Anglo-American Misunderstanding.* Report of a Committee on National Bias in Anglo-American History Textbooks. New York: Hobbs, Dorman & Company, 1966.

Bloom, Benjamin S., *et al.,* eds. *Taxonomy of Educational Objectives: Handbook I: The Cognitive Domain.* New York: David McKay Company, 1956.

Booth, M. B. *History Betrayed?* Longmans' Curriculum Reform Series. London: Longmans, Green and Co., 1969.

Bowes, John S. "Using Documentary Material in the American History Course." *Social Education,* 28 (February 1964): 88–90, 95.

Bragdon, Henry W. "Teaching Writing Through History." *Atlantic Monthly* (November 1959), 118–20.

Branson, Margaret Stimmann. "Using Inquiry Methods in the Teaching of American History." *Social Education,* 35 (November 1971): 776–82.

Brown, Richard H. "History and the New Social Studies." *Saturday Review* (October 15, 1966), 80–81.

Brownsword, Alan W. "What's Wrong with the Teaching of History?" *California Social Science Review*, 6 (December 1966): 10–18.

Brubaker, Dale L., ed. *Innovation in the Social Studies*. New York: Thomas Y. Crowell Company, 1968.

Bruner, Jerome S. *The Process of Education*. Cambridge: Harvard University Press, 1962.

Burston, W. H. *Principles of History Teaching*. London: Methuen & Co., 1963.

———. *Social Studies and the History Teacher*. London: Historical Association, 1962.

———, and Thompson, D., eds. *Studies in the Nature and Teaching of History*. London: Routledge & Kegan Paul, 1967.

Carpenter, P. *History Teaching: The Era Approach*. Cambridge: Cambridge University Press, 1964.

Cartwright, William H., and Watson, Richard L., Jr., eds. *Interpreting and Teaching American History*. Thirty-first Yearbook. Washington D.C.: National Council for the Social Studies, 1961.

Clarke, Arthur C. "History Lesson." *Social Education*, 36 (March 1972): 250–54.

Clarke, Fred. *The Foundations of History Teaching*. London: Oxford University Press, 1929.

Clements, H. Millard, Fielder, William R., and Tabachnick, B. Robert. *Social Study: Inquiry in Elementary Classrooms*. Indianapolis: The Bobbs-Merrill Co., 1966.

Commager, Henry Steele. *The Nature and the Study of History* (With a Concluding Chapter Suggesting Methods for Elementary and Secondary Teachers by Raymond H. Muessig and Vincent R. Rogers). Columbus: Charles E. Merrill, 1965.

Cox, C. Benjamin, and Massialas, Byron G., eds. *Social Studies in the United States: A Critical Appraisal*. New York: Harcourt, Brace & World, 1967.

Crabtree, Charlotte. "Inquiry Approaches: How New and How Valuable?" *Social Education*, 30 (November 1966): 523–25.

Dance, E. H. *History the Betrayer: A Study of Bias*. London: Hutchinson, 1960.

———. *The Place of History in Secondary Teaching: A Comparative Study*. Education in Europe Series. London: George G. Harrap & Company, 1970.

Douch, Robert. *Local History and the Teacher*. London: Routledge and Kegan Paul, 1967.

Elson, Ruth Miller. *Guardians of Tradition: American School-*

books of the Nineteenth Century. Lincoln: University of Nebraska Press, 1964.

Engle, Shirley H. "Decision-Making: The Heart of Social Studies Instruction." *Social Education,* 24 (November 1960): 301–304.

————, ed. *New Perspectives in World History.* Thirty-fourth Yearbook. Washington, D.C.: National Council for the Social Studies, 1964.

Fair, Jean, and Shaftel, Fannie R., eds. *Effective Thinking in the Social Studies.* Thirty-seventh Yearbook. Washington, D.C.: National Council for the Social Studies, 1967.

Fenton, Edwin. "History in the New Social Studies." *Social Education,* 30 (May 1966): 325–28.

————. *The New Social Studies.* New York: Holt, Rinehart and Winston, 1967.

————. *Teaching the New Social Studies in Secondary Schools.* New York: Holt, Rinehart and Winston, 1966.

Ferguson, Sheila. *Projects in History for the Secondary School.* London: B. T. Batsford, 1967.

Findlay, J. J. *History and Its Place in Education.* London: University of London, 1923.

Fink, Lawrence A. *Honors Teaching in American History.* New York: Columbia University, Teachers College Press, 1969.

Goldmark, Bernice. "Another Look At Inquiry." *Social Education,* 39 (October 1965): 349–51.

————, and Schmeider, Morris. "Not History but Historiography." *Social Education,* 31 (March 1967): 201–206.

Gosden, P. H. J. *History for the Average Child: Suggestions on Teaching History to Pupils of Average and Below Average Ability.* Oxford: B. Blackwell, 1968.

Hall, G. Stanley, ed. *Methods of Teaching and Studying History.* Boston: D. C. Heath & Company, 1902.

Hardwick, Francis C., *et al. Teaching History and Geography.* 2nd ed. Toronto: W. J. Gage Limited, 1967.

Herbert, Louis J., and Murphy, William. *Structure in the Social Studies.* Social Studies Readings, no. 3. Washington, D.C.: National Council for the Social Studies [1968].

Hering, William M., Jr. "Social Science, History, and Inductive Teaching." *Social Education,* 32 (January 1968): 34–38.

High, James. *Teaching Secondary School Social Studies.* New York: John Wiley and Sons, 1962.

Hinsdale, Burke Aaron. *How to Study and Teach History.* New York: Appleton, 1894.

Hunt, Erling M. *The Role of History in Today's Schools*. Washington, D.C.: Council for Basic Education, 1966.

———, et al. *High School Social Studies Perspectives*. Boston: Houghton Mifflin Company, 1962.

Hunt, Maurice P., and Metcalf, Lawrence E. *Teaching High School Social Studies*. 2nd ed. New York: Harper & Row, 1968.

Johnson, Henry. *Teaching of History in Elementary and Secondary Schools*. Rev. ed. New York: The Macmillan Company, 1940.

Kane, Michael B. *Minorities in Textbooks*. Chicago: Anti-Defamation League, 1970.

Keating, M. W. *Studies in the Teaching of History*. London: A. and C. Black, 1910.

Keller, Charles R. "Needed: Revolution in the Social Studies." *Saturday Review* (September 16, 1961), 60–62.

Kellum, David F. *American History Through Conflicting Interpretations*. New York: Columbia University, Teachers College Press, 1969.

Keserich, Charles. "Historical Thinking and History Teaching: A Bibliographic Essay." *The History Teacher*, 4 (January 1971): 18–24.

Klapper, Paul. *The Teaching of History*. New York: D. Appleton-Century Company, 1926.

Krathwohl, David R., Bloom, Benjamin S., and Masia, Bertram B. *Taxonomy of Educational Objectives: Handbook II: The Affective Domain*. New York: David McKay Company, 1964.

Krug, Mark M. *History and the Social Sciences*. Waltham, Mass.: Blaisdell, 1967.

Lewenstein, Morris R. *Teaching Social Studies in Junior and Senior High Schools*. Chicago: Rand McNally and Company, 1963.

Lewis, Estella Matilola. *Teaching History in Secondary Schools*. London: Evans Brothers, 1960.

Lichtenberg, Mitchell P., and Fenton, Edwin. "Using AV Materials *Inductively* in the Social Studies." *Audiovisual Instruction*, 2 (May 1966): 330–32.

Lord, Donald C. "The Historian as Villain: The Historian's Role in the Training of Teachers." *The Historian*, 39 (May 1972): 407–20.

Lowe, William T. *Structure and the Social Studies*. Ithaca: Cornell University Press, 1969.

McCully, George E. "History Begins at Home." *Saturday Review* (May 16, 1970), 74–75, 86–88.

McKisack, May. *History as Education.* London: Westfield College, 1956.

Martin, Edward C., and Sandler, Martin W. "Rejuvenating the Teaching of United States History." *Social Education,* 35 (November 1971): 708–39.

Massialas, Byron G., and Cox, C. Benjamin. *Inquiry in Social Studies.* New York: McGraw-Hill Book Company, 1966.

————, and Zevin, Jack. *Creative Encounters in the Classroom: Teaching and Learning through Discovery.* New York: John Wiley & Sons, 1967.

Michaelis, John U., and Johnston, A. Montgomery, eds. *The Social Sciences: Foundations of the Social Studies.* Boston: Allyn and Bacon, 1965.

Morrissett, Irving, ed. *Concepts and Structure in the New Social Science Curricula.* West Lafayette, Ind.: Social Science Education Consortium, 1966.

Morse, Horace T., and McCune, George H. *Selected Items for the Testing of Study Skills and Critical Thinking.* 5th ed. Revised by Lester E. Brown and Ellen Cook. Bulletin no. 15. Washington, D.C.: National Council for the Social Studies, 1971.

Nietz, J. A. *Old Textbooks.* Pittsburgh: University of Pittsburgh Press, 1961.

Noah, Harold J., Prince, Carl E., and Riggs, C. Russell. "History in High-School Textbooks: A Note." *The School Review,* 70 (Winter 1962): 415–36.

Palmer, John R. "Using Historical Research in the Teaching of American History." *Social Education,* 36 (March 1972): 271–79.

Perkins, Dexter. "We Shall Gladly Teach." *American Historical Review,* 62 (January 1957): 291–309.

Pierce, B. L. *Public Opinion and the Teaching of History in the United States.* New York: Alfred A. Knopf, 1926.

Price, Roy A., Hickman, Warren, and Smith, Gerald. *Major Concepts for Social Studies.* Syracuse, N.Y.: Social Studies Curriculum Center, Syracuse University, 1965.

Provus, Malcolm. "Teaching Critical Thinking through History." *School Review,* 62 (October 1955): 393–96.

Reitan, E. A. "Breadth vs. Depth in the Teaching of the Survey Course in World History." *The Social Studies,* 55 (December 1964): 261–64.

Roucek, Joseph S., ed. *The Teaching of History*. New York: Philosophical Library, 1967.

Sanders, Norris M. *Classroom Questions: What Kinds?* New York: Harper & Row, 1966.

Sarkar, Benoy Kumar. *Introduction to the Science of Education and the Inductive Method of Teaching Series*. Trans. B. D. Basu. London: Longmans, Green & Company, 1913.

Scheiber, Harry N. "The California Textbook Fight." *Atlantic Monthly* (November, 1967), 38–47.

Schneider, Donald. "The Historical Method in the Teaching of History." *Peabody Journal of Education*, 40 (January 1963): 199–209.

Scott, Ernest. *History and Historical Problems*. London: Oxford University Press, 1925.

Selakovich, Daniel. *Problems in Secondary Social Studies*. Englewood Cliffs, N.J.: Prentice-Hall, 1965.

Sellers, Charles G. "Is History on the Way Out of the Schools and Do Historians Care?" *Social Education*, 33 (May 1969): 509–16.

Shannon, David A. "The Study of History and the Critical Mind." *Teachers College Record*, 56 (November 1954): 74–83.

Shermis, S. Samuel. "Six Myths Which Delude History Teachers." *Phi Delta Kappan*, 49 (September 1967): 9–12.

Smith, Frederick R., and Cox, C. Benjamin. *New Strategies and Curriculum in Social Studies*. Chicago: Rand McNally & Company, 1969.

Strong, Douglas H., and Rosenfield, Elizabeth S. "What Is History? A Neglected Question." *Social Studies*, 59 (October 1968): 195–98.

The Teaching of History in Secondary Schools. 3rd ed. Incorporated Association of Assistant Masters in Secondary Schools. Cambridge: Cambridge University Press, 1965.

Walworth, Arthur. *School Histories at War*. Cambridge: Harvard University Press, 1938.

Ward, Paul L. *A Style of History for Beginners*. Service Center for Teachers of History Series. Washington, D.C.: American Historical Association, 1959.

Wayland, John W. *How to Teach American History*. New York: The Macmillan Company, 1923.

Wesley, Edgar B. "Let's Abolish History Courses." *Phi Delta Kappan*, 49 (September 1967): 3–8.

————, and Wronski, Stanley P. *Teaching Social Studies in High Schools*. 5th ed. Boston: D. C. Heath and Company, 1964.

West, Edith, ed. *Improving the Teaching of World History.* Twentieth Yearbook. Washington, D.C.: National Council for the Social Studies, 1949.

Williams, G. A., comp. *Guide to Illustrative Material for Use in Teaching History.* London: The Historical Association, 1962.

Index

S

T

Lester D. Stephens

Probing the Past
a guide to the study and
teaching of history

Written especially for the history
teacher, this two-part book combines
a thorough discussion of the nature of
the discipline of history with suggestions on the teaching of history. It
is also appropriate as a textbook in
secondary social studies methods.

Included are sections on . . .

- the relation of history to the social
  sciences.

- the use of visual materials, primary
  sources, interpretation, and textbooks in the teaching of history.

Also . . .

- scores of practical examples.

- abundant illustrations.

- numerous examples of test
  questions.

- many practical suggestions for
  the utilization of instructional
  materials pertinent to the study
  of history.